First World War
and Army of Occupation
War Diary
France, Belgium and Germany

29 DIVISION
88 Infantry Brigade,
Brigade Machine Gun Company
and Trench Mortar Battery
25 January 1916 - 31 January 1918

WO95/2309/7-8

The Naval & Military Press Ltd
www.nmarchive.com
Published in association with The National Archives

Published by

The Naval & Military Press Ltd

Unit 10 Ridgewood Industrial Park,
Uckfield, East Sussex,
TN22 5QE England
Tel: +44 (0) 1825 749494

www.naval-military-press.com
www.nmarchive.com

This diary has been reprinted in facsimile from the original. Any imperfections are inevitably reproduced and the quality may fall short of modern type and cartographic standards.

Contents

Document type	Place/Title	Date From	Date To
Heading	WO95/2309/7		
Heading	29th Division 88th Infy Bde 88th Mach. Gun Coy. 1916 Apr Jan 1918		
Heading	29th Division 88th Infantry Brigade. 88th Machine Gun Company April 1916		
Heading	29 88 Bde M.G Coy Vol 1		
War Diary	Bonneville	01/04/1916	02/04/1916
War Diary	Beauquesne	03/04/1916	03/04/1916
War Diary	Colin Camp	04/04/1916	30/04/1916
Heading	29th Division. 88th Infantry Brigade. 88th Machine Gun Company May 1916		
Miscellaneous	D.A.G 3rd Echelon	31/05/1916	31/05/1916
War Diary	Colincamps	01/05/1916	23/05/1916
War Diary	Englebelmer	23/05/1916	28/05/1916
War Diary	Mailly-Maillet	28/05/1916	31/05/1916
Heading	29th Division. 88th Infantry Brigade. 88th Machine Gun Company June 1916 Operation Orders Attached.		
Miscellaneous	88th Bgde. Machine Gun Coy. War Diary For June 1916	30/06/1916	30/06/1916
War Diary	Mailly-Maillet	01/06/1916	08/06/1916
War Diary	Louvencourt	09/06/1916	15/06/1916
War Diary	Englebelmer	16/06/1916	30/06/1916
Operation(al) Order(s)	Operation Order No. 1 By Captain A Morris Comdg 88th Bgde Machine Gun Company Englebelmer 23.6.16 Appendix "A"	23/06/1916	23/06/1916
Miscellaneous	Operation Order No. 1 By Captain A Morris Comdg. 88th M.G. Company	23/06/1916	23/06/1916
Miscellaneous	Notes Div. Conference		
Operation(al) Order(s)	Operation Order No. 1 By Captain A. Morris Comdg 88th M.G.Coy	23/06/1916	23/06/1916
Operation(al) Order(s)	Operation Order No, 1 By Captain A Morris Comdg. 88th Bgde Machine Gun Company	23/06/1916	23/06/1916
Miscellaneous	4th Division No. GGG 766/61	28/06/1916	28/06/1916
Miscellaneous	29th Divn I.G. 44 28/6/16. 88th Brigade.	30/06/1916	30/06/1916
Miscellaneous	29th Div. I.g. 50 29/6/16. 88th Brigade.	30/06/1916	30/06/1916
Operation(al) Order(s)	29th Division Order No. 41	28/06/1916	28/06/1916
Miscellaneous	Information re Enemy Area Opposite VIII. Corps Front.		
Operation(al) Order(s)	Operation Order No. 1 By Captain A. Morris Comdg 88th M.G. Coy		
Miscellaneous	Fourth Army No. Q.G. 647 VIIIth Corps No. 1272/Q. 29th Division No. A. 406/193. VIII Corps.	27/06/1916	27/06/1916
Heading	29th Division. 88th Infantry Brigade. 88th Machine Gun Company July 1916		
War Diary	Englebelmer	01/07/1916	01/07/1916
War Diary	Knightsbridge	02/07/1916	06/07/1916
War Diary	Englebelmer	07/07/1916	23/07/1916
War Diary	Beauval	24/07/1916	27/07/1916
War Diary	Poperinghe	28/07/1916	29/07/1916
War Diary	Ypres	30/07/1916	31/07/1916
Map			

Heading	88 M.G. Coy Vol 4 July 1916		
Map			
Heading	29th Division 88th Infantry Brigade. 88th Machine Gun Company August 1916		
Miscellaneous	War Diary of 88th Machine Gun Company From 1st August 1916 To 31st August 1916 (Volume V) Vol 5		
Miscellaneous	Brigade Major 88th Brigade.	31/08/1916	31/08/1916
War Diary	Ypres	01/08/1916	09/08/1916
War Diary	Brandhoek	20/08/1916	31/08/1916
Miscellaneous	88th Machine Gun Company		
Map			
Map	All Positions Shown, Map No. 3		
Heading	29th Division 88th Infantry Brigade. 88th Machine Gun Company September 1916		
Heading	War Diary of 88th Machine Gun Company From 1st September 1916 To 30th September 1916 Volume VI		
War Diary	Ypres	01/09/1916	27/09/1916
War Diary	Brandhoek	27/09/1916	27/09/1916
War Diary	Ypres	29/09/1916	30/09/1916
Miscellaneous	88th Machine Gun Company.		
Miscellaneous	88th Machine Gun Company. Appendix "B"		
Operation(al) Order(s)	Operation Order No. 1 By Major. A. Morris. Commanding 88th Machine Gun Company.	28/09/1916	28/09/1916
Miscellaneous	General Idea		
Heading	29th Division. 88th Infantry Brigade. 88th Machine Gun Company October 1916 Operation Orders Attached		
Heading	War Diary 88th Machine Gun Company From 1st October 1916 To 31st October Inclusive Volume 7		
Miscellaneous	88th Brigade.	01/11/1916	01/11/1916
War Diary	Ypres	01/10/1916	04/10/1916
War Diary	Poperinghe	05/10/1916	07/10/1916
War Diary	Saleux	08/10/1916	08/10/1916
War Diary	Corbie	09/10/1916	09/10/1916
War Diary	Montauban	10/10/1916	10/10/1916
War Diary	Somme	11/10/1916	27/10/1916
War Diary	Bernafay Wood	28/10/1916	29/10/1916
War Diary	Pomiers	30/10/1916	30/10/1916
War Diary	Ville	31/10/1916	31/10/1916
Miscellaneous	O.C. 88th Machine Gun Coy. Copy W.Q 88th Bde.	29/09/1916	29/09/1916
Diagram etc	Appendix A		
Map	Sketch Map Showing Part Of Sheet 28. Man Edition 3D		
Miscellaneous	88th Machine Gun Company Relief Orders Appendix B		
Map	Appendix C		
Miscellaneous	A Form. Messages And Signals.		
Miscellaneous	Brigade Orders By Brigadier-General D.E Cayley, C.M.G, Commanding, 88th Inf. Brigade. Appendix D	15/10/1916	15/10/1916
Miscellaneous	Operation Orders By Major A Morris Commanding 88th M.G. Coy. Appendix E	17/10/1916	17/10/1916
Miscellaneous	A Form. Messages And Signals.		
Heading	29th Division 88th Infantry Brigade. 88th Machine Gun Company November 1916		
Heading	War Diary of 88th Machine Gun Company From 1st November 1916 To 30th November 1916 (Volume 1)		
Miscellaneous	Sir Are Major 88th Brigade	01/12/1916	01/12/1916
War Diary	Ville	01/11/1916	14/11/1916
War Diary	Ville & Meaulte	15/11/1916	15/11/1916

War Diary	Meaulte	15/11/1916	18/11/1916
War Diary	Guillemont Les Boeufs	19/11/1916	30/11/1916
Map	Appendix A		
Heading	29th Division 88th Infantry Brigade. 88th Machine Gun Company December 1916		
Miscellaneous	War Diary of 88th Machine Gun Company From 1st December 1916 To 31st December 1916 (Volume No 2) Vol 19		
War Diary	Guillemont & Les Boeufs	01/12/1916	03/12/1916
War Diary	Guillemont Carnoy	03/12/1916	03/12/1916
War Diary	Carnoy	04/12/1916	08/12/1916
War Diary	Carnoy Ville	09/12/1916	09/12/1916
War Diary	Ville	10/12/1916	13/12/1916
War Diary	Ville Crouy	14/12/1916	14/12/1916
War Diary	Crouy	15/12/1916	15/12/1916
War Diary	Molliens Vidame	15/12/1916	31/12/1916
Miscellaneous	Movement Orders By Major A Morris Commanding 88th Machine Gun Company In the Field 8th November 1916	08/11/1916	08/11/1916
Miscellaneous	Movement Orders By Major A. Morris Commanding 88th Machine Gun Company In the Field Tuesday 12th December 1916	12/12/1916	12/12/1916
Miscellaneous	Syllabus Of Training 88th Machine Gun Company.	16/12/1916	16/12/1916
War Diary	Molliens Vidame	01/01/1917	11/01/1917
War Diary	Corbie	12/01/1917	15/01/1917
War Diary	Mansel Camp Carnoy	16/01/1917	17/01/1917
War Diary	Carnoy	18/01/1917	18/01/1917
War Diary	Mansel Camp	18/01/1917	22/01/1917
War Diary	Guillemont Morval	23/01/1917	23/01/1917
War Diary	Guillemont	23/01/1917	24/01/1917
War Diary	Guillemont Morval	25/01/1916	25/01/1916
War Diary	Guillemont	26/01/1916	26/01/1916
War Diary	Guillemont Morval	27/01/1917	30/01/1917
War Diary	Guillemont	31/01/1917	31/01/1917
Miscellaneous	88th Machine Gun Company Programme of Training For Week Ending 6th January 1917	06/01/1917	06/01/1917
Miscellaneous	Operation Orders By Lieut Jelf-Reveley Commanding 88th Company Machine Gun Corps.		
Map			
Miscellaneous	Operation Orders By Lieut Jelf-Reveley Commanding 88th M.G.C		
Miscellaneous	Operation Orders 4 Guns Will Be In Brigade Reserve	05/01/1917	05/01/1917
Miscellaneous	88th Machine Gun Company.	01/07/1917	01/07/1917
Miscellaneous	Movement Orders By Captain C.H. Jelf-Reveley Commanding 88th Machine Gun Company In The Field Tuesday 9th January 1917	09/01/1917	09/01/1917
Miscellaneous	Appendix E Movement Orders By Major A. Morris Commanding 88th Machine Gun Company	22/01/1917	22/01/1917
Operation(al) Order(s)	Operation Order No. 5 By Major A Morris Commanding 88th Machine Gun Company.	25/01/1917	25/01/1917
Operation(al) Order(s)	Appendix G. Operation Orders No. 6 By Major Morris Commanding 88th Machine Gun Coy	28/01/1917	28/01/1917
Heading	War Diary Of 88th Company Machine Gun Corps Period 1st February 1917 To 28th February 1917 (Volume 9) Vol XI		
War Diary	Guillemont	01/02/1917	07/02/1917

War Diary	Mansel Camp	07/02/1917	07/02/1917
War Diary	Coisy	08/02/1917	18/02/1917
War Diary	La Neuville	19/02/1917	20/02/1917
War Diary	Mansel Camp	21/02/1917	21/02/1917
War Diary	Combles	21/02/1917	21/02/1917
War Diary	Haie Wood	21/02/1917	21/02/1917
War Diary	Sector:- Sailly Saillisel	21/02/1917	21/02/1917
War Diary	Combles	22/02/1917	22/02/1917
War Diary	Sailly Saillisel	22/02/1917	26/02/1917
War Diary	Combles Sector:- Sailly Saillisel	27/02/1917	28/02/1917
Heading	War Diary 88 M.G.C Appendix A		
Map	Trench Map No. 1 29th Div (Centre) Area. Scale 1; 10,000. 18.2.17		
Operation(al) Order(s)	Operation Order No. 8 By Major A. Morris Commanding 88th Machine Gun Company In The Field February 25th 1917 Appendix B	25/02/1917	25/02/1917
Heading	War Diary 88th Company M.G. Corps Period 1st March 1917 To 31st March 1917 (Volume 1) Vol 12		
War Diary	Haie Wood Sailly Saillisel	01/03/1917	03/03/1917
War Diary	Meaulte Camp	04/03/1917	05/03/1917
War Diary	Meaulte	06/03/1917	19/03/1917
War Diary	Molliens Vidame	19/03/1917	22/03/1917
War Diary	Molliens Vidame	23/03/1917	28/03/1917
War Diary		29/03/1917	29/03/1917
War Diary	Vignacourt	30/03/1917	31/03/1917
Operation(al) Order(s)	Movement Orders No. 18 By Major A Morris Commanding 88th Company M.G. Corps In The Field	02/03/1917	02/03/1917
Miscellaneous	88th Machine Gun Company. Programme of Training For Week Ending March. 10	11/03/1917	11/03/1917
Miscellaneous	88th Coy Movement Orders By Major A. Morris Commanding Coy Machine Gun Corps In The Field 26th March 19170	26/03/1917	26/03/1917
Heading	War Diary Of 88th Company M.G. Corps Period From 1st April To 30th April 1917 (Volume No. 11) Vol 13		
Miscellaneous	From O.C. 88 Coy M.G.C. To Bde Major 88th Bde.	30/04/1917	30/04/1917
War Diary	Vignacourt Beauval	01/04/1917	01/04/1917
War Diary	Beauval Mondicourt	02/04/1917	02/04/1917
War Diary	Mondicourt	03/04/1917	04/04/1917
War Diary	Brevillers	05/04/1917	06/04/1917
War Diary	Coullemont	07/04/1917	09/04/1917
War Diary	Gouy En Artois	10/04/1917	11/04/1917
War Diary	Arras	12/04/1917	12/04/1917
War Diary	Arras Monchy	12/04/1917	13/04/1917
War Diary	Monchy Le Preux	14/04/1917	17/04/1917
War Diary	Arras	18/04/1917	19/04/1917
War Diary	Monchy Le Preux		
War Diary	Arras	20/04/1917	21/04/1917
War Diary	Monchy Le Preux	22/04/1917	22/04/1917
War Diary	Les Fosses Farm	22/04/1917	23/04/1917
War Diary	Monchy Le Preux	23/04/1917	24/04/1917
War Diary	Arras	25/04/1917	25/04/1917
War Diary	Simencourt	25/04/1917	25/04/1917
War Diary	Gouy En Artois	26/04/1917	26/04/1917
War Diary	Couin Coigneux	27/04/1917	27/04/1917
War Diary	Couin	27/04/1917	30/04/1917

Operation(al) Order(s)	Operation Order No. 10 By Major A Morris Commanding Coy Machine Gun Corps Appendix A		
Map	Guemappe		
War Diary	Rosignol Farm to St Amand	01/05/1917	01/05/1917
War Diary	Arras	02/05/1917	07/05/1917
War Diary	Dainville	08/05/1917	09/05/1917
War Diary	Arras	10/05/1917	15/05/1917
War Diary	Trenches Monchy Le Preux	15/05/1917	19/05/1917
War Diary	South Of The Scarpe To Monchy Preux	20/05/1917	31/05/1917
Operation(al) Order(s)	Operation Order No 80 By Major A Morris Commanding 88 Coy M. 4 Corps. In The Field 28th May 1917	28/05/1917	28/05/1917
Operation(al) Order(s)	Operation Order No 82 By Major A Morris Commanding 88 Coy M. 4 Corps. In The Field 31st May 1917	31/05/1917	31/05/1917
Heading	War Diary 88th Machine Gun Coy From 1st June 1917 To 30th June 1917 (Volume No. 13)		
War Diary	North of Scarpe to Monchy-Le-Preux	01/06/1917	01/06/1917
War Diary	Arras	02/06/1917	04/06/1917
War Diary	Canaples	04/06/1917	25/06/1917
War Diary	Canaples to Doullens	26/06/1917	27/06/1917
War Diary	Proven Area	27/06/1917	30/06/1917
Operation(al) Order(s)	Movement Order No. 84 By Major. A. Morris D.S.O. Commanding 88th Company Machine Gun Corps In The Field Monday 25 June 1917	25/06/1917	25/06/1917
Miscellaneous	Company Orders By		
Miscellaneous	Programme of Training For Week Ending-Saturday 9th June 1917	09/06/1917	09/06/1917
Miscellaneous	Programme of Training For Week Ending-Saturday 10th June 1917	10/06/1917	10/06/1917
Diagram etc	Spanner Machine Gun Emplacement.		
Miscellaneous	88th Company Machine Gun Corps Appendix C	14/06/1917	14/06/1917
Miscellaneous	Programme of Training For Week Ending-Saturday 23rd June 1917 Appendix D	23/06/1917	23/06/1917
Operation(al) Order(s)	Movement Order No. 83 By Major A Morris Commanding 88th Company Machine Gun Corps		
Heading	War Diary of 88th Machine Gun Coy From 1st July 1917 To 31st July 1917 (Volume No. 14)		
War Diary		01/07/1917	31/07/1917
Miscellaneous	Operation Order By Lieut C.H Jelf-Revely Commanding 88th Company Machine Gun Corps In The Field Wednesday 4/7/17	04/07/1917	04/07/1917
Operation(al) Order(s)	Operation Order No 2 By Lieutenant J.F Nichols Commanding 88th Company Machine Gun Corps	26/08/1917	26/08/1917
Miscellaneous	Operation Order No. G/88/3 By Lieutenant A.B.C. Burrell Commanding. Advanced Headquarters 88th Company M.G.C		
Map			
Miscellaneous	Operation Order By Lieut G.F Nichol Commanding 88th Company M.G. Corps. Appendix III	25/07/1917	25/07/1917
Map	1 Section Of Guns		
Miscellaneous	Appendix IV		
Heading	War Diary of 88th Machine Gun Coy From 1st Aug. 1917 To 31st Aug. 1917 (Volume No 14)		
War Diary	In The Field	01/08/1917	31/08/1917

Miscellaneous	Preliminary Operation Orders By Lieutenant J.J. Paskin Commanding, 88th Company Machine Gun Corps In The Field 11th August 1917 Appendix I	11/08/1917	11/08/1917
Miscellaneous	Extracts From 29th Divisional M.G. Barrage Instructions (amended)		
Miscellaneous	Operation Orders By Lieut J.J. Paskin Commanding, 88th Company M.G. Corps in the Field Appendix III	27/08/1917	27/08/1917
Miscellaneous	29th Divisional M.G Barrage.		
Miscellaneous	Amendments to 88th Machine Gun Company. Preliminary Operation Order Dated 11/8/17	11/08/1917	11/08/1917
Operation(al) Order(s)	Operation Orders No. M.G 88/5 By Lieutenant J.J. Paskin Commanding. 88th Company Machine Gun Corps In The Field. 14th August 1917	14/08/1917	14/08/1917
Miscellaneous	Report On Operations From 16/8/17 To 13/8/17 88th Machine Gun Company.	16/08/1917	16/08/1917
Map			
Miscellaneous	Message Pad		
Map			
Miscellaneous	Message Pad		
Map			
Miscellaneous	Message Pad.		
Miscellaneous	War Diary of 88th Machine Gun Company From 1st September 1917 To 30th September 1917 Volume No. 16		
War Diary	In The Field	01/09/1917	29/09/1917
Miscellaneous	Programme of Training 88th Coy M.G. Corps For Week Ending. 8th Sept.		
Miscellaneous	Programme Appendix II		
Miscellaneous	Programme of Training 88th Coy. M.G. Corps For Week Ending 15th Sept.		
Miscellaneous	Operation Order No. M.G88/7 By Captain J.J. Paskin Commanding 88th Infantry Machine Gun Corps In The Field 10th Sept 1917	10/09/1917	10/09/1917
Miscellaneous	Appendix I To Operation Order No. M.G 88/7		
Miscellaneous	Programme of Training 88th Company Machine Gun Corps Commanding 22nd Sep.		
Miscellaneous	M.G Barrage Table		
Miscellaneous	88th M.G. Coy. Order No. M.G. 88/8 By Captain J.J Paskin Commanding 88th M.G.C.	19/09/1917	19/09/1917
Heading	Original War Diary October 1917		
Map	Identification Trace For.		
Heading	War Diary of 88th Machine Gun Company From 1st October 1917 To 31st October 1917 (Volume No. 17)		
War Diary	In The Field	01/10/1917	31/10/1917
Miscellaneous	88th Machine Gun Company. Report On Operations 9th-11th Oct 1917	09/10/1917	09/10/1917
Map			
Miscellaneous			
Heading	War Diary of 88th Machine Gun Company From 1st November, 1917 To 30th November, 1917 (Volume No. 18)		
War Diary	Bienvillers	01/11/1917	30/11/1917
Miscellaneous	88th M.G Coy. Orders No. M.G.88/9 By Capt J.J Paskin Commanding 88th M.G. Coy.		
Miscellaneous	M.G. Barrage Table		
Miscellaneous	88. Coy., M.C.G.	30/11/1917	30/11/1917

Miscellaneous	88th M.G Coy Orders By Capt J.J. Paskin. Commanding 88th M.G. Coy. Appendix I	15/11/1917	15/11/1917
Miscellaneous	88th Machine Gun Coy. Report On Operations 20/11/17-23/11/17 Appendix 2	20/11/1917	20/11/1917
Miscellaneous	88th M.G. Coy. Orders No. M.G. 88/10 B. by Capt J.J. Paskin. Cmdg 88th M.G. Coy.	20/11/1917	20/11/1917
Miscellaneous	88th M.G Coy Orders No. M.G/88/11 Appendix III	26/11/1917	26/11/1917
Miscellaneous	Machine Gun Relief Night 26/27 No. 1917	26/11/1917	26/11/1917
Map			
Heading	War Diary of 88th Machine Gun Coy From 1st Dec. 1917 To 31st Dec 1917 (Volume No. 19)		
War Diary	Marcoing	01/12/1917	06/12/1917
War Diary	Warluzel	07/12/1917	19/12/1917
War Diary	Sains Les Fressin	20/12/1917	31/12/1917
Miscellaneous	War Diary of 88th Machine Gun Company. From 1st January, 1918 To 31st January, 1918 (Volume No. 20)		
War Diary	Sains-Les-Frezzin	01/01/1918	31/01/1918
Miscellaneous	88th M.G. Coy. Orders No. M.G.88/11. Appendix I	27/01/1918	27/01/1918
Heading	WO95/2309/8		
Heading	29th Division 88th Infy Bde 88th Lt Trench Mortar Bty Jly-Dec 1916		
Heading	29th Division. 88th Infantry Brigade. 88th Light Trench Mortar Battery July 1916 Dec. 16		
Miscellaneous	Headquarters, 29th Division. Reference Your A.723 of 12th Instant; 88th Trench Mortar Battery's War Diary for month of July, 1916 herewith.	14/08/1916	14/08/1916
War Diary	France In The Field	01/07/1916	31/07/1916
Heading	29th Division. 88th Infantry Brigade. 88th Light Trench Mortar Battery August 1916		
Heading	War Diary of 88th Trench Mortar Battery From 1st August, 1916 To 31st August, 1916. (Volume No. 2.)		
War Diary	Belgiam In The Field	01/08/1916	16/08/1916
War Diary	Belgiam	17/08/1916	27/08/1916
War Diary	Belgiam In The Field	28/08/1916	31/08/1916
Miscellaneous	88th Trench Mortar Batteries	31/08/1916	31/08/1916
Heading	29th Division. 88th Infantry Brigade. 88th Light Trench Mortar Battery September 1916		
War Diary	Belgiam	01/09/1916	30/09/1916
Miscellaneous	Programme of Training	19/09/1916	19/09/1916
Heading	29th Division. 88th Infantry Brigade. 88th Light Trench Mortar Battery October 1916		
War Diary	Belgiam	01/10/1916	08/10/1916
War Diary	France	09/10/1916	31/10/1916
Heading	29 Division 88 Infantry Brigade Brigade Trench Mortar Battery Nov. 1916 Missing		
Heading	29th Division. 88th Infantry Brigade. 88th Light Trench Mortar Battery December 1916		
War Diary	France	01/12/1916	31/12/1916

29TH DIVISION

88TH INFY BDE

88TH MACH. GUN COY.

1916 APR ~~1917~~ - JAN 1918

29th Division.

88th Infantry Brigade.

88th MACHINE GUN COMPANY

APRIL 1 9 1 6

1
Jan '18

29

11

88 Bde M G Coy

Vol I

Army Form C. 2118.

WAR DIARY

or

~~INTELLIGENCE SUMMARY~~

(Erase heading not required.)

Instructions regarding War Diaries and Intelligence Summaries are contained in F. S. Regs., Part II. and the Staff Manual respectively. Title Pages will be prepared in manuscript.

88 M G Coy
Vol

Place	Date	Hour	Summary of Events and Information	Remarks and references to Appendices
BONNEVILLE	1-4-16		Marched from GORENFLOS to BONNEVILLE.	
BONNEVILLE	2-4-16		remained billeted at BONNEVILLE. 11.30 p.m. rec'd orders to proceed on following day to 31st Division area.	
BEAUQUESNE	3-4-16		marched from BONNEVILLE to BEAUQUESNE. started 9 A.M. arrived 1 P.M. went into billets.	
COIINCAMP	4-4-16		marched from BEAUQUESNE to COIINCAMP. started 9 AM. arrived 3 P.M. billetted. Transport off loaded and returned to COURCELLES-au-BOIS where they billetted.	
COIINCAMP	5-4-16		9 A.M. two sections, each of 4 guns, proceeded to trenches. Took over from 144th M. G. Coy. One section in support lines. One in reserve lines. Company Hqrs & company, less transport & 2 sections, remained in billets.	
	6th		quiet. Machine guns fired long range into SERRE and BEAUMONT-HAMEL and into communication trenches. At night enemy bombarded. One sergeant wounded.	
	7th		quiet. Alternative positions commenced for each gun.	
	8th		quiet.	
	9th		quiet. 3 & 4 sections relieved No's 1 & 2. relief began 9 am. completed 12 noon.	
	10th		quiet.	
	11th		quiet. heavy rain hinders observation of firing by day.	
	12th		"	
	13th		" No's 1 & 2 sections relieved No 3 & 4. hours as before.	Heavy rain day & night rendered observation of fire impossible
	14th		quiet. Very wet.	
	15th		quiet	
	16th		Quiet	
	17th		quiet. No's 3 & 4 sections relieve No 1 & 2. hours as above	

2449 Wt. W14957/M90 750,000 1/16 J.B.C. & A. Forms/C.2118/12.

Army Form C. 2118.

WAR DIARY
or
~~INTELLIGENCE SUMMARY~~
(Erase heading not required.)

Instructions regarding War Diaries and Intelligence Summaries are contained in F. S. Regs., Part II. and the Staff Manual respectively. Title Pages will be prepared in manuscript.

Place	Date	Hour	Summary of Events and Information	Remarks and references to Appendices
COIINCAMP	18/4/16		quiet	
	19		quiet	
	20		quiet	
	21		quiet. No 1 & 2. sections relieved No 3 & 4. at usual hours.	
	22		quiet	
	23		quiet	
	24		quiet	
	25		quiet. No 3 & 4 sections relieved No 1 & 2 sections.	
			} heavy rains day & night rendered observation of fire impossible. [signature]	
	26		quiet	
	27		quiet	
	28		quiet. One gun emplacement hit by H.E. shell & destroyed. No casualties to personnel or gun.	
	29		quiet. Fair number of aerial torpedoes fell near one gun pit, due to construction of new communication trench nearby. No 1 & 2 sections relieved No 3 & 4. Two extra guns sent up to line. i.e 10. guns in trenches, 6 in reserve at COIINCAMP. At 9.30 P.M. rec'd message to say Brigade on right of this area would carry out two raids, to be preceded by artillery bombardment starting at 11.30 P.M. & lasting one hour. Notified the officers i/c M. guns in this area. quiet night in this area. One gun slightly damaged by hostile machine gun fire.	
	30th		quiet.	

2449 Wt. W14957/M90 750,000 1/16 J.B.C. & A. Forms/C.2118/12.

29th Division.

88th Infamtry Brigade.

88th MACHINE GUN COMPANY

MAY 1916

D A G
3rd Echelon

~~O i/c Records,~~
~~Machine Gun Corps.~~
~~Westminster S.W.~~

Herewith appended war diary for the month of May 1916. There is nothing of very great importance to record. We have at present under consideration the isolation of a part of the enemy's line by Machine Gun fire for the purpose of reconnaissance. This will be included in next month's report.

31 - 5 - 16

A Merritt Capt. Comdg.
88th Bgde. M.G. Company.

88 M.G. Coy

Vol 2

29

88th Bgde. M.G. Coy.

Instructions regarding War Diaries and Intelligence Summaries are contained in F. S. Regs., Part II. and the Staff Manual respectively. Title Pages will be prepared in manuscript.

WAR DIARY

~~or~~

~~INTELLIGENCE SUMMARY~~

(Erase heading not required.)

Army Form C. 2118.

Place	Date	Hour	Summary of Events and Information	Remarks and references to Appendices
COLINCAMPS	1/5/16 to 6/5/16	—	Whole area quiet. Only targets available were observation posts & occasional enemy working parties. Night firing on enemy wire, salients & dumps carried out: Enemy's reply invariably a swinging traverse. Alternative emplacements & observation posts constructed.	
"	7/5/16 to 13/5/16	—	Intermittent shelling especially at K23 c 35/30 in front of position at K22d 10/05 & at K34d 20/50. Gun at K34a 90/15 hit by M.G. fire which penetrated loophole. This is the only instance of effective enemy M.G. fire while the Coy. was in this sector. Day & night firing as above. Weather wet; observation difficult.	Map is France 57D N.E.
"	14/5/16 to 20/5/16	—	On the 15th inst. emplacements at K34 d 20/50 & K 34 b 30/50 both hit by shell fire (H.E.). Guns shifted to alternative emplacements & new battle emplacements selected. Concentration of shell fire again noticeable at K23 c 35/30 & K 33 b 80/20. Enemy M.Gs. particularly quiet during day but unusually active from 2000 to 2100. Swinging traverse invariably used by him. Weather good; work carried on without interruption. Co-operation with Lewis Guns increased by comparison of positions, fields of fire etc. Sector quiet by day with artillery & M.G. activity by night.	
"	22/5/16	—	Relieved by 92nd, 93rd, & 94th M.G. Coys. (31st Div.)	
"	23/5/16	—	Moved out of Colincamps to Englebelmer.	
ENGLEBELMER	23/5/16	1900	Arrived Englebelmer.	

A. Moore (?)
Capt. Comdg.
88th Bge. M.G. Coy.

2449 Wt. W14957/M90 750,000 1/16 J.B.C. & A. Forms/C.2118/12.

88th Bge. M.G. Coy.

Instructions regarding War Diaries and Intelligence Summaries are contained in F. S. Regs., Part II. and the Staff Manual respectively. Title Pages will be prepared in manuscript.

WAR DIARY

~~or~~

~~INTELLIGENCE SUMMARY~~

(Erase heading not required.)

Army Form C. 2118.

Place	Date	Hour	Summary of Events and Information	Remarks and references to Appendices
ENGLEBELMER	24/5/16	—	Relieved 87th Bge. M.G. Coy. in Right Sector of 29th Div. front: 8 guns in firing line & 4 in redoubt line. Found the line quiet.	
"	24/5/16 to 27/5/16	—	Began work on alternative positions, range charts, night firing tables, reconnaissance etc. At 2200 on 27th inst. carried out night firing scheme against enemy works at Q11c 60/50 to Q11c 90/90, from position at Q17c 40/35. Enemy retaliated by shell fire. The operation was successfully carried out & reported upon favourably by G.S. 29th Div.	Map is 57D SE. 1+2. (parts of)
"	28/5/16	—	Relieved by 87th Bge. M.G. Coy.	
"	"	1900	Moved out of Englebelmer towards Mailly-Maillet	
MAILLY-MAILLET	"	2000	~~Arrived &~~ billeted.	
"	29/5/16	—	Relieved 86th Bge. M.G. Coy.	
"	29/5/16 to 31/5/16	—	Found line relatively quiet. Proceeded with reconnaissance etc.	

A.L. Morris Capt. Comdg.
88th Bge. M.G. Company.

2449 Wt. W14957/M90 750,000 1/16 J.B.C. & A. Forms/C.2118/12.

29th Division.

88th Infantry Brigade

88th MACHINE GUN COMPANY

J U N E 1 9 1 6

Operstion Orders attached.

88M G Coy
Vol 3

88th Bgde. Machine Gun Coy.

War Diary for June 1916.

D. A. G. 3rd Echelon.

War Diary for the month of June appended.

I would like to draw your attention to two points

1 The prevention of enemy traffic entering Beaumont Hamel by night by machine gun fire These facts were ascertained by observation of independent infantry units.

2. The accuracy obtained by means of indirect fire from which excellent results have been procured.

30-6-16

A.M. Morris Captain Comdg
88th M. G. Coy.

88th Bge. Machine Gun Coy.

Instructions regarding War Diaries and Intelligence Summaries are contained in F. S. Regs., Part II. and the Staff Manual respectively. Title Pages will be prepared in manuscript.

WAR DIARY
or
~~INTELLIGENCE SUMMARY~~
(Erase heading not required.)

Army Form C. 2118.

88th BRIGADE MACHINE GUN COMPANY.

Place	Date	Hour	Summary of Events and Information	Remarks and references to Appendices
MAILLY-MAILLET.	1-6-16	—	Work on strengthening of emplacements & construction of alternatives proceeded with.	
		2.10 am	Traversed enemy wire by arrangement with O.C. firing line to catch enemy patrols.	
"	2-6-16	—	Traffic on roads into BEAUMONT HAMEL stopped by M.G. fire. Indirect fire has been directed on these roads at irregular intervals after dark on previous nights. Report from 4th Worcester Regt. (O.C. left sector firing line) of decrease & finally of stoppage of traffic.	
"	3-6-16	7.15 pm. 10 pm.	Fire from redoubt line on BEAUMONT HAMEL & enemy support trenches. " " support " " " " " Earlier in the day an enemy M.G. was observed firing. The artillery was notified & observed fire as directed at Q4d 86/00: a hit was registered.	
"	4-6-16	Midnight 3rd to 1 am. 4th	Guns in redoubt line & White City sector supported a raid on enemy trenches at Q4d 85/00. They isolated the sector selected for attack by flanking fire on both sides. This was successfully accomplished.	57D S.E. 1&2 (parts of).
"	5-6-16	—	At irregular intervals during the night the guns traversed the damaged wire & trenches which the enemy would seek to repair after the bombardment of the previous night.	
"	6-6-16	—	Last night's operations repeated effectively while indirect fire was continued from redoubt guns on BEAUMONT HAMEL & its approaches. The observed results in diminution of traffic & hampering of enemy work amply justified these operations. Work on alternative emplacements carried on continually favoured by good weather conditions.	
"	7-6-16	—	Enemy working party observed behind Beaumont Hamel; fire opened & party immediately dispersed & did not attempt to renew work. BEAUMONT HAMEL and approaches kept under intermittent fire during the night.	
"	8-6-16	—	Relieved by 86th M.G. Coy. Proceeded to LOUVENCOURT.	
		7 pm.	Arrived at Louvencourt.	

A.Morris Captain Comdg.
88th M.G. Coy.

2449 Wt. W14957/M90 750,000 1/16 J.B.C. & A. Forms/C.2118/12.

88th Bgd. M.G. Coy.

Instructions regarding War Diaries and Intelligence Summaries are contained in F. S. Regs., Part II. and the Staff Manual respectively. Title Pages will be prepared in manuscript.

WAR DIARY

~~or~~

~~INTELLIGENCE SUMMARY~~

(Erase heading not required.)

Army Form C. 2118.

88th BRIGADE MACHINE GU[N] COMPANY. No. .... Date........

Place	Date	Hour	Summary of Events and Information	Remarks and references to Appendices
LOUVENCOURT	9-6-16	—	Overhauling of guns & stores. Section training.	
"	10-6-16	—	Section training. Special attention to instruction in gas.	
"	11-6-16	—	Ditto. Ditto. Training hindered by inclement weather.	
"	12-6-16	—	Brigade Training: The attack. 2 Guns detailed to each of the attacking units: 8 Guns forming a reserve of fire.	
"	13-6-16	—	Brigade Training continued by rt. half Coy. Left half Coy. carried out firing practice on the range at FORCEVILLE.	
"	14-6-16	—	Brigade Training: The attack as on the 12th & including the assault.	
"	15-6-16	—	Relieved 87th M.G. Coy. in rt. sector of divisional area.	
ENGLEBELMER	16-6-16	—	12 Guns in Bgd. area. 80 ammn. carriers added to strength of Coy: These obtained in sections of 20 from each unit in the Bgd. Proceeded to train these men in belt filling by hand & by machine. 5 per. gun detailed in view of probable operations. The additional labour thus available utilised to complete all preparations of emplacements & ration dumps, ammunition dumps, dugouts etc.	
"	17-6-16	—	Activity in the line normal. Fire at intervals on enemy wire & communication trenches. Attention devoted to completion of work in progress.	
"	18-6-16	—	Work on Yellow Line (redoubt line of 8 gun positions) to be occupied by this Coy. pushed forward & completed. Enemy aeroplanes & artillery active — we sustained one casualty from shrapnel.	

A. Morris Captain Comdg
88th Brigade M.G. Coy.

2449 Wt. W14957/M90 750,000 1/16 J.B.C. & A. Forms/C.2118/12.

88th Bge. Machine Gun Coy.

Instructions regarding War Diaries and Intelligence Summaries are contained in F. S. Regs., Part II. and the Staff Manual respectively. Title Pages will be prepared in manuscript.

WAR DIARY
or
~~INTELLIGENCE~~ ~~SUMMARY~~

(Erase heading not required.)

Army Form C. 2118.

Place	Date	Hour	Summary of Events and Information	Remarks and references to Appendices
ENGLEBELMER	19-6-16 20 " " 21 " " 22 " "	— — — —	These days were occupied by preparations for the operations in view. Night firing was maintained on enemy wire & lines of approach. Meantime the Yellow Line was stocked with food, water & ammunition in view of the bombardment. Forward ammunition dumps selected & stocked with spare belts (filled) & belt filling machines. Reconnaissance of these dumps, Bge. dumps & Divisional ammn. dump carried out by officer in charge ammn. supply, Sgt. Major & all available N.C.Os. On the 21st & 22nd insts. a reconnaissance was also made of the concentration point selected for concentration of reserve guns prior to the advance, by which all Officers & N.C.Os became thoroughly acquainted with the rendez-vous & the approaches to it.	
"	23-6-16	—	Eight positions in the firing line were taken over by the 87th M.G. Coy. We retained the four in the Yellow Line & took over four in the Yellow Line of the left sector from the 86th M.G. Coy. The eight guns detailed to Units as per operation orders appended joined these units at Louvencourt. The Headquarters of the Coy. remained at Englebelmer being in telephonic communication with both sectors of the Yellow Line. Operation orders published.*	* Appendix "A".
"	24-6-16 25 " " 26 " " 27 " " 28 " "	— — — — —	These were U, V, W, X & Y days respectively. During these days of bombardment by our artillery the guns of the Coy. kept up intermittent fire on the enemy's wire especially at night. Fire was all indirect by means of traversing & elevating dials, their operation at night being greatly facilitated by the use of the electric torches now issued. A "silent period" was observed each night to allow of reconnoitring of enemy wire & raiding of enemy trenches to be carried out. All arrangements made for protection, ammunition supply, food & water supply & communication proved satisfactory. Weather conditions very unfavourable; heavy rains daily; trenches very wet. On the 28th inst. orders were received that operations would be postponed 48 hours.	

2449 Wt. W14957/M90 750,000 1/16 J.B.C. & A. Forms/C.2118/12.

A.W. Morris Captain Comdg
88th M.G. Coy

Army Form C. 2118.

88th BRIGADE MACHINE GUN COMPANY.

No. .... Date ....

WAR DIARY

or

~~INTELLIGENCE~~ SUMMARY

(Erase heading not required.)

88th Bge. Machine Gun Coy.

Instructions regarding War Diaries and Intelligence Summaries are contained in F. S. Regs., Part II. and the Staff Manual respectively. Title Pages will be prepared in manuscript.

Place	Date	Hour	Summary of Events and Information	Remarks and references to Appendices
ENGLEBELMER	29-6-16	–	Bombardment continued as on previous day. Conditions slightly improved but ground still sodden. "Y1" day.	
"	30-6-16	–	"Y2" day. From minute observation of the enemy's line we observed ~~that~~ a portion of it was occupied as officers' dugouts. After preliminary reconnaissance by day we moved forward the machine guns under cover of darkness & engaged ~~the target~~ with four guns, obviously with very good results as these dugouts do not show now any signs of being inhabited.	

A. Morris Captain Comdg
88th M.G. Coy.

2449 Wt. W14957/M90 750,000 1/16 J.B.C. & A. Forms/C.2118/12.

Appendix "A".

Operation Order No I   Copy No 6

By

Captain A. Morris Comds

88th Bgde Machine Gun Company

Englebelmer

Ref Trench Map 57D S.E.   23.6.16

I Information (a) Own Troops;

The 88th Bgde will advance to take the German 3rd Line.

(b) The Enemy;

Are entrenched.

II Intention The G.O.C. intends to use all the available Machine Guns of the Brigade to cover the right Flank and afford covering fire when possible to the advancing troops. Machine Guns allotted to units will reach the consolidated position as soon as possible in order to meet the counter attack. The Reserve guns will be in position at Artillery Lane (approximately) and will go forward on the first available opportunity for defensive purposes.

III Distribution No I Section will be at the disposal of Officers Commanding

Lt H.A. Bingley, Wor: The Worcestershire and Essex Regiments:

" C.S. Parsons, Essex Commanders as per margin.

Fire control commander as per margin.

Lt C.H. Kelf-Reveley-Nfld. No 2 Section has been allotted to the Officers Commanding.

" R.F.L. Owen Hampshire Newfoundland and Hampshire Regts: Commanders as per margin

Capt H.S. Windeler. Fire control commander as per margin.

Lt Johnston No 3 + 4 Sections form the Brigade Reserve under Capt A. Morris.

" J. Chalmers

IV Formations The formations to be adopted will be :- (1) Lines of Sections in File or single file. (2) Lines of Teams in file at 50 paces interval and 250 yards distance.

V Ammunition Will be brought forward by specially detailed Ammunition carriers. Distribution as follows:-

		No of Boxes per gun
No 3 & 5 of each gun 2 Boxes each	=	4
5 Ammunition Carriers 2 Boxes each	=	10
Total Boxes per gun	=	14

Officer in charge of Ammunition Supply 2Lt W.H. Fay — In addition there will be 3 full Belts per gun as already detailed making a total of 4250 rounds per gun. When the Guns are actually in position 2 ammunition carriers per gun will be retained to bring back empty belt boxes. The remaining 3 Ammunition Carriers per gun will be sent back to Lt Fay who will march them to the rear. Ammunition carriers will wear a distinguishing mark

6 Communication — Will be by telephone if possible, otherwise by flag or Orderly who will wear the distinction armlet as issued.

The following signals will be used :- A = We want ammunition
W = We want water.

7 Oil & Discs — Spare oil will be carried in the spare parts box. Every man will wear a tin triangular disc with a Red Line on obverse and reverse sides from apex to centre of base of the triangle.

8 Water & Tools — The N.C.O of each team will carry a two gallon petrol tin of Water in his pack as practiced. Every man will be in possession of a pick or a spade, the ratio being 2 picks to each gun. the remainder spades.

9 Range finders & Range Cards — The range finders will be carried by Sgt Newman & the Coy. Sgt Major. Range cards made from the map have been issued to all concerned.

10 Reports — Will be sent to 88th M.G. Coy Headquarters, ARTILLERY LANE.

11 Transport — The Transport of the Company will remain at ACHEUX.

A Morris Captain

Issued at 2100 — Commanding 88th Bgde M.G. Coy

Copy No 1 Operation Order file — By Orderly
" 2 Brigade Major 88th Bgde — " "
" 3 Fire control Commander — " "
" 4 Ammunition Supply Officer — " "
" 5 O.C. 88th M.G. Company — " "
" 6 D.A.G. 3rd Echelon — By Post
" 7 O i/c Records M.G. Corps — " "
91 York Street Westminster

Copy No I

Operation Order No I
By
Captain A. Morris Comdg.
88th M. G. Company.

Englebelmer.

Ref. Trench. Map. 57 D S.E 23. 6. 16

1 Information (A) Own troops

~~The 88th Brigade will advance to take the~~

The 88th Brigade will advance to take the German 3rd line.

(B) The Enemy

Are entrenched.

2. Intentions

The G. O. C. intends to use all the available machine Guns of the Brigade to cover the right flank and afford covering fire when possible to the advancing troops. Machine Guns allotted to units will be reach the consolidated position as soon as possible in order to meet the counter attack. The reserve guns will be in position at ARTILLERY LANE (approximately) and will go forward the first available opportunity for defensive purposes.

3. Distribution

2/Lieut N.O Bingley Worcestershire
Lieut C.S. Parsons Essex

No I Section will be at the disposal of O's Commanding The Worcestershire and Essex Regiments
Commanders as per margin

2 Lieut Reveley Newfoundland
Lieut Owen Hampshire

No 2 Section has been allotted to the O's C. Newfoundland and Hampshire Regts. Commanders as per margin

Fire Control Commander
Captain. H.S Windeler

Notes Div: Conference

Stokes Bombs

Field Coy Commanders

C.O's not to be under Machine Gun
under
Captain. H.S. Windeler
Fire Control Commander

Each Machine Gun should have

Fort Jackson
Whittington Avenue
88th

Our Guns are only allotted for
protection of battalions
4 Guns accompanying each line

They are all under Windeler
Fire Control Command

Pam 34 plant
35 ouiter 80+
50 Machine Guns
14 boxes per gun

88th M.G. Coy.

Precis on Preparations for Operations.

I. Ammunition. Each gun in yellow line will have 10,000 S.A.A. for immediate use & at the moment of advance will be in possession of 4250 S.A.A. in belts.
Each gun with the Bge. units will have in its possession 4250 S.A.A. at moment of advance.
A reserve of S.A.A. is dumped at
A reserve of 72000 is on wheels at Ecclesx

2. Dumps. Each gun in yellow line has its own dumps beside it for water, rations & ammun.

3. Rations. Are provided for 4 days in Vodoulet line + each man has his day's ration & iron ration in his possession.

4. Water – Reserve of 80 gallons in Vodoulet line
5. Accomodation – Stores & 20 men in cellar at 104.
20 men in cellar at 105.
Hq. in Elephant in Orchard behind 105.

6. Oil – sufficient for several days carried in sp. pts. boxes.
7. Targets – As per map from yellow line & as per range cards for Artillery Lane.

8. Bearing right hand corner Bois d'Hollande.
Magnetic 1° 30 N.W. from
True bearing 15° – 6 W.

Distribution

2 Lieut. Johnston
2 Lieut Chalmers.

The Nos 3 and 4 Sections form the Brigade reserve. under Capt A Morris.

4. Formations

The formations to be adopted will be
(I) Lines of Sections in file or single file
(ii) Lines of teams in file at 50 paces interval and 250 yards distance.

5 Ammunition.

Will be brought forward by specially detailed ammunition carriers distribution as follows.

Officer in charge of Ammunition Supply.

2 Lieut. W. H. Fry.

	No of Boxes per gun
No's 1 and 3 of each gun 2 boxes each =	4
5 ammunition carriers " " =	10
Total boxes per gun =	14

In addition there will be 3 full belts per gun. as already detailed making a total of 4,250 rounds per gun. When the guns are actually in position 2 ammunition carriers per gun will be retained to bring back empty belt boxes. The remaining three ammunition carriers will be sent back to Lieut. Fry who will march them to the rear. Ammunition carriers will wear a distinction mark.

6. Communication – Will be by telephone if possible otherwise by flag or orderly who will wear the distinction armlet as issued.

The following signals will be used.

A = We want Ammunition
W = " " Water.

7. Oil and Discs.

Spare oil will be carried in the spare part box. Every man will ~~be~~ wear a tin triangular disc with a red line on obverse and reverse sides from apex to centre of base of the triangle.

8 Water and Tools.

~~Every man will~~ The N.C.O of each team will carry a two gallon petrol tin of water in his pack as practised. Every man will be in possession of a pick or a ~~shovel~~ spade The ratio being 2 picks to each gun the remainder spades.

9. Range Finders and Range Cards.

The Range finders will be carried by Sgt Newman and the Coy Sgt Major. Range cards made from the map have been issued to all concerned.

10. Reports will be sent to 88th M.G. Company Headquarters. Artillery Lane.

Issued at 2100

Copy No I Operation Order File
" No 2 Brigade Major
" No 3 Fire Control Commander ~~Captain H.S. Wardle~~
" No 4 Ammunition Supply Officer
" No 5 O.C. 88th M.G. Coy.

A.Morris Captain Comdg.
88th Machine Gun Company.

By orderly.
2150.

II Transport. The transport of the body [illegible] [illegible] at [illegible].

(Copy No 6)

1

Operation Order No. I.

By

Captain A. Morris Comdg.

88th. M.G. Coy.

Englebelmer.

Ref. French Map 57D. S.E. 23-6-16.

I. Information. (a) Own troops;

The 88th. Bge. will advance to take the German 3rd. line.

(b) The Enemy;

Are entrenched.

II. Intention. The G.O.C. intends to use all the available Machine Guns of the Bge. to cover the right flank & afford covering fire when possible to the advancing troops. Machine guns allotted to units will reach the consolidated position as soon as possible in order to meet the counter attack. The reserve guns will be in position at ARTILLERY LANE (approximately) & will go forward on the first available opportunity for defensive purposes.

III. Distribution. No. I Section will be at the disposal of O.s

Lt. N.O. Dingley, Worcestershire. Commanding The Worcestershire & Essex Regts:

Lt. C.S. Parsons, Essex. Commanders as per margin.

Fire control commander as per margin.

Lt. C.H. Jeff-Rowley, N.F.L.D. No. 2 Section has been allotted to the O.s C.

Lt. R.F.L. Owen, Hampshire. Newfoundland & Hampshire Regts: Commanders as per margin.

Capt. H.S. Windeler. Fire control commander as per margin.

Lt. Johnston. No. 3 & 4 Sections form the Brigade Reserve

Lt. J. Chalmers. under Capt. A. Morris.

IV. Formations. The formations to be adopted will be:

(i) Lines of Sections in file or single file.

(ii) Lines of teams in file at 50 paces interval and 250 yards distance.

5. Ammunition. Will be brought forward by specially detailed ammunition carriers.

Officer in charge of Ammunition Supply: 2nd Lt. W. H. Fry.

Distribution as follows:

		No. OF BOXES PER GUN.
Nos. 3 & 5 of each gun 2 boxes each	=	4
5 ammunition carriers 2 boxes each	=	10
Total boxes per gun	=	14

In addition there will be 3 full belts per gun as already detailed making a total of 4250 rounds per gun. When the guns are actually in position 2 ammunition carriers per gun will be retained to bring back empty belt boxes. The remaining 3 ammn. carriers per gun will be sent back to 2nd Lt. Fry who will march them to the rear. Ammunition carriers will wear a distinguishing mark.

6 Communication. Will be by telephone if possible, otherwise by flag or orderly who will wear the distinction armlet as issued.

The following signals will be used:

A. - We want ammunition.

W. - We want water.

7. Oil & Discs. Spare oil will be carried in the spare parts box. Every man will wear a tin triangular disc with a red line on obverse & reverse sides from apex to centre of base of the triangle.

8. Water & Tools. The N.C.O. of each team will carry a two gallon petrol tin of water in his pack as practised. Every man will be in possession of a pick or a spade, the ratio being 2 picks to each gun, the remainder spades.

9. Rangefinders & Range Cards. The rangefinders will be carried by Sgt. Newman & the Coy. Sergt. Major. Range cards made from the map have been issued to all concerned.

10 Reports. Will be sent to 88th M.G. Coy. Headquarters, Artillery Lane.

11. Transport. The transport of the Coy. will remain at Acheux.

A Morris Lieut Comm'd.
88th M.G. Coy.

Issued at 2100.

Copy No 1 Operation order file
" 2 Brigade Major 88th Brigade
" 3. Fire Control Commander
" 4. Ammunition Supply officer
" 5. O.C. 88th M.G. Coy
" 6. D.A.G. 3rd Echelon
" 7. O i/c Records M.G. Corps
91 York. Street Westminster

Coy orderly.
2150 hrs

Coy Post

4 Guns each time

[illegible] to each

Bea [illegible]

Zero [illegible]

2 pm 2.40

from Station Road — 2nd line

7 day [illegible]

4.2 forming up [illegible]

MGs! Machine Guns going to regiments

Mailly. Headquarters

Essex Right of Q.17.22
Left Q to 16.6
Right
Left

Mary Redan Trench
Dragoon

Right of Newfoundland Regt
Left of Essex

Station alley

After crossing

2 from Station Road
to 2nd line.

On crossing the German 2nd line
a partial wheel will be made
at 2.30 advance will [illegible]
to Puisieux Road.
at 3.10 advance to the assault

Operation Order No I Copy No

By

Captain A. Morris Comdg

88th Bgde Machine Gun Company

Englebelmer

Ref Trench Map 57D S.E. 23.6.16

I Information (a) Own Troops;

The 88th Bgde will advance to take the German 3rd Line.

(b) The Enemy;

Are entrenched.

II Intention The G.O.C. intends to use all the available Machine Guns of the Brigade to cover the right Flank and afford covering fire when possible to the advancing troops. Machine Guns allotted to units will reach the consolidated position as soon as possible in order to meet the counter attack. The reserve guns will be in position at Artillery Lane (approximately) and will go forward on the first available opportunity for defensive purposes.

III Distribution No I Section will be at the disposal of Officers Commanding

Lt. N.O. Bingley, Wors: The Worcestershire and Essex Regiments:

" C.S. Parsons, Essex Commanders as per margin.

Fire control commander as per margin.

Lt C.H. Fell-Reveley NFLD. No 2 Section has been allotted to the Officers Commanding.

" R.F.L. Owen Hampshire Newfoundland and Hampshire Regts: Commanders as per margin

Capt. H.S. Windeler. Fire control commander as per margin.

Lt Johnston No 3 & 4 Sections form the Brigade Reserve under Capt. A. Morris.

" J. Chalmers

IV Formations The formations to be adopted will be :- (1) Lines of Sections in file or single file. (2) Lines of Teams in file at 50 paces interval and 250 yards distance.

V Ammunition Will be brought forward by specially detailed Ammunition carriers. Distribution as follows :-

		No of Boxes per gun
No 3 & 5 of each gun 2 Boxes each	=	4
5 Ammunition Carriers 2 Boxes each	=	10
Total Boxes per gun	=	14

Officer in charge of Ammunition Supply 2/Lt W.H. Fay — In addition there will be 3 full Belts per gun as already detailed making a total of 4250 Rounds per gun. When the Guns are actually in position 2 ammunition carriers per gun will be retained to bring back empty belt boxes. The remaining 3 Ammunition carriers per gun will be sent back to Lt Fay who will march them to the rear. Ammunition carriers will wear a distinguishing mark

6 Communication — Will be by telephone if possible, otherwise by Flag or Orderly who will wear the distinction armlet as issued.
The following signals will be used :- A = We want ammunition W = We want water.

7 Oil & Discs — Spare oil will be carried in the spare parts box. Every man will wear a tin triangular disc with a Red Line on obverse and reverse sides from apex to centre of base of the triangle.

8 Water & Tools — The N.C.O of each team will carry a two gallon petrol tin of Water in his pack as practiced. Every man will be in possession of a pick or a spade, the ratio being 2 picks to each gun. The remainder spades.

9 Range finders & Range Cards — The range finders will be carried by Sgt Newman & the Coy. Sgt Major. Range cards made from the map have been issued to all concerned.

10 Reports — Will be sent to 88th M.G. Coy Headquarters, Artillery Lane.

11 Transport — The Transport of the Company will remain at Acheux.

Issued at 8100

Captain
Commanding 88th Bgde M.G. Coy

Copy No 1	Operation Order file	By Orderly
" " 2	Brigade Major 88th Bgde	" "
" " 3	Fire control Commander	" "
" " 4	Ammunition Supply Officer	" "
" " 5	O.C. 88th M.G. Company	" "
" " 6	D.A.G. 3rd Echelon	By Post
" " 7	O/C Records M.G. Corps 91 York Street Westminster	" "

S E C R E T .   4th Division No. GGG 766/61

29th Division.

The following signals will be fired by 10th Brigade by day if necessary :-

2 White lights from a Very Pistol in quick succession -
"Held up by machine Gun fire"

1 White light -
"Held up by uncut wire".

(Signed) H.G.N. FELLOWES, Capt.
for Lieut-Colonel,
General Staff 4th Division.

28/6/16.

-2-

29th Divn G.S.
G.S.S. 55/5 d/t 28/6/16

88th Brigade.

For information.

(Signed) W.M. ARMSTRONG Capt.
for Lieut-Colonel, G.S.
29th Division.

28/6/16.

-3-

HEADQUARTERS,
88th INFANTRY BDE.
No. B 354
Date 29 . 6 . 16

O. C.,
88th Machine Gun Company.

For information.

Thos H Loone Captain,
Brigade Major, 88th Brigade.

29/6/16.

29th Divn.
I.G.44.
28/6/16.

SECRET.

88th Brigade.

1. Daily Intelligence Summaries will be ~~ee~~ discontinued in their present form from the 28th instant till further orders.

2. During operations Brigades will render situation reports every hour by priority telegram, commencing 3-30 a.m. on the 29th. In addition to these every event of importance must be reported by telegram immediately.

3. All items of intelligence should be reported at once, such as :-

(a) Identification.

(b) Important matters obtained from documents.

(c) Information as to arrival of reserves.

(d) Number of prisoners and guns taken.

(e) Morale of the enemy.

(Sgd) W.M. ARMSTRONG Captain,G.S.

28th June 1916. 29th Division.

-2-

O. C.,

88th Machine Gun Coy.

The above for your information.

G.B. Arnold 2nd Lieut.

30/6/16. Intelligence Officer, 88th Brigade.

88th Brigade. 29th Div. I.G. 50 29/6/16.

In continuation of this office I.G. 50 the following additional instructions are issued for the use of Intelligence Officers:-

(1) Identity Discs will not be removed from Prisoners.

(2) Papers and SOLDBUCHS will be left on private soldiers prisoners until they reach Divisional Compounds.

(3) N.C.O's will be relieved of all documents as soon as clear of the battle zone.

(4) Officers will be releived of all documents immediately on capture.

(5) Documents taken from Officers and N.C.O's will be carried by their escort to the Divisional Compounds.

(6) Identity Discs will be removed from the dead with their SOLDBUCHS and ~~and~~ Documents.

(Sgd) W.M. ARMSTRONG, Capt. G.S.

29th June 1916. 29th Division.

-2-

O. C.,

88th Machine Gun Company.

For your information.

G. B. Arnold 2nd Lieut.

30/6/16. Intelligence Officer 88th Brigade.

S E C R E T. COPY NO. 6.

29th DIVISION ORDER NO. 41.

28th June, 1916

1. With reference to C.G.S. 55/3 of 27th instant, Zero will be postpondd 48 hours.
   29th June will be called "Y" 1 Day.
   30th June will be called "Y 2" Day.
   1st July will be "Z" Day.

2. No alteration in the present dispositions of the Division will be made.

3. (a) The artillery programme will be carried out as for to-day, special attention being paid to the following :-

   (i) The prevention of all hostile movements and work both by day and night; the night bombardments must therefore be fully maintained.

   (ii) The completion of wire cutting.

   (iii) Counter-battery work, advantage being taken of all favourable weather to destroy hostile batteries.

   (b) Concentrated bombardments will take place as follows:-

   "Y 1" Day.....................4-00 p.m. to 5-20 p.m.
   "Y 2" Day.....................8-00 a.m. to 9.20 a.m.

4. With reference to para 3 (a) of 29th Division Order No. 39 a reconnaissance of wire on the enemy's front will be carried out between the hours named below:-

   "Y" night.....................11.30 a.m. to 12.30 p.m.
   "Y 1" night...................10.30 a.m. to 11.30 a.m.
   "Y 2" night...................11.00 a.m. to 12 midnight.

5. The programme for "Z" day will be as originally arranged.

6. Watches will be synchronised by the General Staff at 9.0 a.m. and 7.0 p.m. on "Y 1" and "Y 2" days.

7. Please acknowledge.

(Sgd) C.G. FULLER,
Lieut.Colonel. G.S.
29th Division.

Issued at 10.30p.m.

Copies 1 - 3 General Staff
4 86th Brigade
5 87th Brigade
6 88th Brigade
7 C. R. A.
8 C. R. E.
9 Officer i/c Signals
10 A.A. & Q.M.G.
11 O.C. 252nd Tunnelling Coy.
12 O.C. 1/2nd Monmouth Regt.

Forwarded for information

[illegible]

Information re Enemy Area opposite VIII.Corps Front.

BEAUCOURT SUR ANCRE

There is an Ammunition Depot at R7d 20.89

From M.CADET Fortuna Maire of BEAUCOURT refugeed at St OUEN,house of M.MOUTARDIER schoolmaster.

GRANDCOURT

German Officers Club at R9b 16.10

Ammunition limbers are parked at R 9c 30.90 to R 8d 90.72

Ammunition Depot at R 9b 40.15 to R 9b 20.15.

Entrance to Subterranean CAVES at R 9d 36.82. This subterranean is quite important;old books mention it,but no further details could be obtained.

From M.CARON late curé of GRANDCOURT,now at FLESSELLES.

MIRAUMONT

At point R 5a 48.98 is the entrance to a subterranean passage which reaches BEAUREGARE DOVECOTE. The entrance has been closed by M. DUBOURGUIER. The passage is big enough to contain a horse and cart.

At R 5c 18.46 there is an entrance to a subterranean gallery, 100 metres in extension,4 to 5 metres high & 3 metres wide. This gallery was made in 1880.

At point L 25 d 12.88. is the entrance to a Chalk Quarry ; at the entrance,under a mound it is from 8 to 10 metres high. There are several passages,all of which run in the direction of IRLES church at about G 31b 91.78. There is no exit at IRLES.
As one goes Eastward the galleries get smaller,but all the way through,there is ample room for a man to walk.

From M.DUBOURGUIER Doyen de VILLERS-BOCCAGE and from Lieut.CAFFIN and Pte.Eugene ARRACHART 16th French Territorial Infantry Regt. 11th Coy.

Information gained by Interpreter M.H.Reis.

Copy No I

Operation orders No I by Captain A Morris Comdg 88th M.G. Coy.

Ref: Trench map 57 D S.E   Englebelmer.

I Information
(a) own troops

(b) Enemy

II Intention Heavy tripods will be used in the advance.

III Distribution

Worcestershire Regt = 2 guns under Lieut H.O. Dingley; ~~Essex~~ Regt 2 guns under Lieut C.S. Parson	No I Section is allotted to the Assaulting line. as per margin. No I Section
Newfoundland Regt 2 guns under 2 Lieut C.H. Reveley; Hampshire Regt 2 guns under Lieut R.F.L. Owen	No 2 Section is allotted to the reserve line as per margin. No 2 Section. Fire Control Commanders as per margin.

Fire Control Commanders Captain N.S. Windeler.

No 3 Section under 2 Lieut H.B. Johnston; No 4 Section under 2 Lieut and A/adjt J. Chalmers	No 3 and 4 Section will form the Brigade Machine Gun Reserve. Commander Captain A. Morris

IV Ammunition

1

By ammunition carriers and spare numbers under the command of an officer named in the margin

2/Lieut. W. H Fry.

	No. of boxes
Nos 3 and 5 of each gun	~~4~~
5 Ammunition Carriers	10
3 loose belts in pack for each gun	14
Total per gun 14	

3,500 rounds.
~~3,500~~ 750 = 4250

Detail has been issued verbally.

The ammunition carriers on ~~having~~ delivering the box ammunition will be marched back to bring up reserve ammunition.

These men will carry forward the heavy tripods under darkness

V Water

Each non-commissioned officer of each gun will carry a two gallon petrol tin filled with water in his pack. This will allow for the replenishment of ~~water~~ barrel casing twice.

VI Spare parts, bill and range finder

No 4 ~~will~~ of each gun will carry the spare parts ~~wallet~~. Box

The range finder will be carried by N.C.O as per margin, Officers

Sgt Newman.

(ii) Belt filling machines will be with the reserve guns.

VII Transport

VIII Communication Signals

Visual stations of passive in the event of no Telephonic communication.

Fourth Army No. Q.G. 647.
Vlllth Corps No. 1872/Q.
29th Division No. A. 406/193.

Vlll Corps.

It has been brought to notice that some units are demanding components over and above their immediate require:ments. Stocks at the Base for extra components do not admit of spares being retained with units, and therefore Corps must ensure that demands are limited to actual requirements.

Sd/ H.C. SUTTON, Maj.Gen.,

27/6/16. D.A. & Q.M.G., Fourth A.

(2)

Headquarters,

88th Brigade.

For information.

Sd/ P. FRASER, Major,

28/6/16. D.A.Q.M.G., 29th Division.

(3)

Officer Commanding,

88th M. G. Company.

HEADQUARTERS,
88th INFANTRY BDE.
No. A 1058
Date.

For information and compliance.

[signature] Captain,

29/6/16. Staff Captain, 88th Infantry Brigade.

29th Division.

88th Infantry Brigade.

88th MACHINE GUN COMPANY

JULY 1916

Army Form C. 2118.

Instructions regarding War Diaries and Intelligence Summaries are contained in F. S. Regs., Part II. and the Staff Manual respectively. Title Pages will be prepared in manuscript.

WAR DIARY
or
~~INTELLIGENCE SUMMARY~~

(Erase heading not required.)

88th Brigade Machine Gun Coy.

Place	Date	Hour	Summary of Events and Information	Remarks and references to Appendices
ENGLEBELMER	1-7-16	7.30am	Headquarters left ENGLEBELMER & proceeded to Concentration point in our front trench at Q17b70/60. The "UP" trench (WIGHTINGTON AVE) was clear & had not been damaged by bombardment but its parapets were being subjected to continuous M.G. fire. From KNIGHTSBRIDGE forward progress was interrupted by wounded & in a few places trenches were	MAP 57D S.E. 1&2.
		8.20am	damaged by shell fire. Concentration point was reached at 8.20 am. & the	
		8.30am	concentration of the eight reserve guns was complete at 8.30am. Officers in charge of sections at once reconnoitred our front trench with a view to finding suitable points at which their teams could leave the trench & pass through our own wire. During the reconnaissance they found that enemy M.Gs. & snipers had all the lanes in our wire covered. The Brigade attacked at 8.50 am. but was held up by M.G. fire. The Company was ordered to remain where it was till further orders. The nearest available dugouts were used for cover for men & guns, the enemy shelling now being very heavy on the front line. Orders to move were issued	
		2.30pm	at 2.30 pm. when the reserve half company was ordered to take up gun positions in the front system with a view to defense. An hour later the guns from the units were ordered to rejoin the Company at HYDE PARK CORNER. As they assembled they were detailed to occupy positions for defensive purposes. When all were in position the Company had six guns in the redoubt line & ten in the front line. Casualties: During the day we lost two N.C.Os. of the Company & two ammunition carriers (attached). Coy. Hq. were fixed at KNIGHTSBRIDGE & telephonic communication was established	

2449 Wt. W14957/M90 750,000 1/16 J.B.C. & A. Forms/C.2118/12.

A.W. Morris Capt. Comdt
88th M. G. Coy

Instructions regarding War Diaries and Intelligence Summaries are contained in F. S. Regs., Part II. and the Staff Manual respectively. Title Pages will be prepared in manuscript.

WAR DIARY
or
~~INTELLIGENCE SUMMARY~~

(Erase heading not required.)

Army Form C. 2118.

88th Brigade Machine Gun Coy.

Place	Date	Hour	Summary of Events and Information	Remarks and references to Appendices
			with the redoubt line. Everything was prepared with a view to a probable counterattack that night; each gun was supplied with 6500 S.A.A. rounds & a tin of reserve water while spare numbers were accommodated in deep dugouts, while all precautions were taken against gas.	
KNIGHTSBRIDGE	2-7-16	—	The night of 1st/2nd passed without other incident than the heavy shelling of our lines both by high explosive & heavy shrapnel. Our guns had orders to prevent the enemy from repairing his wire. Fire was limited by the fact that we had many wounded in NO MANS LAND, many of them near the enemy wire, & by the work of our stretcher bearers & rescue parties. As a result of the shelling on this date we lost four ammn. carriers wounded. During the day the enemy were observed bringing up gas cylinders. Orders for the probable counterattack were again issued but except for very heavy shelling the night passed without incident.	
	3-7-16	—	The work of clearing the trenches was carried on. The guns kept intermittent fire on the enemy wire which he did not attempt to repair. Operations were very	
	4 " "	—	much hampered on the 4th & 5th by very heavy rains which rendered conditions	
	5 " "	—	in the trenches very trying. On the 4th inst. we lost an N.C.O. killed & a man & an ammn. carrier wounded. The enemy shell fire was very heavy: it was responsible for all our casualties. On the 5th inst. we took over more front from the 4th Division which necessitated bringing two more guns forward from the redoubt line. We then had 12 guns in the front system. The four in the redoubt line were relieved the same night by the 86th M.G. Coy. & returned to Billets in Englebelmer.	

A. M. Morris Captain Comdg
88th M. G. Coy

Instructions regarding War Diaries and Intelligence Summaries are contained in F. S. Regs., Part II. and the Staff Manual respectively. Title Pages will be prepared in manuscript.

WAR DIARY

~~or~~

~~INTELLIGENCE SUMMARY~~

(Erase heading not required.)

88th Brigade Machine Gun Coy.

Army Form C. 2118.

Place	Date	Hour	Summary of Events and Information	Remarks and references to Appendices
KNIGHTSBRIDGE.	6-7-16	—	Weather conditions improved. Reorganisation of trenches was completed the 48th Div. taking over part of the right of our line thus allowing us to relieve two guns at Shooters' Hill. We were thus left with the guns in the line & six in reserve. Coy. HQ. removed from Knightsbridge to Englebelmer.	
ENGLEBELMER.	7-7-16 to 12-7-16	—	Owing to the activity of our patrols & wiring parties there was very little M.G. activity during this period. Improvements in overhead cover of new emplacements were carried out. Enemy wire Y RAVINE & the HAWHTORN CRATER were the chief targets engaged. Enemy activity was confined to shelling of our front system. Trenches were damaged but no emplacements were hit during this period. On the 12th inst. the six guns in reserve relieved six guns in the front line. A new position in A. Street was selected & occupied its object being to cover the point of MARY REDAN.	
"	13-7-16	—	In compliance with Bgde. Operation Order No. 14 dated 13th July a fire programme was arranged for the ten guns in the line. Orders were issued for a barrage of the German front system from Q17a 90/80 to Q11c 50/40, 1st rapid fire on the whole front at 3.15am. 2nd violent bursts till 3.45 am, 3rd fire at irregular intervals throughout the day. The front to be raided by the Hampshire Regt. from Q10 d 80/98 to Q10b 80/25 was also specially covered with a view to heavy fire after the raid. Fire programme after daylight was fixed as follows: One belt at each of the following periods by each gun, — 5am, 6.25am, 7.10am, 9 am, 9.15am, 10.50am, 1.30pm, 1.50pm, 3.5pm.	57D SE 1+2
"	14-7-16	—	The scheme as detailed above was successfully carried out. Enemy retaliation was very severe. Several gun positions were damaged but we had only one casualty (slightly wounded). One direct hit resulted in the destruction of an emplacement, the gun therein being put out of action & several ammn. boxes destroyed. A gun from reserve was sent to replace the one rendered unserviceable & the programme duly completed.	

A. Morris Capt. Comdg
88th M.G. Coy.

88th BRIGADE MACHINE GUN COMPANY. No. .... Date ....

2449 Wt. W14957/M90 750,000 1/16 J.B.C. & A. Forms/C.2118/12.

Army Form C. 2118.

WAR DIARY
or
~~INTELLIGENCE SUMMARY~~

(Erase heading not required.)

Instructions regarding War Diaries and Intelligence Summaries are contained in F. S. Regs., Part II. and the Staff Manual respectively. Title Pages will be prepared in manuscript.

88th Brigade Machine Gun Coy.

Place	Date	Hour	Summary of Events and Information	Remarks and references to Appendices
ENGLEBELMER	14-7-16	—	The enemy retaliated heavily during the night but caused us no further damage. The trenches suffered severely but the dugouts + emplacements escaped.	
"	15-7-16	—	The orders issued for the day were "Intermittent bombardment lasting for 3 minutes will take place in conjunction with 4th Division at 11.30 am. 2 pm. + 5 pm. today. Bombardment will be accompanied by heavy bursts of machine gun fire." This was carried out. Enemy retaliation during the day was weak but towards night it became vigorous.	
"	16-7-16	—	The following scheme was prepared:— 11 pm to 11.10 pm; 11.45 pm to 11.50 pm; 12.15 am to 1.0 am; 1.5 am to 1.20 am; 1.25 am to 1.40 am; 1.50 am to 2 am; Cease fire at 2 am. } of ½ belt should be used for each period for each gun. Particular attention must be paid to Wagon Road & the Y Ravine. This programme was duly carried out.	
"	17-7-16	—	The following orders were issued:— "There will be a discharge of gas tonight. All guns will engage the enemy's line so as to drown the noise of escaping gas except the A.A. gun which will not fire. There will be no fire south of a point 200 yds. north of point 03 (Q17b 05/35). The fire will commence at Zero (an hour to be notified later) & will on no account continue after 1.30 after Zero." This scheme was not carried out. The wind was adverse making gas discharge impossible. Enemy shelling was very heavy. Englebelmer was most heavily shelled.	57D S.E. 1 + 2.
"	18-7-16	—	The Company was relieved by the 87th M.G. Coy. + returned to Hq. at Englebelmer.	

2449 Wt. W14957/M90 750,000 1/16 J.B.C. & A. Forms/C.2118/12.

A. Morris Capt Comd 88th M. G. Coy

Army Form C. 2118.

Instructions regarding War Diaries and Intelligence Summaries are contained in F. S. Regs., Part II. and the Staff Manual respectively. Title Pages will be prepared in manuscript.

WAR DIARY
or
INTELLIGENCE ~~SUMMARY~~

(Erase heading not required.)

88th Machine Gun Company.

Place	Date	Hour	Summary of Events and Information	Remarks and references to Appendices
ENGLEBELMER	19-7-16	–	Overhaul of all guns, spare parts, ammn. etc. Worn barrels replaced & damaged guns repaired. Hot baths procured for the whole Company at [illegible]. Extract from Divisional Order received:– "The 88th Bge. will make emplacements for eight machine guns in rear positions in the area bounded on the right by the line Q 18 c 29 – PROSPECT POINT, & on the left by the Southern boundary of the Left Brigade Sector." "In addition to the above emplacements Brigades will select forward positions & if necessary construct emplacements for their remaining eight machine guns per Brigade. These positions should enable a heavy machine gun fire at short range to be brought to bear on the enemy's front line trenches." In accordance with above a reconnaissance of the new area was made & positions selected.	
"	20-7-16	–	Work was begun on the rear gun positions in new area. See attached trench map.	Appendix A.
"	21-7-16	}	Work on these positions continued. Enemy comparatively quiet, Englebelmer shelled each night with both H.E. & Shrapnel.	
"	22-7-16	}		
"	23-7-16		The Coy. was relieved by the M.G. Coy. at 5 pm. & route marched to Beauval arrived BEAUVAL at 11.30 pm.	
BEAUVAL	24-7-16		The Company went into billets in Beauval.	
"	25-7-16		Route march with the Brigade	
"	27-7-16		The Coy. moved to POPERINGHE. Entrained at CANDAS, one section with its guns, stores & baggage accompanying each Battalion of the Brigade.	
POPERINGHE	28-7-16		Remained at Poperinghe. Arranged baths for all ranks.	

A.Morris Capt Comdg
88th M.G. Coy

2449 Wt. W14957/M90 750,000 1/16 J.B.C. & A. Forms/C.2118/12.

Instructions regarding War Diaries and Intelligence Summaries are contained in F. S. Regs., Part II. and the Staff Manual respectively. Title Pages will be prepared in manuscript.

WAR DIARY
or
INTELLIGENCE SUMMARY

(Erase heading not required.)

Army Form C. 2118.

Place	Date	Hour	Summary of Events and Information	Remarks and references to Appendices
POPERINGHE	29-7-16	9 p.m.	Entrained for YPRES. Arrived at Ypres & took over from the 16th M.G. Coy. at 11 pm. Relief was completed by 1.30 am. We took over 15 gun positions.	
YPRES	30-7-16	—	Positions occupied as shown on attached map. They have been sited with a view to defensive measures only. The enemy line cannot be covered as in previous sectors. The flatness of the ground makes command difficult. 6A & 6B positions can only be approached at night. Trenches are shallow. Communication trenches are not traversed. Enemy aeroplanes are active & he has an extensive balloon observation system. The sector generally is quiet except for an occasional small calibre shell. No movement has been noticed. Rations & water must be taken up by night & all work carried out is likely to be night work.	Appendix B.
"	31-7-16	—		

A. Morris Captain Comdg
88th M.G. Coy

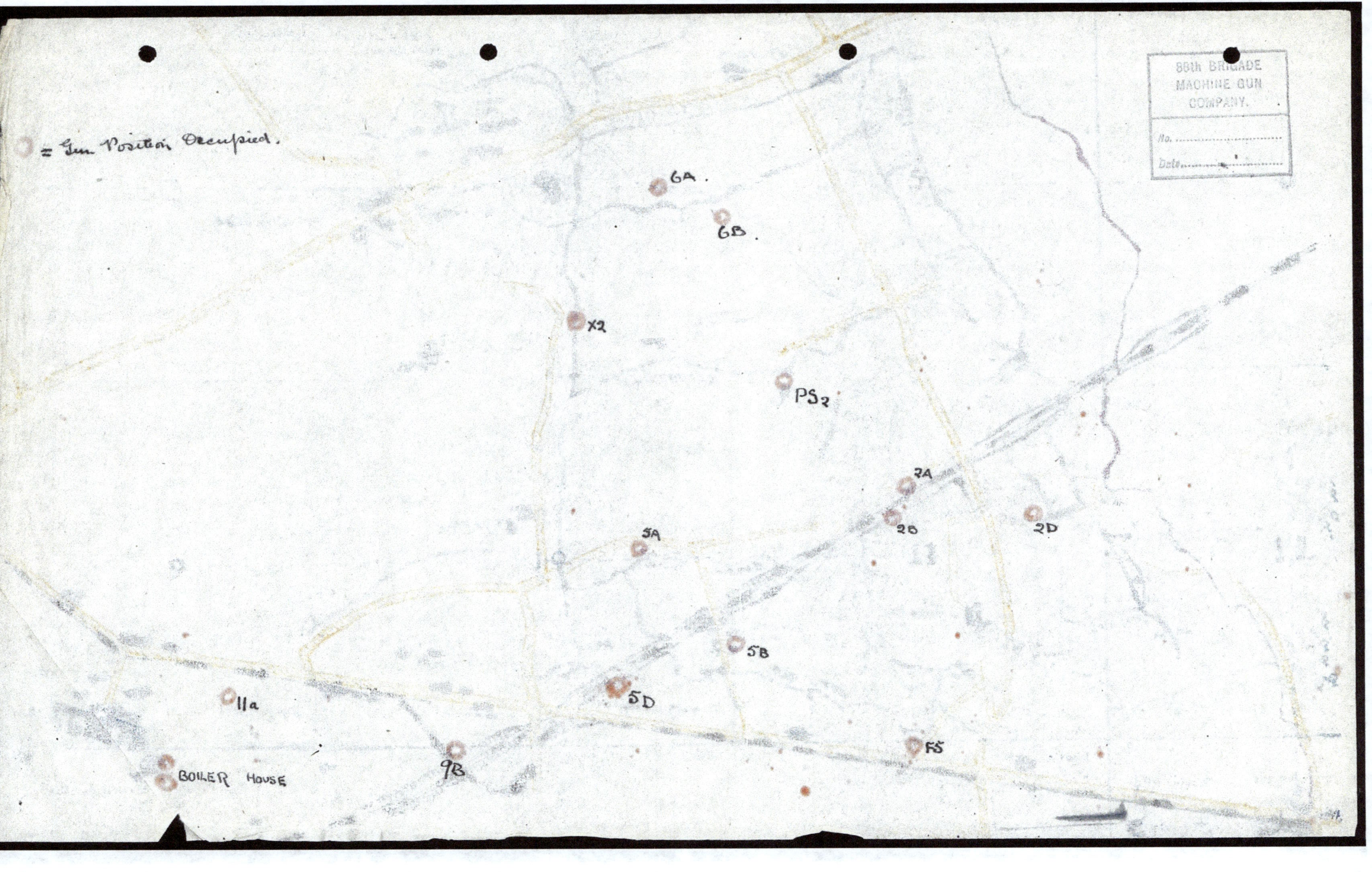
88th BRIGADE
MACHINE GUN
COMPANY.
No.
Date
= Gun Position Occupied.
6A
6B
X2
PS2
2A
2B
2D
5A
5B
5D
11a
9B
F5
BOILER HOUSE

88 M G Coy

29 Vol 4

July 1916

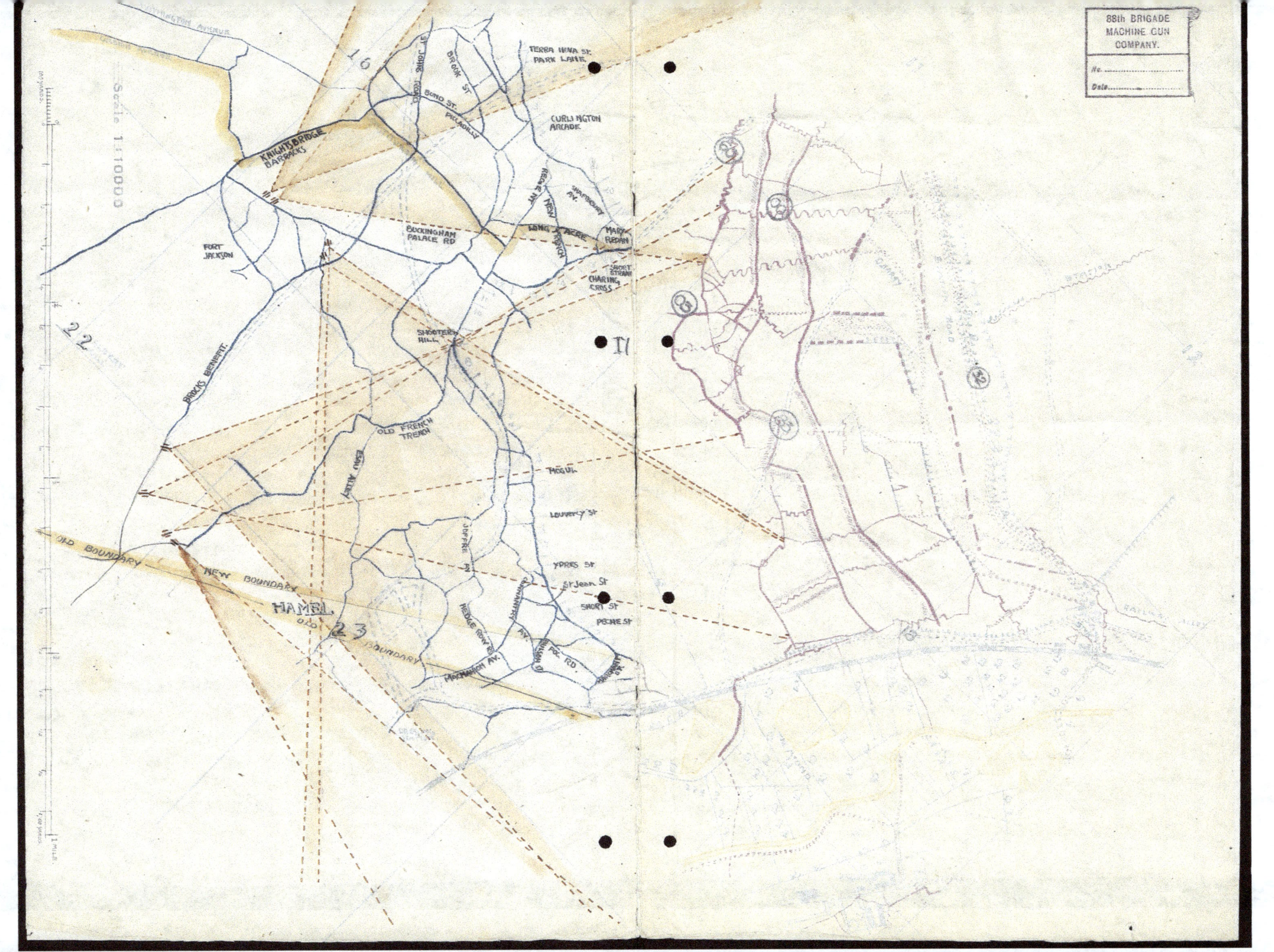

88th BRIGADE
MACHINE GUN
COMPANY.
No.
Date.
Scale 1:10000
KNIGHTSBRIDGE BARRACKS
ST JOHNS ROAD
BROOK ST
BOND ST.
PICCADILLY
TERRA NOVA ST.
PARK LANE
CURLINGTON ARCADE
REGENT ST.
NEW TRENCH
LONG ACRE
MARY REDAN
BUCKINGHAM PALACE RD
SHORT STRAND
CHARING CROSS
FORT JACKSON
SHOOTERS HILL
BRICKS BENEFIT
OLD FRENCH TRENCH
ESAU ALLEY
MOGUL
LOUVERCY ST
JOFFRE AV
YPRES ST
ST JEAN ST
SHORT ST
PEARSE ST
HEDGE ROW
MACMAHON AV.
OLD BOUNDARY
NEW BOUNDARY
HAMEL
1 MILE

" 29th Division.

88th Infantry Brigade.

88th MACHINE GUN COMPANY

AUGUST 1916

Vol 5

Confidential.

War Diary

of

88th. Machine Gun Company.

From 1st. August 1916 To 31st. August 1916.

(Volume V.)

Brigade Major
88th Brigade.

Herewith attached War Diary for the month of August. There has been no usual development in operations from which lessons may be learnt in Machine Gun Tactics. The exceptions being.

1. Retaliation
On taking over this sector the part of the Roulers railway in our area was only to be used subject to the enemy's sufferance. Fresh emplacements were made which controlled his communications and registered and fired upon with the result that his fire was neutralised.

2. Unaimed Fire or Indirect
There are great possibilities of indirect fire facilitated so much by the use of the Elevating and Traversing Dials. A definite fire programme engaging the enemy's line by day and by night has had considerable moral effect. The dictated has become the dictator hence superiority of fire action

31-8-16 A Moore Capt Comdg
88th M. G. Coy

Army Form C. 2118.

Instructions regarding War Diaries and Intelligence Summaries are contained in F. S. Regs., Part II. and the Staff Manual respectively. Title Pages will be prepared in manuscript.

WAR DIARY
or
INTELLIGENCE SUMMARY
(Erase heading not required.)

Place	Date	Hour	Summary of Events and Information	Remarks and references to Appendices
YPRES	1-8-16	–	15 guns in the sector + 1 at Coy. Hq. The condition of the sector demanded (a) a redistribution of guns for defensive + particularly for offensive purposes; (b) building suitable emplacements on the sites selected (c) provision of dugouts for the gun crews (d) drainage. The enemy showed very little offensive action so that continuous night work seemed possible. (a) redistribution was accordingly made.	
	2-8-16	–	The old positions to be retained were cleaned out + the loopholes readjusted where necessary overnight. Targets were registered from these positions during the day. Enemy activity was confined to M.G. fire on railway during the night + whizzbangs on "Duckboards" during the day.	MAP ATTACHED. No I
	3-8-16	–	Covered emplacements on new sites begun at X_2, 6C + F5. Nature of ground + position of enemy necessitated all material being carried up by night + all work carried out under cover of darkness. Registered on points O8 + 34 during the day + engaged enemy line from pt. 67 to pt. 86 from 5B + 5D.	
	4-8-16	–	With a view to covering the MENIN RD. a position was sited in front of HELLFIRE CORNER + work begun on it overnight. Working parties were allotted to the Coy. by Brigade as the amount of work to be done could not be overtaken by the gunners. These were sent to Section Officers nightly according to the amount of work to be carried out in each section area. Two other new alternatives were	

2449 Wt. W14957/M90 750,000 1/16 J.B.C. & A. Forms/C.2118/12.

A Morris Capt Coy

Army Form C. 2118.

Instructions regarding War Diaries and Intelligence Summaries are contained in F. S. Regs., Part II. and the Staff Manual respectively. Title Pages will be prepared in manuscript.

WAR DIARY
or
INTELLIGENCE SUMMARY
(Erase heading not required.)

MACHINE GUN COMPANY.

Place	Date	Hour	Summary of Events and Information	Remarks and references to Appendices
			begun – RAILWAY AVE. & PS 2: No positions seemed to have had alternatives	
YPRES	4-8-16	–	previously. Night firing programme carried out on BELLEWARDE lines.	
	5-8-16	–	Registered from indirect positions by means of forward observation officers.	
"			Carried out night firing programme against HOOGE, employing guns at 5B & F5. Retaliated on Roulers Railway after enemy M.G. had searched from WEST LANE barricade to HELL FIRE corner. This carried out at request of O.C. infantry Battn. in the line.	
"	6-8-16	–	M.G. work on Divisional strong point at White Chateau arranged with engineers & begun at night. This is the most commanding defensive position in the area & is being supplied with two gun positions. Open alternative begun at WEST LANE BARRICADE. Programme of night firing against communication trenches in BELLEWARDE area. Enemy machine guns active at night. We retaliated.	
"	7-8-16	–	New covered emplacements begun at H21 + S21 in RAILWAY WOOD. These positions were sited to enfilade No man's Land in front of left Battn. as shown in map. Other work continued. Night firing on Railway & HOOGE. Enemy quiet except for intermittent shelling of Duckboards & Railway Wood. Aeroplanes active on both sides.	Map attached. No. III
"	8-8-16	–	Registered from new positions. Owing to spell of good weather observation of strike of bullets was comparatively easy. Good observation obtained from H21 + S21 [illegible] of indirect [illegible] from West Lane Barricade & PS 2.	

A Morris Capt Comdg

2449 Wt. W14957/M90 750,000 1/16 J.B.C. & A. Forms/C.2118/12.

Instructions regarding War Diaries and Intelligence Summaries are contained in F. S. Regs., Part II. and the Staff Manual respectively. Title Pages will be prepared in manuscript.

or

INTELLIGENCE SUMMARY

(Erase heading not required.)

Place	Date	Hour	Summary of Events and Information	Remarks and references to Appendices
YPRES	9-8-16	–	Work interrupted by changing over teams & by enemy gas attack. As the Company was to have a 20 day spell in the line hence the interchange of teams. This was in progress when enemy sent over gas. Subsequent enquiry brought out the following: The men took their gas helmets into use immediately so that we had no casualties from the delay in using helmets. Both P.H.G.s & Box Respirators were in use by different sections & both proved effective in keeping out the gas. The box pattern was the better in this that the men using it could see what they were doing while those using the P.H.G. were practically blind. Any stores lost were lost by teams wearing P.H.Gs. Reliefs were ultimately completed without immediate casualties. Next day several men were suffering from "drift" but all cases were slight. Guns at H21, S21, RS2 + X2 covered the front affected by gas, the first two enfilading enemy line from Pt. 54 north.	
	10-8-16	–	All work pushed forward. Dugout begun at West Lane Barricade. Alternatives for H21 + S21 sighted. Fire programme between 2pm + 6pm. Good observation was obtained on communication trenches beyond Pt. 91.	
	11-8-16	–	The alternatives as sighted above commenced. The work in progress on this date was as follows:— Covered emplacements at: White Chateau, Menin Rd., 5C, Railway Avenue, F4, H21 alternative, S21 alternative + X2. Open emplacements at: F5. F4 alternative; 2B alternative; RS.2 alt. + 6C alternative.	

2449 Wt. W14957/M90 750,000 1/16 J.B.C. & A. Forms/C.2118/12.

A.Morris Capt Comd 9

Instructions regarding War Diaries and Intelligence Summaries are contained in F. S. Regs., Part II. and the Staff Manual respectively. Title Pages will be prepared in manuscript.

or

INTELLIGENCE SUMMARY

(Erase heading not required.)

Place	Date	Hour	Summary of Events and Information	Remarks and references to Appendices
YPRES	11-8-16	–	Dugouts at: Menin Rd, West Line Barricade, H21 & S21. Indirect fire programme from 2B & 2D on communication trenches behind pts. 39 & 67.	
"	12-8-16	–	Wiring in front of Railway Farm. Menin Rd. position registered on wire across Menin Rd.	
"	13-8-16	–	P.S2 & F5 completed with alternatives & ammunition stores. Guns registered from these new emplacements & observation obtained. Two hostile aeroplanes engaged. Enemy shelling increased over whole area, with special attention to Hell Woods & White Chateau. This last was given away by a cable trench being dug by Signals Section to it. Enemy put both shrapnel & 5.9s on it with great accuracy. He also showed more attention to Ypres, particularly the Menin Gate & the Square. His machine guns were also active in the Potijze Sector their night firing on Haymarket & the X trenches being very accurate.	
"	14-8-16	–	Completed Menin Rd position. Enemy shelling of White Chateau continued but no damage done to gun positions. Potijze Rd. heavily shelled. Constructed an antiaircraft mounting in ramparts at Ypres & mounted a gun there in accordance with Divisional Orders.	
"	15-8-16	–	6B & alternative, H31, S21, & 5C completed. 5C registered on pt. 86. Engaged hostile aeroplane from X2. White Chateau & Potijze Rd. again shelled.	

A. Morris Capt Comdg

2449 Wt. W14957/M90 750,000 1/16 J.B.C. & A. Forms/C.2118/12.

Army Form C. 2118.

Instructions regarding War Diaries and Intelligence Summaries are contained in F. S. Regs., Part II. and the Staff Manual respectively. Title Pages will be prepared in manuscript.

WAR DIARY
or
INTELLIGENCE SUMMARY

(Erase heading not required.)

Place	Date	Hour	Summary of Events and Information	Remarks and references to Appendices
YPRES	16-8-16	–	Railway Avenue completed & registered on point 85. Fire programme by 5C, 5B & 2B on second line at pt. 85. Reconnaissance of gun positions in Ypres ramparts with a view to occupation in the event of emergency whilst in reserve. Four sets of positions were given to Section Officers to reconnoitre & sixteen ultimately selected to be occupied. These were entered with their cones of fire on map & copies issued to all officers & submitted to Bgde.	Maps attached No. II
"	17-8-16	–	X2, H2, & S21 alternatives & F4 completed & duly registered. Dugout at Menin Rd. completed. Hostile aircraft engaged.	
"	18-8-16	–	Wiring of Railway Farm completed. Enemy artillery active against Potyze & Menin Rds.	
"	19-8-16	–	The Company was relieved by 86th M.G. Coy & proceeded to BRANDHOEK. Took over M.G. camp from 87th M.G. Coy.	
BRANDHOEK	20-8-16	–	Found work necessary at camp as follows: Drainage, new incinerators, refitting of huts, replacing of duck boards, new cookhouse, road making at transport lines, new wagon standing & drainage.	
"	21-8-16	–	Programme of training as submitted to Bgde. carried out. Working party supplied for work at transport lines; this party to be permanent while Coy. is in camp. Commenced new incinerator to west of camp.	See copy attached.
"	22-8-16	–	Training as per programme. Worked on road in transport lines & extended wagon standing.	

A. Morris Capt. Comdg.

2449 Wt. W14957/M90 750,000 1/16 J.B.C. & A. Forms/C.2118/12.

Instructions regarding War Diaries and Intelligence Summaries are contained in F. S. Regs., Part II. and the Staff Manual respectively. Title Pages will be prepared in manuscript.

WAR DIARY
or
INTELLIGENCE SUMMARY
(Erase heading not required.)

Place	Date	Hour	Summary of Events and Information	Remarks and references to Appendices
BRANDHOEK	23-8-16	–	as programme. Permanent fatigue supplied to load bricks at Vlamertinghe in order to supply material for wagon standing, cookhouse etc. Attached one gun team to duty at RRVLERSBURG. Deepened main camp drain.	
"	24-8-16	–	Collected bricks, corrugated iron & timber for new cookhouse. Completed incinerator. Training as programme.	
"	25-8-16	–	Commenced new ablution well & cookhouse & refitted certain huts. Working parties as above & training continued. Officers made reconnaissance of roads to west & north of YPRES in accordance with Brigade Orders.	
"	26-8-16	–	Officers' reconnaissance of crossings of KIMMELBEEK carried out. Second incinerator completed ~~to east of~~ camp. Duck board walks throughout camp repaired. Transport work & training programme continued.	
"	27-8-16	–	Church parades.	
"	28/29	–	Prepared guns & stores for trenches & moved into line to relieve 86th M.G. Coy. Left camp 8 pm. Relief completed 1.30 am. Found the sector very quiet & relief was carried out without interruption. 12 guns in position in the line; 4 kept in ramparts as Divisional Reserve in accordance with Corps orders. Distribution as per attached maps.	Maps showing distribution of guns is attached. No III

A.W. Morris Capt Comdg

2449 Wt. W14957/M90 750,000 1/16 J.B.C. & A. Forms/C.2118/12.

WAR DIARY
or
INTELLIGENCE SUMMARY
(Erase heading not required.)

Instructions regarding War Diaries and Intelligence Summaries are contained in F. S. Regs., Part II. and the Staff Manual respectively. Title Pages will be prepared in manuscript.

Place	Date	Hour	Summary of Events and Information	Remarks and references to Appendices
YPRES	30-8-16	–	Working party supplied to R.Es. for work on Elation; this to be permanent till work is completed. Very heavy rains, trenches very wet. Attention to drainage throughout the sector. Fire programme prepared in accordance with Bde. Orders in conjunction with proposed gas attack. Guns at H21, S21, 5D, F4 & F5 selected to operate in conjunction with gas & artillery as in following table: Zero = 1.30 am. Zero – Gas discharge commences. 0.10 – Bombardment by Heavy & Divisional Artillery commences. Machine Guns fire bursts of rapid fire. 0.20 – Gas discharge ceases. 0.40 – Bombardment by artillery ends & machine guns cease fire. 1.00 – Patrols move out. Wind proved unfavourable for gas; operations therefore postponed. Gas alarm at 10.30 pm. 29th inst. Remained on "alert" till 12 midnight but no gas reached this sector.	
"	31-8-16	–	Dugout at H21 commenced. Gas attack again postponed owing to wind being unfavourable.	

A Morris Capt Comdg

- 88th Machine Gun Company -

Programme of Work.

Saturday	Sunday	Monday	Tuesday	Wednesday	Thursday	Friday	Saturday	Sunday	Monday
11 am Cleaning of Guns and Stores	Holiday	6.30 to 7.30 am Running, Walking & Physical Exercises — 9.30 to 10 am Handling of Arms — 10 to 10.30 am Gas Helmet drill — 10.30 am to 12.30 pm Laying & Holding — 2 to 3 pm Lecture by O.C. Coy Visual Training & Judging Distance	6.30 to 7.30 am Running, Walking & Physical Exercises — 9.30 to 10 am Ceremonial — 10 to 10.30 am Gas Helmet drill — 10.30 am to 12.30 pm Stoppages & Mechanism — 2 to 3 pm Lecture by O.C. Coy Fire Orders Part I	6.30 to 7.30 am Running, Walking & Physical Exercises — 9.30 to 10 am Section Drill. — 10 to 10.30 am Gas Helmet drill — 10.30 am to 12.30 pm Elevating & Traversing drill — 2 to 3 pm Lecture by O.C. Coy Fire Orders Part II	7 to 7.30 am Running, Walking & Physical Exercises — 9.30 to 10 am Section Drill — 10 to 10.30 am Gas Helmet drill — 10.30 am to 12.30 pm Bombing — 2 to 3 pm Lecture by O.C. Coy	8.30 am Range — 2 to 3 pm Lecture by O.C. Coy	7 to 7.30 am Running, Walking & Physical Exercises — 9.30 to 10 am Gas Helmet drill — 10 to 10.30 am Inspection of Gas Helmets — 10.30 am to 12.30 pm Inspection	Divine Service	7 to 7.30 am Running, Walking & Physical Exercises — 9.30 to 12.30 General cleaning up of Camp & Preparing Guns etc. for Trenches — 8 pm parade for Trenches

A. Morris Capt. Comdg

MAP: No 1; SHOWING
DISTRIBUTION OF GUNS 1/8/16.
Bellewaarde beek.
88th
MACHINE GUN
COMPANY.
Date 31/8/16.
Bond St.
Haymarket
Piccadilly.
Railway
Mud Lane.
Union Street.
6A.
6B.
X2.
PB2
2A
2C
5A.
5B.
5D
9B
11A
F6.
Reserve Gun at
Schoolmaster's House 11B

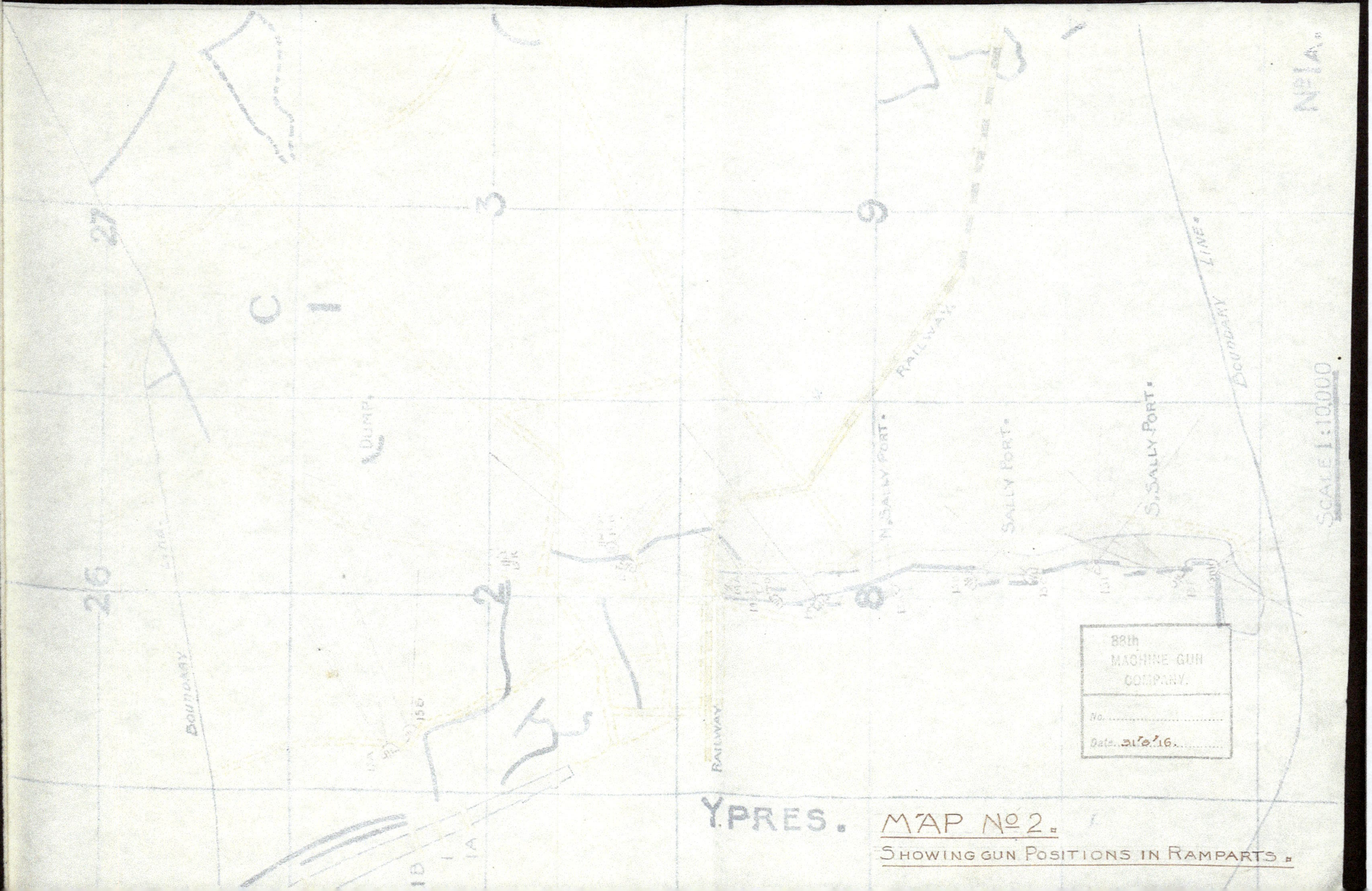

YPRES. MAP Nº 2.

SHOWING GUN POSITIONS IN RAMPARTS.

Nº 1A.

SCALE 1:10,000

88th MACHINE GUN COMPANY.

No. ....

Date 31.8.16.

BOUNDARY LINE

RAILWAY

N. SALLY PORT

SALLY PORT

S. SALLY PORT

DUMP

RAILWAY

BOUNDARY LINE

C

1

3

9

27

26

2

8

1B

1A

156

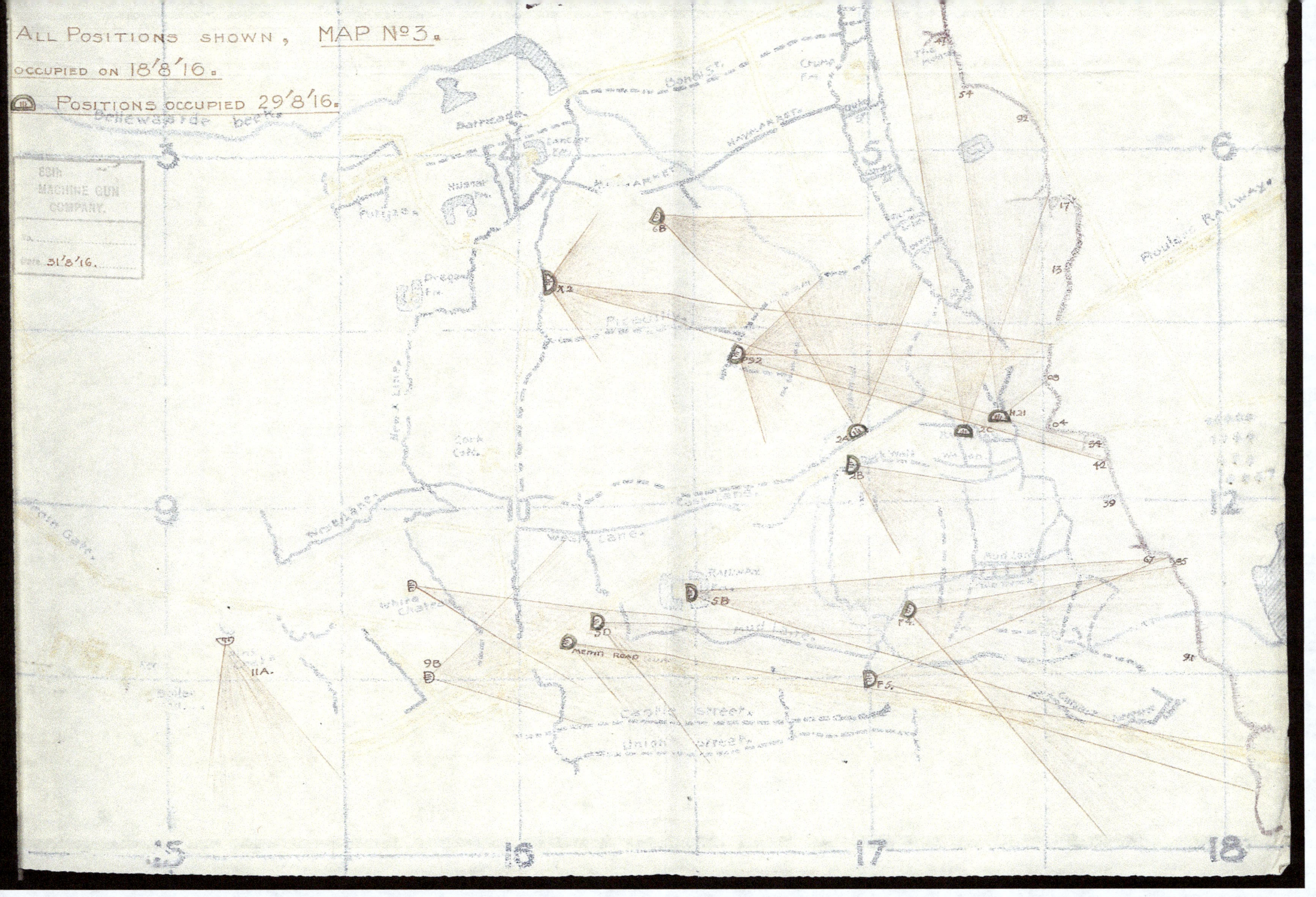

All Positions shown, occupied on 18/8/16.
MAP No 3.
Positions occupied 29/8/16.
Bellewaarde beek
Barricade
Hussar Fm.
Railway
West Lane
Union Street
Castle Street
Menin Road
White Chateau
Cork Cott.
New X Lane
Rouler Railway
Bond St.
Haymarket
6B
X2
92
2A
2B
2C
H21
5B
5D
F4
F5
9B
11A
5
6
9
12
15
16
17
18
80th Machine Gun Company.
Date 31/8/16.

29th Division.

88th Infantry Brigade.

88th MACHINE GUN COMPANY

SEPTEMBER 1 9 1 6

Confidential –

War Diary
of
88th. Machine Gun Company.

From 1st. September 1916 to 30th. September 1916.

"Volume VI".

Vol 6

Army Form C. 2118.

WAR DIARY
or
INTELLIGENCE SUMMARY
(Erase heading not required.)

Instructions regarding War Diaries and Intelligence Summaries are contained in F. S. Regs., Part II. and the Staff Manual respectively. Title Pages will be prepared in manuscript.

Place	Date	Hour	Summary of Events and Information	Remarks and references to Appendices
YPRES	1-9-16	—	Distribution of guns as in maps attached to Volume V.	MAP 28 N.W.
		1.40am–2.10am	Guns H21, S21, F4, F5 + D5 operated during discharge of gas by us. 3 guns engaged enemy machine gun + silenced it. New targets registered. 4 antiaircraft mountings constructed on Ypres ramparts for use by guns in Divisional Reserve.	
	2-9-16	—	Engaged enemy lines at pts. 67-91; 42-08; 17-54; + by indirect fire communication trenches behind pt. 85. Worked on new dugout at H21 + completed it. Drainage + latrines improved at all positions. Material sent up for work at P.S.2. Bricks collected + sent down to transport lines for use in extension of wagon standing. Experienced the first heavy rain since coming into the salient. Noted effect on drainage arrangements + dugouts + directed improvements accordingly. 3 gas alarms during the night: no casualties.	
	3-9-16	—	Programme expending 4000 rds. carried out against the following Targets: Pts. 31, 34 + 27; pt. 06; vicinity of pts. 64 + 87. Work in progress at S21 + F4, deepening, revetting + laying duckboards in trenches. Working parties supplied each night to R.E. for work on White Chateau. Improvements carried out at Coy. Hq. in construction of cookhouse, washouse + latrines, erection of a rabbit wire screen, ventilation of cellars by means of airshafts + in improving drainage.	
			G R Thomson Lieut.	

2449 Wt. W14957/M90 750,000 1/16 J.B.C. & A. Forms/C.2118/12.

Instructions regarding War Diaries and Intelligence Summaries are contained in F. S. Regs., Part II. and the Staff Manual respectively. Title Pages will be prepared in manuscript.

Army Form C. 2118.

WAR DIARY
or
INTELLIGENCE SUMMARY

(Erase heading not required.)

Place	Date	Hour	Summary of Events and Information	Remarks and references to Appendices
YPRES	4-9-16	–	Enemy trenches engaged behind points 42 + 08; pt. 91; + pt. 17. Enemy aeroplane engaged from X2: another by all four guns in ramparts; the latter driven off. New dugout at P.S.2 completed, trench boards put down + parapet improved. Worked on parapet of S21 trench. Sap at F4 continued, deepened + revetted. Arranged with R.Es. to build concrete emplacement at F5 the labour being supplied by the M.G. Coy + the skilled labour by the engineers. Compared zones of fire of ~~the~~ guns of this unit with those of 4th Division on the right with a view to co-operation.	
	5-9-16	–	Enemy second line trenches from EITHEL FRITZ FME. to OSCAR FME. engaged. " " " " " 12a 35/85 to 12a 65/10. " " " " " " OSKAR FME. to RLY. Work continued at PS2, S21, F4 + F5. Vicinity of 2A + 2B shelled probably owing to new trench under construction there; 2A slightly damaged.	
	6-9-16	–	The following targets were engaged in a night firing programme: Enemy communication trenches leading to HOOGE. T-Roads at C 30 c 05/10. Trenches + light railway at 6C 70/85. Work continued during night on trenches leading to H21 + S21 – drainage + rebuilding of parapets. Working parties supplied to R.Es. for White Chateau + F5. W R Thomson Lieut.	

2449 Wt. W14957/M90 750,000 1/16 J.B.C. & A. Forms/C.2118/12.

Army Form C. 2118.

WAR DIARY
or
INTELLIGENCE SUMMARY
(Erase heading not required.)

Instructions regarding War Diaries and Intelligence Summaries are contained in F. S. Regs., Part II. and the Staff Manual respectively. Title Pages will be prepared in manuscript.

Place	Date	Hour	Summary of Events and Information	Remarks and references to Appendices
YPRES	7-9-16	–	Programme including I6c 00/35 to I12a 55/45; C30c 05/10, I12b 60/55, J7a 20/55; Frontline at C29d 70/00 – 40/60; I5b 85/25; C29a 80/00. Infantry reported sounds of enemy transport galloping + men shouting as result of this firing. New emplacements sited + constructed at PS3 + No. 2 Crater with the object of covering enemy line from pt. 59 to pt 34. Further work on S21, H21, F4 + PS2. Material transported for girder emplacement at PS2 + for concrete emplacement at F5. Labour parties detailed for night work on all these.	
	8-9-16	–	Targets engaged: J7a 10/55, C29a 40/20, C29a 20/80, C29c 95/00; junction of trenches + light railway at 6c 75/85; communication trenches to Hooge. All work progressed. Enemy activity very slight in all departments except his trench mortars. Weather conditions favourable to furtherance of work on the lines, drainage, revetting + construction of new trenches carried on throughout the sector in both German + own lines. Fire programme issued as per attached copy.	APPENDIX "A"
	9-9-16	–	Sector very quiet. At no time does enemy activity interrupt work. Work in progress: trenches at S21 + F4: Concrete emplacement at F5: Girder emplacement at PS2. Working parties are despatched nightly to these points.	

G R Thomson Lieut

85th MACHINE GUN COMPANY.

2449 Wt. W14957/M90 750,000 1/16 J.B.C. & A. Forms/C.2118/12.

Instructions regarding War Diaries and Intelligence Summaries are contained in F. S. Regs., Part II. and the Staff Manual respectively. Title Pages will be prepared in manuscript.

WAR DIARY
or
INTELLIGENCE SUMMARY

(Erase heading not required.)

Army Form C. 2118.

Place	Date	Hour	Summary of Events and Information	Remarks and references to Appendices
YPRES	9-9-16	—	Targets engaged: WESTHOEK X Rds. at I 7 b, X Rds at J 7 a 20/55 & at C 30 c 05/10. Searched enemy front line from C 29 d 40/00 to d 40/60. Engaged strong pts. at I 5 b 40/10 & I 5 b 15/40. From left sector engaged junction at 6 c 70/45 & enemy support line from 6 c 00/33 to 12 a 60/40.	
	10-9-16	—	The use of Forward Observation Posts having been approved by G.O.C. Division, sites were selected for these with a view to control of guns by 'phone code signals & estimates of instruments & wire required sent forward. Targets engaged: Road crossing railway at J 1 a 85/65; communication trench at I 12 d 80/20; support line behind pt. 91; junction at 6 b 70/80 & line at I 12 a 35/77 to 12 a [illegible]/50; WESTHOEK X Rds., Rd. from I 12 b 70/55 to J 7 a 20/60; [illegible]; Rd. from C 30 c 10/15 to C 30 c 50/35; front line from C 29 d 40/00 to C 29 d 40/60. Roads & communication trenches were engaged at night. Anti-aircraft: Two Bosche machines engaged; one driven off from our parts by combined fire of three guns.	
	11-9-16	—	Targets engaged: Enemy support trench I 6 a 10/90 to 80/00 engaged by two guns. Junction at I 6 c 70/80, I 5 b 50/10, Cross Rds. C 30/c 05/10, Westhoek Cross Rds., Birr Cross Rds. [illegible]. Work was continued on positions & O.P.	
	12-9-16	—	The carrying out of the fire programme resulted in some retaliation from enemy M.Gs. which traversed railway from Hell Fire Corner to Cambridge Rd. & P.S.2 trench. Enemy guns seemed to be firing from longer range than previously possibly on account of activity of our trench mortars. Enemy mortars also active & damaged trenches round forward guns. Repair of the damage along	

G.R. Thomson Lieut.

2449 Wt. W14957/M90 750,000 1/16 J.B.C. & A. Forms/C.2118/12.

Instructions regarding War Diaries and Intelligence Summaries are contained in F. S. Regs., Part II. and the Staff Manual respectively. Title Pages will be prepared in manuscript.

WAR DIARY
or
INTELLIGENCE SUMMARY
(Erase heading not required.)

Army Form C. 2118.

Place	Date	Hour	Summary of Events and Information	Remarks and references to Appendices
YPRES	12-9-16	–	with usual work on emplacements carried out during the night. Fire according to programme was continued the following targets being engaged: Bend on Menin Rd. behind pt. 91; Cross Rds. at J7a 80/20; railway at J1a 85/65; Junction at I6c 70/80 engaged by three guns; Westhoek x Rds., Cross Rds. at J7a 20/55 + I6c 20/80.	
	13-9-16	–	Wiring in front of Railway Avenue position. Working parties supplied each night to R.Es. for work on White Chateau + F5. O.P. at S21 continued. Owing to work in hand all gunners employed when off sentry on work at positions. Fire programme again drew retaliation. Enemy M.G. located: fire of two guns turned on it + effectively silenced it. Roads + railway engaged as on previous nights.	
	14-9-16	–	Enemy shelled new work throughout the sector. Increased activity in all arms. Working parties continuously sniped + shelled while trench mortars + howitzers were busy against new parapets especially at P32 + Railway Wood. Gun positions escaped without damage but much repair was needed to parapets. Engaged targets at hours stated in programme: Little Fritz Farm; Hooge; Junction at I6c 70/80 by three guns.	
	15-9-16	–	Work carried on throughout the area. F.O.P. in Railway Wood completed. In view of Divisional Operation against enemy front ordered for night of 15th/16th the necessary arrangements were made. The guns were ordered to create a defiladed zone between lines (a) Crater No 6 + I6c 10/15 (b) Crater No 3 + Point 04.	

W.P. Thomson Lieut.

Army Form C. 2118.

WAR DIARY
or
INTELLIGENCE SUMMARY
(Erase heading not required.)

Instructions regarding War Diaries and Intelligence Summaries are contained in F. S. Regs., Part II. and the Staff Manual respectively. Title Pages will be prepared in manuscript.

Place	Date	Hour	Summary of Events and Information	Remarks and references to Appendices
YPRES	15-9-16	–	The necessary guns were detailed for the work. All working parties east of the Canal were cancelled & arrangements made for all Transport to be clear of Ypres on the return journey by 10.30pm. "Zero" was fixed for 11pm.	
"	16-9-16	–	The machine gun work in connection with the operation during the night was effectively carried out. Reports showed that the barrage created was accurate & effective the raiding frontage being kept defiladed throughout while the flanks were kept under incessant fire. Enemy retaliation was weak & caused little damage in the sector.	
"	17-9-16	–	The necessary wiring was done to enable the Railway Wood guns to be controlled by telephone from the O.P. The control of three guns was practised & proved absolutely successful. The officer in the O.P. could bring fire to bear where & when he desired & could at the same time observe the fire effect. All fire orders were sent in code & no conversation was allowed over the line in view of the enemy listening apparatus known to be in operation. Fire orders for the night were "to keep the gaps in the enemy wire formed by previous night's bombardment under intermittent fire to prevent his repairing it." Guns were detailed accordingly so	

G R Thomson Lieut.

2449 Wt. W14957/M90 750,000 1/16 J.B.C. & A. Forms/C.2118/12.

Instructions regarding War Diaries and Intelligence Summaries are contained in F. S. Regs., Part II. and the Staff Manual respectively. Title Pages will be prepared in manuscript.

WAR DIARY
or
INTELLIGENCE SUMMARY
(Erase heading not required.)

Army Form C. 2118.

Place	Date	Hour	Summary of Events and Information	Remarks and references to Appendices
YPRES	14-9-16	–	as to engage all points bombarded. Work was renewed throughout the sector. Enemy activity still slight & conditions generally good.	
	18-9-16	–	The Railway Wood Sector was heavily bombarded from 8 am to 9.30 am by H.E. & Mortars. Much damage was done to the new trench system. Gun positions escaped but dugouts suffered, two being blown in. The Coy. had only one casualty. The 86th Coy. relieved the 88th between ~~the~~ hours of 11 pm & 3 am.	
	19-9-16	–	Moved into camp at BRANDHOEK.	
	20-9-16 } 27-9-16 }	–	In Divisional Reserve. Attached is scheme of training carried out during this period. Attached also copy of special scheme carried out by officers. Special attention paid throughout period in reserve to cleanliness of men & of clothing. Sport & recreation encouraged as much as possible, football, boxing & concerts being arranged. Work was carried on in camp – ditches dug, drains deepened, roads bricked & new cookhouse built. A working party was also supplied daily for work in Transport lines, where a drainage	APPENDIX "B" " "C"

W. P. Thomson Lieut.

Army Form C. 2118.

WAR DIARY
or
INTELLIGENCE SUMMARY

(Erase heading not required.)

Instructions regarding War Diaries and Intelligence Summaries are contained in F. S. Regs., Part II. and the Staff Manual respectively. Title Pages will be prepared in manuscript.

Place	Date	Hour	Summary of Events and Information	Remarks and references to Appendices
BRANDHOEK			scheme was completed, sheds tarred & standings improved. All guns were overhauled by artificer & necessary repairs carried out. In the daily training special attention was paid to Gas Helmet drill with the new Small Box Respirator & to training. In the range exercises in dial reading, fire control, stoppages & loading, were carried out both with & without the respirators being worn by the gunners. The Company moved up to relieve the 80th M.G. Coy. on the evening of the 28th inst.	
YPRES	29-9-16	–	General cleaning up of emplacements & dugouts. Fire programmes arranged & special orders issued for use of certain guns required to cooperate in raid on night of 30th/1st.	
	30-9-16	–	The following targets were engaged: Westhoek / Zonnebeke Road, Light Railway & junction at I 6 c 75/80; road from Verlorenhoek to C 30 d 05/60, Hooge, & Menin Rd. from Hooge to J 13 b 05/20. The sector was very quiet generally except for the ranging of our howitzers on enemy wire. Work for the night had to be abandoned on account of prospective operations.	
			W R Thomson Lieut.	

APPENDIX "A"

- 88th Machine Gun Company -

Fire Programme

The following programme as tabulated below will be carried out by all Guns capable of Offensive action whilst in the Line. The order of Fire will be strictly adhered to and there will be no deviation as regards alterations of time or ammunition expenditure without reference to the Company Commander

Date	Time by Day	Time by night	Number of Rounds	Remarks
Monday	0400	2345	250	Arrangements will be made by Section Officers
Tuesday	0425	2215	250	with the Commanding Officers in whose area
Wednesday	0515	0135	200	they are operating and the Targets explained to them.
Thursday	0320	0210	150	There will be no Fire on the Enemys first line
Friday	0525	0115	100	trenches but on those tactical points and communications
Saturday	0555	2305	125	in rear which he is compelled to use.
Sunday	0635	2400	100	

88th MACHINE GUN COMPANY. No. .... Date ....

W R Thomson Lieut. ~~Captain~~

Commanding 88th Machine Gun Company

APPENDIX "B"

- 88th Machine Gun Company.

Tuesday	Wednesday	Thursday	Friday	Saturday	Sunday	Monday	Tuesday	Wednesday	Thursday
General Cleaning up of Camp Guns Rifles etc.	8 am Fitting and Testing of Small Box Respirators and Gas Helmets at Divisional Gas School — 1-30 pm Baths	8 to 8-30 am Physical Training 9 to 9-30 am Drill and Inspection of Gas Helmets 9-30 to 10 am Mechanism 10 to 10-30 am Stoppages 10-30 am to 12 noon Section drill 2 to 3 pm Judging distance 3 to 4 pm Range taking	8 to 8-30 am Physical Training 9 to 9-30 am Drill and Inspection of Gas Helmets 9-30 to 10 am Stoppages 10 to 10.30 am Mechanism 10-30 to 11 am Handling of Arms 11am to 12 noon Standard tests 2 to 3 pm Bomb Throwing 3 to 4 pm Section Drill	8 to 8-30 am Physical Training 9 to 10 am Standard Tests 10 to 10-30 am Stripping and assembling of Gun 10-30 to 11 am Stoppages 11am to 12 noon Cleaning of Ammunition 2 to 3 pm Revolver instruction for No. ones and Twos. 2 to 2.30 pm Drill and inspection of Gas helmets 2.30 to 4 pm Judging distance and Range Taking	Holiday	8-30 am Range Revolver Practice	8 to 8-30 am Physical Training 9 to 9-30 am Cleaning and assembling Gun also practice in Stripping 9-30 to 10 am Inspections of Guns Rifles and Revolvers 10 to 10-30 am Section drill 10-30 to 11 am Handling of arms 11am to 12 noon Standard Tests 2 to 2.30 pm Drill and Inspection of Gas Helmets 2.30 to 4 pm Visual Training and Range Taking	8 to 8-30 am Physical Training 9 to 9-30 am Inspection of Gas Helmets 9-30 to 10 am Stoppages 10 to 10-30 am Mechanism 10-30 to 11 am Mounting and dismounting Gun 11 am to 12 noon Lecture by O.C. Company 2 to 3 pm Bomb Throwing 3 to 4 pm Judging Distance	8 to 8.30 am Physical Training — 9am to 12 noon Tactical Scheme —

88th MACHINE GUN COMPANY. No. ...... Date. ......

A.R. Thomson Lt. for Major Commanding
88th Machine Gun Company

APPENDIX C

Operation Order No I
By
Major A. Morris; commanding
88th Machine Gun Company.

In the Field.
28/9/16.

Reference
Hazebrouck 5A.

Information.

1. (a) Enemy – A hostile force has advanced through Ypres and are holding the line Chateau De Trois Tours, H.5. Central – Cross Roads H12.C.2.7. Estimated enemy strength as per margin.

Enemy's Estimated Strength.
1 Battery Artillery
1 Brigade Infantry
2 Squadrons Cavalry.

(b) Own Troops. – The 88th Brigade are on the left flank and hold the line B.27.C.9.3. to H.10.a.3.5. (Ypres Road exclusive). The 87th Brigade is on the right.

2. Intentions. – The G.O.C. intends 4 guns to be with the leading battalions and 8 guns in reserve.

3. Distribution – as per margin.
No I Section will accompany the Hampshire Regt.
No 2 " " " " Newfoundland ".
Nos 3 and 4 Sections will be in reserve at Vlamertinghe church.

No 1 Section under 2Lt C.S. Parsons.
No 2 Section under Lt. Owen.
Nos 3 + 4 in Reserve under 2Lt Thomson

4. Communication – will be by cyclist orderly; Reports will be sent to Vlamertinghe church.

5.

6. Special Order –. Scouts report that the enemy artillery are getting into positions in rear of the Chateau De Trois Tours. They are heavy guns and will take some time to get into position. No 4 Section will move forward and get into position at the chateau as per margin and engage the enemy, – every endeavour being made to knock out the gun crews. Nos I & 2 Sections will remain with the unit to which they have been detailed and form an interlaced cone of fire over the Brigade frontage.

Sheet 28.
H.5.a. 40·50

7. Preliminary Reconnaissance. Details of avenues of approach, water supply etc. as the result of " " will be communicated to all ranks.

Issued at 08.00

A Morris Major Comdg
88th M.G. Coy

P.T.O.

Copy No 1 Operation Order File.
" No 2. G. S. O. 2.
" No 3 Brigade Major
" No 4. Transport Officer.
" No 5. No 1 Section
" No 6. No 2 Section
" No 7. O.C. Reserve Section.

GENERAL IDEA

A hostile Force (Brown) has advanced through YPRES and a White Force is despatched to engage it from POPERINGHE (Encounter Battle).

SPECIAL IDEA.

The White Force having advanced to VLAMERTINGHE scouts report that the enemy are holding a line - CHATEAU DES TROIS TOURS - H.5.central - CROSS ROADS H.12.c.2.7

The 88th Brigade is on the left flank and occupies a front from B.27.c.9.3 to H.10.a.3.5 (exclusive of YPRES ROAD) 2 Battalions in front line, 2 Battalions in support dividing line between Right and Left Battalions, is the POTTENHOEK to BRIELEN Road.

The 87th Brigade is on ~~our~~ the Right.

The objective of 88th Brigade is from CHATEAU DES TROIS TOURS to FARM H.5.central inclusive.

The G.O.C. 88th Brigade orders 4 guns to be attached to each leading Battalion and 8 to be in Reserve.

EXERCISES.

1. The G.O.C. informs you that the Left flank is the dangerous flank and orders 4 guns from the Reserve to be detailed to protect that flank.

As O.C. Company state your orders.

2. As O.C. Section with Right Battalion give your orders and state action taken.

3. As O.C. Section with Left Battalion give your orders and state action taken.

4. As O.C. Section protecting left flank give your orders and state action taken.

29th Division.
88th Infantry Brigade.

88th MACHINE GUN COMAPANY

OCTOBER 1916

Operation Orders attached

CONFIDENTIAL

War Diary

of

88th Machine Gun Company

from 1st October 1916 TO 31st October inclusive

VOLUME 7

88th Brigade.

Herewith War Diary of the 88th Machine Gun Company for the Month of October 1916.

There were a few lessons learnt from the recent operations by the 88th Brigade, which may be summarised as follows.

1. The introduction of the mobile section as an experiment. It was entirely successful.

2. The closer co-operation between machine guns and infantry. The proper system now seems to be established and a perfect understanding seems to exist between the two arms. The regiments welcomed the machine gun fire and advanced through our guns with the greatest of confidence. The promotion and cultivation of this spirit is satisfactory.

3. The indubitable and established superiority of our gun and personnel over the enemy. The enemy formerly enjoyed advantage in numerical superiority which no longer exists.

R.W. Morris Major Comdg
88th Machine Gun Coy.

1 - 11 - 16

Army Form C. 2118.

Instructions regarding War Diaries and Intelligence Summaries are contained in F. S. Regs., Part II. and the Staff Manual respectively. Title Pages will be prepared in manuscript.

WAR DIARY
or
INTELLIGENCE SUMMARY

(Erase heading not required.)

Place	Date	Hour	Summary of Events and Information	Remarks and references to Appendices
YPRES	1-10-16	–	On night of 30th/1st, 5 guns as detailed in APPENDIX "A" co-operated in raid by 86 Bde. against Point O4. Enemy retaliation was very slight so that [illegible] guns were never in difficulties but carried out their programme without interruption.	APPENDIX "A".
	2-10-16	–	Targets engaged: Westhoek, Eelsar Fme., X Rds. J13d 20/70, J13a 50/40, J14d 00/05; HOOGE, Menin Rd. J13 d 05/90, X Rds. I12b 60/60 to J7a 30/05, Station Bly. J14 60/40, Light Rly. Trenches from I6c75/80 to I6c60/40, [illegible] & Wieltje Rd. Enemy M.G. fire very feeble. He did not reply to our fire to any extent. The sector as a whole was extremely quiet. Slight aerial activity. We engaged one machine which returned to its own lines immediately.	BELGIUM
	3-10-16	–	Targets again engaged as above eliciting replies from two enemy guns but these ceased fire on being engaged. The enemy absolutely inactive in all arms. Work on emplacements & dugouts continued without interference from him throughout the sector.	
	4-10-16	–	Relieved by The 165th M.G. Coy. Copy of "Relief Orders" attached. One officer & one N.C.O. sent in advance by relieving unit. These shown our line & made acquainted with emplacements, routes, methods of relief, enemy's line etc. Other arrangements made for incoming unit as per "orders". Officer & N.C.O. sent as advance party to new area from ~~this unit~~. On relief the Company moved into billets in Poperinghe.	APPENDIX "B".

A.W. Morris Major Comd.
88th M.G. Coy

2449 Wt. W14957/M90 750,000 1/16 J.B.C. & A. Forms/C.2118/12.

WAR DIARY
or
INTELLIGENCE SUMMARY
(Erase heading not required.)

Instructions regarding War Diaries and Intelligence Summaries are contained in F. S. Regs., Part II. and the Staff Manual respectively. Title Pages will be prepared in manuscript.

Place	Date	Hour	Summary of Events and Information	Remarks and references to Appendices
POPERINGHE	5-10-16	–	In Poperinghe. Cleaning guns &c prior to packing for transport to new area. Limbers loaded & all transport prepared for move (movement order attached)	Appendix F.
"	6-10-16	–	Entrained at Proven en route for new area.	
"	7-10-16	–	Detrained at Saleux at 10 am. Route marched to Corbie & arrived there at 9 p.m.	
SALEUX.	8-10-16	–		
CORBIE.	9-10-16	–	Rested the Coy. in billets. At 8 pm. orders to proceed to the line were received. The Coy. travelled by motor bus leaving Corbie 12 midnight & arriving at Montauban 5 am.	
MONTAUBAN	10-10-16	–	Marched to bivouac allotted. Transport followed by road leaving Corbie at 8 am. & arriving in lines at Montauban at 4 pm. Orders to relieve the 37th M.G. Coy. were received at 9 am. the 88th Brigade being attached to the 12th Division. The Commanding Officer made a reconnaissance of the new area during the day & arranged all details of relief with O.C. 37th M.G. Coy. Relief started at 5 pm. & was complete by 10 p.m. Disposition of guns as follows: Front line 8 guns of which 5 were actually in position & three in reserve in dugout in Guedecourt. Support line 4 guns. Reserve at Coy. Hq. 4 guns.	

A Morris Major Cmdg
88th M. G. Coy

2449 Wt. W14957/M90 750,000 1/16 J.B.C. & A. Forms/C.2118/12.

Instructions regarding War Diaries and Intelligence Summaries are contained in F. S. Regs., Part II. and the Staff Manual respectively. Title Pages will be prepared in manuscript.

WAR DIARY
or
INTELLIGENCE SUMMARY

(Erase heading not required.)

Place	Date	Hour	Summary of Events and Information	Remarks and references to Appendices
SOMME	11-10-16	–	Found the sector under heavy shell fire particularly the village of Gueudecourt. Great activity was apparent in all arms. Details of the proposed advance came in at 7 p.m. Copy of operations orders attached. These were issued to Section Officers by 11 p.m. The special idea involved was that three guns should be held as a mobile reserve of fire specially detailed to engage enemy machine guns which had survived the artillery bombardment.	Appendix C
"	12-10-16	–	Zero was fixed for 2.5 p.m. Our artillery barrage along our front was most accurate & effective. Special targets could not have been engaged by our machine guns owing to the dust & smoke obscuring our front. The locality of enemy machine guns however was given away by their sound. Our mobile guns immediately came into action against these. From shell holes in NO MAN'S LAND they succeeded in completely neutralising the effect of their fire thus giving our infantry every chance of getting forward. Our other guns meantime kept up their barrage on enemy communications & afforded covering fire to the advancing troops. The attack was completely successful the objective of the Brigade being reached & consolidated. The 5 guns detailed went forward & took up position in the captured trench their disposition being two guns on each flank & one placed centrally. An interlaced zone of fire was thereby formed along our Brigade frontage while our flanks were provided for. Orders were issued to	

A.L. Morris Major Cmd
58th M.G. Coy

2449 Wt. W14957/M90 750,000 1/16 J.B.C. & A. Forms/C.2118/12.

Instructions regarding War Diaries and Intelligence Summaries are contained in F. S. Regs., Part II. and the Staff Manual respectively. Title Pages will be prepared in manuscript.

WAR DIARY
or
INTELLIGENCE SUMMARY

(Erase heading not required.)

Place	Date	Hour	Summary of Events and Information	Remarks and references to Appendices
SOMME	12-10-16	(cont.)	the section in support to move up at dusk to their new support position in the old front line, two reserve guns being sent to take their place in the old support line.	
"	13-10-16	–	Consolidation in our new line was completed. The casualties in the Company during the action of the 12th inst. were 10 O.R. Water + rations were conveyed during the period by pack mules. Communication to support line was by telephone + forward of that point by orderly.	
"	14-10-16	–	Heavy enemy shelling of our new support lines. He seemed to leave the front line alone + concentrate on the old line through Gueudecourt which he shelled continually. The remaining two reserve guns were moved up to old support line prior to relief. At dusk the reserve section + one of the support guns relieved the four guns in the firing line these going back to reserve in the old support line.	
"	15-10-16	–	Enemy shelling again heavy + his aircraft active. He made no attempt to counterattack. Copy of Bgd. Orders of this date attached.	Appendix D.
"	16-10-16	–	Two reserve guns mounted to deal with enemy aircraft which had become exceptionally active resulting in great improvement in accuracy of enemy shell fire.	

A M Morris Major Comd
86th M. G. Coy

2449 Wt. W14957/M90 750,000 1/16 J.B.C. & A. Forms/C.2118/12.

WAR DIARY
or
INTELLIGENCE SUMMARY
(Erase heading not required.)

Instructions regarding War Diaries and Intelligence Summaries are contained in F. S. Regs., Part II. and the Staff Manual respectively. Title Pages will be prepared in manuscript.

Place	Date	Hour	Summary of Events and Information	Remarks and references to Appendices
SOMME	17.10.16		Details of a proposed further advance arrived at 2 pm and operation orders (copy of which are attached) were sent out to section officers by 4 pm. The mobile guns as in the last attack proving a great assistance to the advancing infantry were again used in this advance.	Appendix E.
"	18.10.16	—	Zero was fixed for 3.40 am. The Artillery barrage was perfect. No German machine guns opened fire to the four mobile guns to engage. All the Corps guns kept up their barrage on enemy's communications [illegible] fire to assault infantry. Half an hour after Zero these four guns together with the 5 other guns detailed in operation orders went forward to the new position, a few enemy bombers were found in the new trench, these were disposed of and positions were taken up as follows. 4 guns on left of Brigade on exposed flank 1 centre of left Battn 2 in centre of Brigade 2 on right flank of Brigade [struck through]. The attack was completely successful the objectives of the Brigade being reached & consolidated. The positions of the guns immediately after the attack were as follows. 9 guns in front line 4 in support 3 in reserve which were used for anti-aircraft purposes. In the actual advance our casualties were 1 O.R. wounded. The enemy shelling on the new position was not heavy. [struck through] Heavy sniping was experienced. At 2 pm the 3 Reserve guns teams moved up and relieved 4 guns in Support who in turn relieved 4 guns in the firing line. Our dispositions now being 9 guns firing line 3 in Support & 4 in Reserve. Rations water & Ammunition were being carried in relays to the front line part of the distance pack animals being utilised	
	19.10.16		Operation Orders were received for relief of the Company by the 87th M.G.C. on the 20th inst. at 3 pm. Orders were sent to section officers to supply the necessary guides for the following day. The front line experienced heavy shelling throughout the day.	

A. Morris Major Comg
88th M.G. Coy

2449 Wt. W14957/M90 750,000 1/16 J.B.C. & A. Forms/C.2118/12.

Instructions regarding War Diaries and Intelligence Summaries are contained in F. S. Regs., Part II. and the Staff Manual respectively. Title Pages will be prepared in manuscript.

WAR DIARY
or
INTELLIGENCE SUMMARY
(Erase heading not required.)

Place	Date	Hour	Summary of Events and Information	Remarks and references to Appendices
	20.10.16		Relief of the Company commenced at 5 pm and continued throughout the night. The relieving Company experiencing transport difficulties.	
	21.10.16		The last teams were finally relieved at 11 pm and the Company went into bivouacs near BERNAFAY WOOD S22D. Our total casualties for the time in the line and the two attacks consisted of 1 Officer + (3) O.Ranks killed (13) O.R. wounded + (5) missing.	B.L. WATTS 2nd LIEUT.
	22.10.16		The Company proceeded to clean all guns ammunition which had become exceedingly muddy owing to the state of the ground + the wet weather.	
	23.10.16		The Company still in Reserve in bivouacs in the battle zone the shelters are improvised being on conquered territory. The men on the whole although physically fatigued are strongly imbued with the offensive spirit on account of their magnificent achievement for the recent operations. The Commanding Officer + Adjutant + Section Officers + Senior N.C.Os of the Company made a Reconnaissance of the Support Lines of the Divisional Area with a view of affording covering fire to our advancing troops in the next attack.	
	24.10.16		The Company still in reserve is being reinforced + reorganised for future operations.	
	25.10.16		The Company still in reserve, guns being overhauled usual routine parades. Weather conditions at the present time are adverse to immediate operations.	
	26.10.16		The Company still in reserve in the battle zone	
	27.10.16		The Company are ordered to move into positions already selected in order to cover the advance of future operations. The guns numbering 12 are extended over the Divisional area.	

A.L. Morris Major Comdg
88th M.G. Coy

Instructions regarding War Diaries and Intelligence Summaries are contained in F. S. Regs., Part II. and the Staff Manual respectively. Title Pages will be prepared in manuscript.

WAR DIARY
or
INTELLIGENCE SUMMARY

(Erase heading not required.)

Place	Date	Hour	Summary of Events and Information	Remarks and references to Appendices
BERNAFAY WOOD	28.10.16		Company still in bivouacs waiting for final movement orders. Slight improvement in weather conditions. Previous orders cancelled.	
	29.10.16		Movement orders came through for a move on the following day. Transport loaded ready for the road	
POMIERS	30.10.16		Company paraded at 9.30 am and marched to POMIERS CAMP arriving there at 2 pm where we bivouaced for the night. Roads were very heavy. Rations issued to individual men	
VILLE	31.10.16		Company paraded at 9.30 am marched to VILLE via FRICOURT, MEAULTE. Billeting parties were sent ahead at 8 am. Transport leaving at the same time via CARNOY, MAMETZ, FRICOURT, MEAULTE, arrived at VILLE 2 pm where billets were awaiting us. Transport arrived an hour afterwards. Days ration issued as yesterday.	Map of FRANCE AMIENS 17 1/100,000

W Morris Major Comdg
8th Machine Gun Coy

2449 Wt. W14957/M90 750,000 1/16 J.B.C. & A. Forms/C.2118/12.

Confidential

G 37

29 Sept 16.

O.C. 88th Machine Gun Coy.
Copy to HQ 88th Bde

Reference Programme for operations on the night of 30th inst. your guns are required to fire from 8.55 p.m to 9.30 p.m with the object of keeping down enemy patrols & fire from the area shot over.
The following guns should be used:—

6 B	range 1600x ;	traverse 100°–105°
5 A ALT open E	1000x	55°–70°
X 2	1500x	90°–95°
2 B	8–900x	90°–100°
F 5 open E	1000x	50°–60°.

A. C. [illegible] Capt
for Bde Major
86th Inf Bde

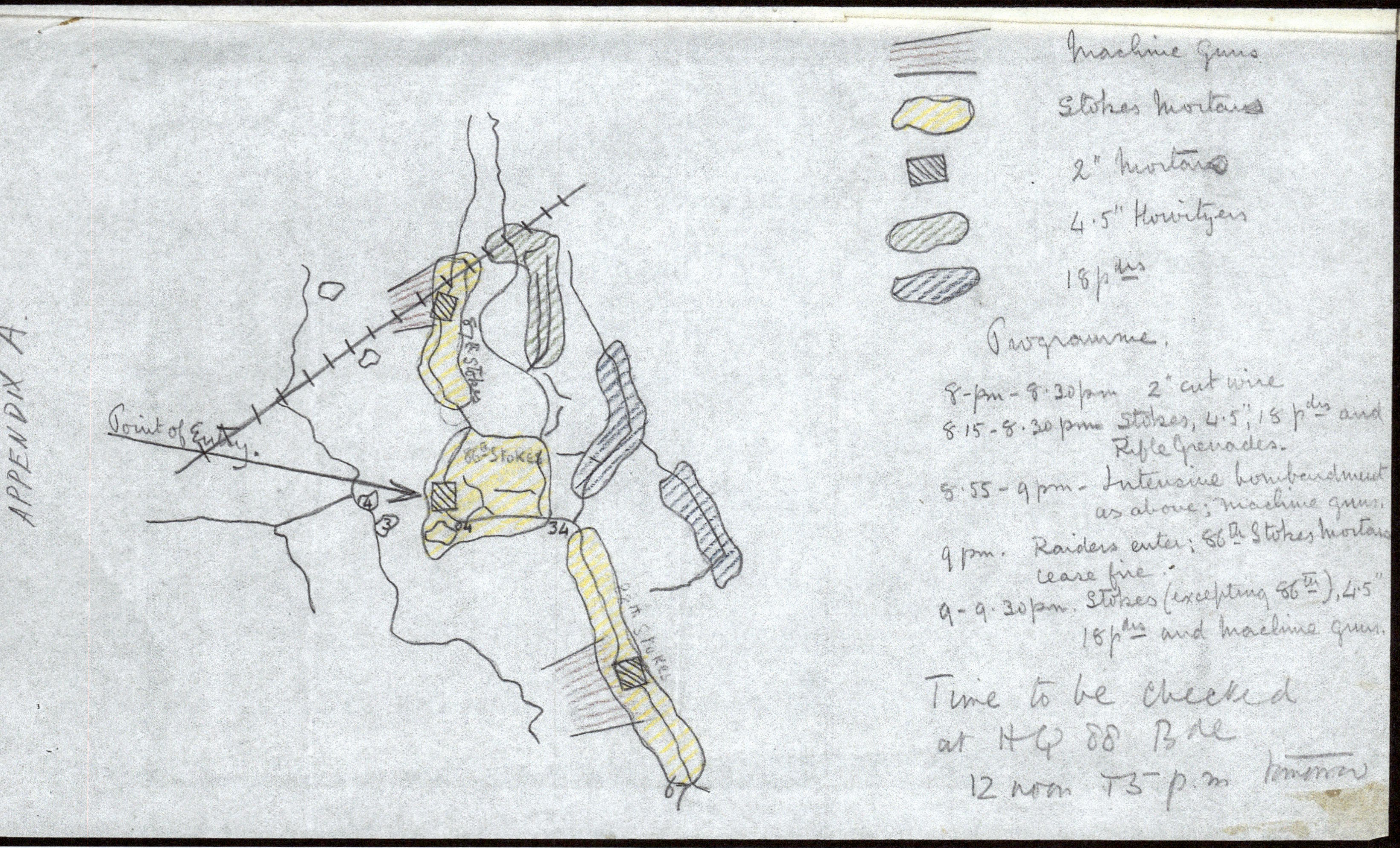

APPENDIX A.
Point of Entry.
87th Stokes
86th Stokes
4
3
94
34
67
Machine Guns
Stokes Mortars
2" Mortars
4.5" Howitzers
18 pdrs
Programme.
8 pm - 8.30 pm 2" cut wire
8.15 - 8.30 pm Stokes, 4.5", 18 pdrs and Rifle Grenades.
8.55 - 9 pm - Intensive bombardment as above; machine guns.
9 pm. Raiders enter; 86th Stokes Mortars cease fire.
9 - 9.30 pm. Stokes (excepting 86th), 4.5" 18 pdrs and machine guns.
Time to be checked at HQ 88 Bde 12 noon T3 p.m tomorrow

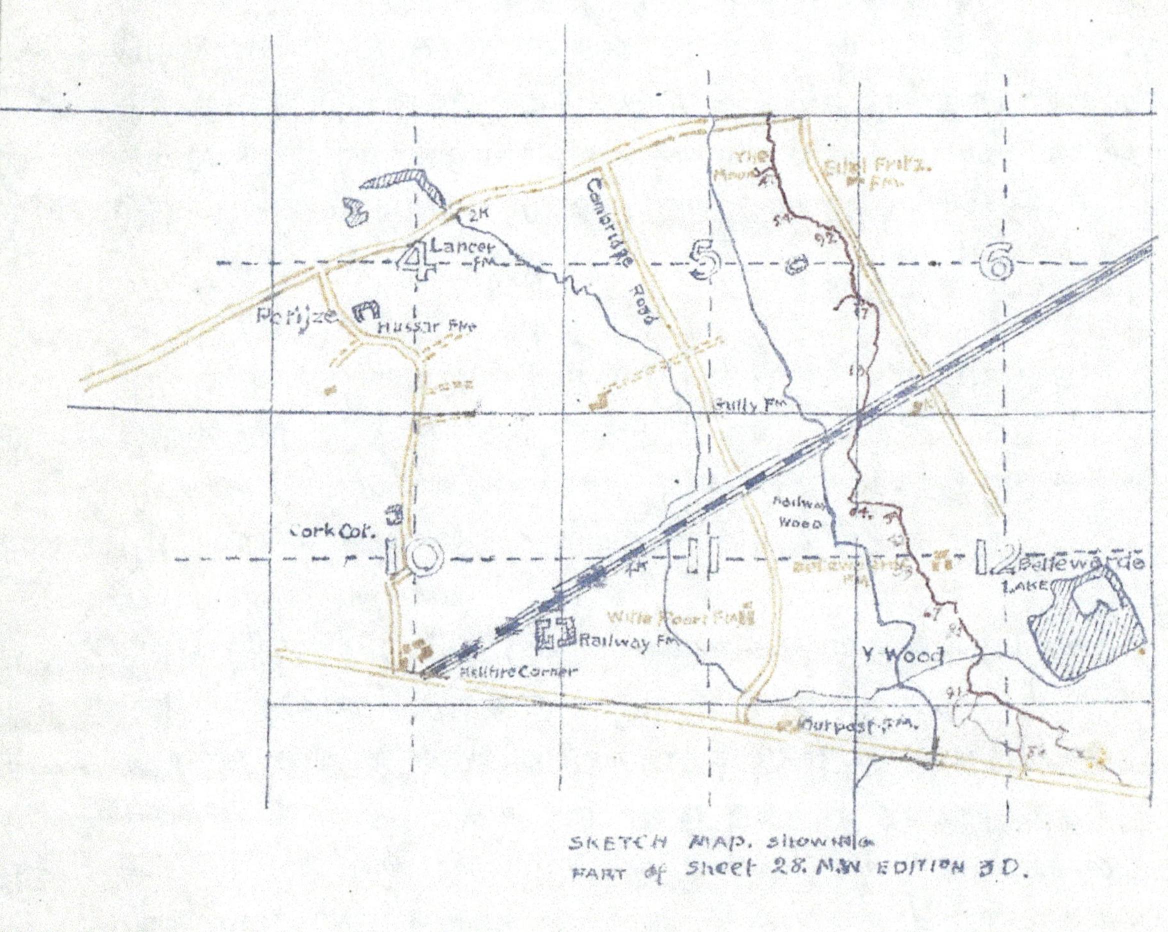

SKETCH MAP. SHOWING
PART of Sheet 28. N.W EDITION 3D.

APPENDIX B

88th Machine Gun Company
Relief Orders

The company will be relieved by the 165th Company on the night of 4/5
The Transport Officer will arrange with the Transport Officer 165th Company, a guide for their Transport.

I 4 Guides from Ramparts will be at Menin Gate at 7-30pm.
3 " " Potijze will be at Junction of Potijze and Menin Road at 7-00pm
Guides for all other Guns will be at Company Headquarters at 7-30pm.
These guides will be the No 3s of each gun who will remain with the incoming teams till the following day.

IV The N.C.O i/c each gun will get a receipt for everything handed over, these receipts will be handed to Section Officers who will forward them to the Company Orderly Room on the next day
Range cards will be included in these receipts

V 10 Belt Boxes per gun (except from Ramparts) should reach Company Headquarters. Ecole between the hours of 5pm and 7pm on the 4th inst.

VI On relief each team will return to Company Headquarters and load material on Limbers except (a) teams from CB. X2. and PS2. who will load at Potijze cross roads. (b) Rampart teams who will load at Ramparts. Well clear of Menin Road.

VII Section Officers will give relieving Officers all necessary information regarding the positions

VIII All Headquarter Baggage will be ready for loading by 8pm

IX 7 Limbers, 1 G.S. Wagon (from Hants) 1 Mess Cart and 1 Water Cart will be required as follows at 8-30pm.
At Company Headquarters 4 Limbers, 1 G.S. Wagon. 1 Mess Cart, 1 Water Cart.
" Potijze Cross Roads 1 Limber
" Ramparts 2 "

X No IV Section on Relief will join No II Section at Ramparts and await Coy.

XI The company will entrain at Asylum and detrain at Poperinghe where it will be met by the Q.M.S & proceed [illegible] Billets. Dress:- Marching Order with packs.

XII Lieut Parsons will remain at Ecole till the 5th inst. No 3s will report to him by 6pm on that date at the Ecole, The complete party will proceed by train to Poperinghe where a guide will meet them

Jas. Chalmers 2nd Lieut & Act Adjt.
88th Machine Gun Company

A. Morris Major Comd
88th M.G. Coy

APPENDIX C

Scale 1/10,000
13
14
15
19
20
21
Line Trench
Bank
Luisenhof Farm
Willow trees
Juice Alley
Luisenh Tr.
Bayonet Trench
Barley Trench
Scoyds
Bread Trench
Bacon Trench
Scabbard
Bayonet Tr.
Stormy Tr.
Gresse Trench
Cloudy Tr.
Mild Tr.
Hill Trench
Gird
Gird Trench
Gird Support
Factory Corner
Grove Alley
Cander Tr.
Seven Dials
Gross Lane
North Road
Rainbow Tr.
Great Bear
Gorden Tr.
British Trenches
True North
110
120

"A" Form. Army Form C. 2121.

MESSAGES AND SIGNALS.

No. of Message ....

Prefix .... Code .... m.	Words	Charge	This message is on a/c of:	Recd. at .... m.
Office of Origin and Service Instructions. Appendix C.	Sent At .... m. To .... By		Copy No IV Service. (Signature of "Franking Officer.")	Date .... From .... By ....

TO { Operation Orders by Major A. Moore Comdg. 88th M.G. Coy. 11th October 1916.

Sender's Number.	Day of Month.	In reply to Number.	AAA
*			

I. Information. A. Own Troops: The 88 Bge. will attack on the right flank of the 12th Division at "Zero" (an hour to be notified later) tomorrow the 12th inst.

B. Enemy: The enemy has no recognised system of defence as in the earlier stages of the advance.

2. Distribution. A. The machine guns of the 88th Coy will participate as follows:
The five guns in the front line will afford covering fire to the advancing troops until the summit of the safety margin has been reached. The enemy's line on the 88 Bge. frontage will be engaged 200 (two hundred) yards beyond Barley Trench*. These five guns will maintain a continuous fire forming a barrage. Commander as per margin.

From * BARLEY TRENCH - N.14 b 5.4 - 15.a.6.0 - 15.d.10.75 - 16.c.4.8.

Place BREAD TRENCH - N.15.a.3.8 - 15.d.75.00 - 22.a.0.6.

Time

The above may be forwarded as now corrected. (Z)

Censor. Signature of Addressor or person authorised to telegraph in his name.

* This line should be erased if not required.

225,000. W 14042—M 44. H. W. & V., Ld. 12/15.

"A" Form. Army Form C. 2121

MESSAGES AND SIGNALS.

No. of Message ....

Prefix .... Code .... m. Office of Origin and Service Instructions.	Words / Charge; Sent At .... m. To .... By	This message is on a/c of: .... Service. (Signature of "Franking Officer.")	Recd. at .... m. Date .... From .... By ....

TO

Sender's Number.	Day of Month.	In reply to Number.	AAA
*			

B. Mobile Guns: 3 guns (commanded as far [illegible]) will be utilised to neutralise the effect of enemy machine gun fire by forming a [illegible] effective zone at the [illegible] from which the fire is most intense. The O/C Mobile Guns will keep observation on the enemy's line & act according to the operation order for location of enemy machine guns. Consolidation. When the infantry has reached its objective the signals will be [illegible] which will consist of Yellow Flares. Two guns will go forward under Lt. Owen ~~[illegible]~~ half an hour after the Yellow Flares has gone up taking opportunity of a lull in the barrage. Lt. C. S. [illegible] & the three mobile guns will move forward at ~~[illegible]~~ dusk.

From

Place

Time

The above may be forwarded as now corrected. (Z)

Censor. Signature of Addressor or person authorised to telegraph in his name.

* This line should be erased if not required.

225,000 W 14042—M 44. H. W. & V., Ld. 12/15.

"A" Form. Army Form C. 2121

MESSAGES AND SIGNALS.

No. of Message..........

Prefix .... Code .... m.	Words	Charge	This message is on a/c of:	Recd. at .... m.
Office of Origin and Service Instructions.	Sent		.... Service.	Date ....
	At .... m.			From ....
	To			
	By		(Signature of "Franking Officer.")	By ....

TO

Sender's Number.	Day of Month.	In reply to Number.	AAA
*			

4. Support Guns: Targets as already arranged will be engaged. Fire will be opened at Zero and will be continued until one hour after the Yellow Flares have been sent up. In the event of an enemy counter attack developing the guns will reopen on the same targets.

5. Reserve guns will remain at Coy. Hq at the disposal of the Bde. Commander.

6. Reports: Disposition reports will reach this office as soon as possible with explanatory diagram attached.

7. Watches: Watches will be synchronised at No 4 section headquarters by ration carriers tonight.

8. Water & Rations: Men will be in possession of iron rations & unconsumed portion of the day's rations. Water will be sent up by men of the reserve section guided by orderlies who bring in disposition reports.

From

Place

Time

The above may be forwarded as now corrected. (Z)

Censor. Signature of Addressor or person authorised to telegraph in his name.

* This line should be erased if not required.

225,000 W 14042—M 44. H, W & V., Ld. 12/15.

"A" Form.

Army Form C. 2121.

MESSAGES AND SIGNALS.

No. of Message ....

Prefix .... Code .... m.	Words	Charge	This message is on a/c of:	Recd. at .... m.
Office of Origin and Service Instructions.	Sent		.... Service.	Date ....
	At .... m.			From ....
	To			
	By		(Signature of "Franking Officer.")	By ....

TO

Sender's Number.	Day of Month.	In reply to Number.	AAA
*			

9. Communication: Messages will be sent to O.C. No 1 Section (in Fire Trench) who will forward them.

10 Movement of Support Section: No 2 Section will move forward to the present firing line after dark tomorrow evening if the operation is successful. A guide for this purpose will be provided.

11 Implements: Tools will be taken forward by all consolidating teams.

12 Acknowledge.

A.H. Moore Major Comndg.
88 T.M. Company

Copy No I Operation Order File
" II O.C. Support Section.
" III O.C. No. I Section.
" IV O.C. No. II Section.
" V War Diary.

From

Place

Time

The above may be forwarded as now corrected. (Z)

.... *Censor.* Signature of Addressor or person authorised to telegraph in his name.

* This line should be erased if not required.

225,000. W 14042—M 44. H. W. & V., Ld. 12/15.

Note: The hour of Zero will be obtained by Os.C. Nos 1 & 2 Sections from the nearest Coy HQ in the line.

Appendix D.

B R I G A D E   O R D E R S

by

Brigadier-General D.E. CAYLEY, C.M.G., Commanding, 88th Inf. Brigade.

****

15th October, 1916.

1. No Brigade Orders were published on the 14th instant.

2. OPERATIONS.

The G.O.C. wishes to place on record his appreciation of the gallant conduct of the 1st Essex Regiment and the Newfoundland Regiment in the attack on October 12th. They set a splendid example to the rest of the Division in this their first real chance against the Germans. The Newfoundland Regiment especially distinguished themselves, shewing qualities of the greatest dash and determination.

Though he deplores the heavy casualties, he thinks it is some satisfaction to feel that these two Regiments inflicted far heavier casualties on the enemy.

He would like to congratulate the 88th Machine Gun Company too for their splendid dash and for the invaluable work they did on this occasion.

3. RETURNS.

Units will please render to this office as early as possible, but not later than 0900 on the 17th instant -

(a) a certificate, saying they are complete in Iron Rations.

(b) the numbers in and out of trenches.

(c) a list of Interpreters and Interpreters' horses on their ration strength.

Thos H Gooze Captain,

Staff Captain, 88th Infantry Brigade.

APPENDIX E.

OPERATION ORDERS
BY
Major H. Morris Commanding
88th M.G. Coy.

…mation

1. A. Own Troops. The 88th Brigade will attack at or about dawn tomorrow morning the 18th October 1916 at zero (zero hour to be notified later. The objective of the Brigade is GREASE TRENCH from the Cross roads (N20. D.6.9½) inclusive to N21b. 2.2. the assaulting troops will be composed of The Worcestershire Regt The Hampshire Regt.

B. Enemy The enemy's morale has broken inferior in numbers with a little determination he can be completely routed.

Distribution

Lieut Leighton

2. The four of the five guns now in HILT TRENCH will form the mobile section under Lieut Leighton he will watch for the opening of enemy machine gun fire and put a combined effective zone over the area from which it comes. Prior to zero the mobile section will take up a position in selected points in NO MANS LAND or otherwise from which the enemy's line can be controlled, the limit of frontage being as already laid down in para 1.

2nd Lt Johnston

The four guns in front of GUEUDECOURT under 2/Lt Johnston will afford covering fire to the advancing troops until the summit of the safety margin has been reached

These four guns will maintain a continuous fire forming a barrage not nearer than 200 yards in rear of BARLEY TRENCH. With the remaining gun in HILT TRENCH these will go forward on consolidation under 2nd Lieuts Johnston & Watts two guns on either flank of the right Battalion of the Brigade and one at the junction of companies in the captured position. The guns in support commanded as per margin will move forward

[Lieut] Owen three quarters of an hour after zero to what at present forms our front line. Particular attention being paid by this section to the five Cross Roads (N20 D 6. 9½) to watch for enemy movement. The supports guns will assist in forming the barrage on BARLEY TRENCH

[L]ieut Parsons. Three guns will be in Reserve under Lieut Parsons

[Co]nsolidation When the infantry has reached its objective signals will be sent up which will consist of Flares (color to be

3. notified later. The guns as heretofore detailed will go forward on receipt of this signal and take up positions as previously enumerated.

Patrols Will possibly be going out tonight during periods of

4. silence. The time to be obtained by Section Officers from the nearest Company Commander of Infantry.

Water & Rations 5. — Men will be in possession of Iron Rations & the unconsumed portion of the day's rations. WATER Empty tins must be returned to Company H.Q. tonight they will be refilled & sent up to Support Section & taken forward by them to HILT TRENCH where teams will send for their water.

Mobile Guns (Special) 6. — The four guns under Lieut Leighton will support the left Battn in consolidation particular attention being paid to the left flank.

Use of captured guns 7 — All possible use will be made of captured guns

Synchronisation of watches 8. — To be obtained from the nearest unit.

Communications 9. — Messages will be sent to the O.C. Support guns GIRD TRENCH who will forward them.

Implements 10. — As many tools as possible will be taken forward by consolidating teams

Reserve Ammunition 11. — Is being sent to GIRD TRENCH tonight from here it will be drawn when required

12. Please acknowledge

[signature] Commanding 88th M.G.C

Issued at Delville Valley 4 pm 17.10.16.

"A" Form.

Army Form C. 2121

MESSAGES AND SIGNALS.

No. of Message ....

Prefix .... Code .... m. | Words | Charge

Office of Origin and Service Instructions.

Sent At .... m. To .... By ....

This message is on a/c of: .... Service.

Appendix F,

(Signature of "Franking Officer.")

Recd. at .... m. Date .... From .... By ....

TO { Movement Orders.

Sender's Number.	Day of Month.	In reply to Number.	AAA
* —	9	—	

(1) Parade outside Coy. Hq. at ~~[illegible]~~ 12 midnight. Sections at full strength.

(2) Members of Reserve Section not actually acting as gun numbers will remain under command of Baggage Officer (Lt. Langton).

(3) Rations: Will be issued for 24 hrs to all ranks proceeding Tangier [illegible]. 2 dixies per Section + 1 for Officers' Mess will be carried. Coy. Cook (Cpl. Budden) & Officers' Mess Cook will accompany the Company.

(4) Signallers: Three signallers will [illegible] with the Coy. taking one bicycle.

(5) Equipment. Guns in French bags: all other parts & clean material: tripod ~~[illegible]~~ & belt boxes will be carried.

From

Place

Time

(6) N.C.O's will carry two belt boxes each.

The above may be forwarded as now corrected.

(Z)

Censor.

Signature of Addressor or person authorised to telegraph in his name.

(7) Transport [illegible] separately

* This line should be erased if not required.

225,000 W 14042—M 44. H. W & V., Ld. 12/15.

[illegible signature]

"A" Form.

Army Form C. 2121

MESSAGES AND SIGNALS.

No. of Message ....

Prefix .... Code .... m.	Words	Charge	This message is on a/c of:	Recd. at .... m.
Office of Origin and Service Instructions.	Sent		.... Service.	Date ....
	At .... m.			From ....
	To			
	By		(Signature of "Franking Officer.")	By ....

TO { 1 Movements Orders (Transport).

Sender's Number.	Day of Month.	In reply to Number.	AAA
* —	9	—	

(1) Route: Bronfay – Heilly – Dernancourt – Meaulte – Fricourt – Pommiers

If weather permits the horse track North of Heilly, Dernancourt, Meaulte – Fricourt will be used.

(2) 500 yds. interval between Battns. & Regtl. Transport will be kept. Halts will be made for 10 mins. at 10 mins to each clock hour. Units will halt & move off independently at these times.

(3) Guides will rendezvous outside at Bde. H.q. at 7.30 am.

(4) Order of March: Worcesters
Warwicks.
Bde. Hq.
M.G. Coy. Transport

(5) Worcesters start from end of their area nearest Place de la Republic at 8 am.

From

Place

Time

The above may be forwarded as now corrected.

B.T. .... Censor.

(Z) .... at Corbie 6

Signature of Addressor or person authorised to telegraph in his name.

* This line should be erased if not required.

225,000. W 14042—M 44. H. W & V., Ld. 12/15.

"A" Form.
Army Form C. 2121

MESSAGES AND SIGNALS.

No. of Message ....

Prefix .... Code .... m.	Words	Charge	This message is on a/c of:	Recd. at ....m.
Office of Origin and Service Instructions.	Sent		..........Service.	Date ....
	At..........m.			From ....
	To			
	By		(Signature of "Franking Officer.")	By ....

TO

Sender's Number.	Day of Month.	In reply to Number.	AAA
*			

(7) Dinners will be cooked en route.

(8) Transport parades at 7 a.m.

(9) Animals will be fed at 5.30 a.m.

J. Miller [illegible]

[illegible]

From

Place

Time

The above may be forwarded as now corrected. (Z)

Censor. Signature of Addressor or person authorised to telegraph in his name.

* This line should be erased if not required.

225,000. W 14042—M 44. H. W. & V., Ld. 12/15.

29th Division.

88th Infantry Brigade.

88th MACHINE GUN COMPANY

NOVEMBER 1 9 1 6

Confidential

War Diary

of

88th Machine Gun Company

From 1st November 1916 to 30th November 1916

(VOLUME I)

Brigade Major
88th Brigade

There seems nothing to be learnt from the period embracing the last month with the exception that all ranks now recognise that we have established superiority ~~of~~ over our enemy.

This is especially clear as regards Machine Guns. It is manifest that the enemy can no longer use his machine guns with the same impunity as in the ~~[illegible]~~ earlier stages of the war.

There has been a considerable decrease in his machine gun fire as regards effect.

A. Morrison Major Cmdg
88th M. G. Coy

1-12-16

Army Form C. 2118.

WAR DIARY
or
INTELLIGENCE SUMMARY

(Erase heading not required.)

Instructions regarding War Diaries and Intelligence Summaries are contained in F. S. Regs., Part II. and the Staff Manual respectively. Title Pages will be prepared in manuscript.

Place	Date	Hour	Summary of Events and Information	Remarks and references to Appendices
VILLE	1/11/16		Company resting in billets, cleaning of guns & spare parts, general cleaning of clothing & equipment	
"	2.11.16		In billets usual parades, kit inspections	
"	3.11.16		In billets Company training	
"	4.11.16		Still resting ordinary parades	
"	5.11.16		Billets ceremonial parades	
"	6.11.16	noon	Company with transport inspected by Brigadier General D.E. Cayley C.M.G.	
"	7.11.16		Billets usual parades. Improvement of billets, making incinerators, wash houses &c	
"	8.11.16		Bathing parade.	
"	9.11.16		Usual parades Company training.	
"	10.11.16		Usual parades	
"	11.11.16		Route march VILLE, TREUX, BUIRE.	
"	12.11.16		Parades & inspections	
"	13.11.16		Usual parades	
"	14.11.16		Thorough cleaning of guns & ammunition, preparatory to going into the line.	[illegible signature]

2449 Wt. W14957/M90 750,000 1/16 J.B.C. & A. Forms/C.2118/12.

Army Form C. 2118.

Instructions regarding War Diaries and Intelligence Summaries are contained in F. S. Regs., Part II. and the Staff Manual respectively. Title Pages will be prepared in manuscript.

WAR DIARY
or
INTELLIGENCE SUMMARY
(Erase heading not required.)

Place	Date	Hour	Summary of Events and Information	Remarks and references to Appendices
VILLE + MEAULTE	15.11.16		Movement orders received an advance party of one Officer and N.C.Os preceded the Company by three hours. The Company moved off at 9 am marched with transport to SANDPITS CAMP near MEAULTE and remained the night under canvas.	
MEAULTE	16.11.16		Preliminary reconnaissance of the new line by the Commanding Officer Adjutant + Section Officers, The Company remained in SANDPITS. Operation Orders received that half teams should relieve the 24th M.G.C on the night of 16/17th accordingly	
	16.11.16		Half teams under Section officers moved off at 9 am ROUTE MAMETZ, MONTAUBAN, GUILLEMONT arriving at GUILLEMONT STATION at 2 pm where they rested an hour and moved off to their respective positions at 5 pm. All packs being left at the Transport lines. The rest of the Company remaining at SANDPITS.	[illegible] 88 M.G. Coy
	17.11.16		The remainder of the Company moved to GUILLEMONT route as previously mentioned arriving at 1 pm, the remainder of the 24th M.G.C. being relieved and Headquarters established at GUILLEMONT STATION. Disposition of the guns as follows. Four guns in the front line (two in AUTUMN TR. two in DEWDROP TR.) Four in Support JOHN BULL TRENCH. Four in Reserve FIERS LINE Four at Coy Hq. Transport moved to CARNOY	Appendix 1/1
	18.11.16		Weather cold no proper accomodation for the men, shelling normal	FRANCE 57c S.W.

2449 Wt. W14957/M90 750,000 1/16 J.B.C. & A. Forms/C.2118/12.

WAR DIARY
or
INTELLIGENCE SUMMARY
(Erase heading not required.)

Army Form C. 2118.

Instructions regarding War Diaries and Intelligence Summaries are contained in F. S. Regs., Part II. and the Staff Manual respectively. Title Pages will be prepared in manuscript.

Place	Date	Hour	Summary of Events and Information	Remarks and references to Appendices
GUILLEMONT LES BOEUFS	19.11.16		Weather changing from cold to wet and the front trenches & the sunken road close to LES BOEUF being barraged every evening, the four guns in the advanced positions relieved at 7 am by the Section at Coy Hq the latter leaving at 3.30 am, taking with them 48 hours rations and water. Ammunition etc being handed over with the exception of the guns.	[illegible] Capt
" "	20.11.16		Wet weather, the trenches in a bad condition, communication at the present time is very difficult and entails a great deal of labour on the personnel in the carrying of their guns & tripods. Water and rations being taken to the FLERS LINE by pack animals and thence carried by the men.	
" "	20.11.16		A most regrettable incident happened to the Company on this date a whole gun team was annihilated and the gun tripod & spare parts blown up, this was due to the enemy observing new work in communicating and heavily barraged the sector in which the gun was situated, with the unfortunate result as above stated. A further remarkable incident in connection with this sad affair was the death of Cpl Gillingham who had been through the whole campaign since the beginning of hostilities in the East & was present at the historic landing of the incomparable 29th Division at Cape Helles in ~~March~~ April 1915. He went through the whole campaign without a days absence from duty until he paid the final tribute to his country before LE TRANSLOY tolled in the	

Army Form C. 2118.

Instructions regarding War Diaries and Intelligence Summaries are contained in F. S. Regs., Part II. and the Staff Manual respectively. Title Pages will be prepared in manuscript.

WAR DIARY
or
INTELLIGENCE SUMMARY

(Erase heading not required.)

MACHINE GUN COMPANY. No. .... Date ....

Place	Date	Hour	Summary of Events and Information	Remarks and references to Appendices
			performance of his duty. This N.C.O. won the Military Medal for his gallantry in action in the attack on the	
GUILLEMONT	20.11.16		enemy trenches before GUEDECOURT on October 12th 1916. This attack with that of 18th Octr 1916 was successful	
LES BOEUFS			in the outset in both of which the 88th M.G.C. participated & played a prominent part.	
	21.11.16		At 3.30 am. the section at Coy Hq relieved the section in FLERS LINE who in turn relieved the front four guns the latter relieving those in JOHN BULL TRENCH that section returning to Coy Hq.	
"	22.11.16		Guns advanced a trench which had been observed for a considerable period in the vicinity of JOHN BULL TRENCH this commanded the valley & the entrance to LES BOEUFS from the North it also afforded direct enfilade fire on LES BOEUFS in the event of an enemy ~~counter~~ attack being in any way successful. Improvement of trenches, building of gun emplacements & dug outs.	
"	23.11.16		at 3.30am section in rear relieved section in FLERS LINE who relieved those in front line on relief came to JOHN BULL TRENCH relieved section to Coy Hq.	
"	24.11.16		Enemy barraged LES BOEUFS heavily at 8 P.M. Enemy shelling with considerable activity. GINCHY CORNER shelled intermittently	
"	25.11.16		The relief of C Section in advanced positions by those in FLERS LINE. The relieved section came back into Reserve. This taking place in the early morning as usual.	
"	26.11.16		The revetting of trenches and building of shelters. The heavy shell fire to which the ground	

2449 Wt. W14957/M90 750,000 1/16 J.B.C. & A. Forms/C.2118/12.

WAR DIARY
or
INTELLIGENCE SUMMARY
(Erase heading not required.)

Instructions regarding War Diaries and Intelligence Summaries are contained in F. S. Regs., Part II. and the Staff Manual respectively. Title Pages will be prepared in manuscript.

Place	Date	Hour	Summary of Events and Information	Remarks and references to Appendices
GUILLEMONT			has been subjected, makes the revetting of all trenches a necessity	
LES BOEUF	27.11.16		Relief of the forward section by ~~the~~ the section in FLERS LINE. Relief being carried out in this way that the men have not so far to walk to the front line instead of coming straight from Reserve. 48 hours rations being taken by the relieving section, saving the employment of ration parties each night. Weather wet and foggy	
" "	28.11.16		On notification that our present frontage was being extended. Reconnaissance of the new line by the C.O. & Adj. and new gun positions sited, and arrangements made for deep dug outs being provided for gun teams.	
" "	29.11.16		Relief of forward section by that in FLERS LINE completed by 8 am, slight improvement in the weather conditions	
" "	30.11.16		Gun teams move into new positions sited on the 28th inst. Working on the positions & improvements to surrounding trenches. Weather cold but fine. Shell fire normal	

2449 Wt. W14957/M90 750,000 1/16 J.B.C. & A. Forms/C.2118/12.

APPENDIX A
Transloy
Trench
Cemetery Circle
Hail Tr.
Pollax
Sleet
Fall Tr.
Autumn Tr.
Bennet Tr.
Mirage
Spectrum
Summer
Boriska
Frosty
Ozone Avenue
Dewdrop Winter Trench
Dewdrop
Snow
Antelope Tr.
Slush
Rainy
Thunder
Cold Tr.
German Tr.
Windy
Maitland
Burnaby Trench
Musty
Windy
Mid Lane
Thistle Trench
Shamrock Trench
Flank Aven
Trench
Ozone
Lesboeufs
Windmill
Odour Tr.
Fluff Trench
CORPS BOUNDARY
"Future"
No 6. 18-11-16
Shewing Derelict Trenches
Scale 1:10000

29th Division.

88th Infantry Brigade.

- ---------

88th MACHINE GUN COMPANY

DECEMBER 1916

W249

Confidential —

War Diary

of

88th Machine Gun Company

From 1st December 1916 To 31st December 1916

(Volume 7 of ?)

Army Form C. 2118.

Instructions regarding War Diaries and Intelligence Summaries are contained in F. S. Regs., Part II. and the Staff Manual respectively. Title Pages will be prepared in manuscript.

WAR DIARY
or
INTELLIGENCE SUMMARY

(Erase heading not required.)

Place	Date	Hour	Summary of Events and Information	Remarks and references to Appendices
GUILLEMONT & LES BOEUFS	1.12.16		Relief of the front Sections by those in Reserve, the former taking over the latters place at Coy Hq. One gun from FLERS LINE taking up position in THISTLE Trench (N.34c 35.65.) and the remaining guns in FLERS LINE took up and occupied the following positions in the vicinity of that line T8d 80.75. T9c 15.60 T9c 40.80. After the completion of this relief the position of our guns being FALL TRENCH N35c 9.4. SUMMER TRENCH N35c 3.9. OZONE TRENCH N34b 6.2 WINTER TRENCH N35c 35.10 THISTLE TRENCH N34c 35.65 COW TRENCH T3a central T3a 7.3. T3b 2.8 OX TRENCH T9b 45.75 FLERS LINE as formerly stated. Enemy shelling throughout the day normal but between 5 pm & 8 pm he heavily barraged LES BOEUFS & the vicinity. Operation	FRANCE 57c S.W. Map Référence
" "	~~1.12.16~~		orders received that the Company was being relieved by the 87th M.G.C. on the 3rd inst. & that half teams ~~with~~ would be sent ahead to arrive at Brigade Headquarters at 3 pm on Saturday 2nd December	

R. W. [illegible] Major
88th M.G. Cy

2449 Wt. W14957/M90 750,000 1/16 J.B.C. & A. Forms/C.2118/12.

Instructions regarding War Diaries and Intelligence Summaries are contained in F. S. Regs., Part II. and the Staff Manual respectively. Title Pages will be prepared in manuscript.

WAR DIARY
or
INTELLIGENCE SUMMARY
(Erase heading not required.)

Place	Date	Hour	Summary of Events and Information	Remarks and references to Appendices
GUILLEMONT LES BOEUFS	2.12.16		Guides arrived at Coy Headquarters at 11 am according to orders issued to Section Officers late last night. Half teams from the 87th Company arrived at Headquarters 12 noon and moved off to their respective positions at 3 pm on relief half teams proceeded to Coy Hq as per orders. The construction of Deep Dugouts started in the COW TRENCH under supervision of the R.E's.	
	3.12.16		The remainder of the 87th Company arrived at 12 noon. Sections on relief after reporting completion of relief & handing in certificates of trench stores to Company Headquarters proceeding to camp CARNOY WEST. The last section leaving and relief completed by 11 pm. The Company housed in Niessen huts. Tripods & belt boxes handed over to the incoming unit.	
	~~4.12.16~~		~~Cleaning of guns~~ The total number of casualties while the Company was in the line being 8 killed 5 wounded & 9 to hospital. For the period the Company was in the line there appeared to be great artillery activity on the	

[illegible] Major

Instructions regarding War Diaries and Intelligence Summaries are contained in F. S. Regs., Part II. and the Staff Manual respectively. Title Pages will be prepared in manuscript.

WAR DIARY
or
INTELLIGENCE SUMMARY
(Erase heading not required.)

Place	Date	Hour	Summary of Events and Information	Remarks and references to Appendices
GUILLEMONT – CARNOY	3.12.16	–	part of the enemy, he registered definite zones which were easily avoided after a little experience on certain sectors he seemed to be particularly obtuse as his registration was perfect though non effective	
CARNOY	4.12.16		Cleaning of guns spare parts belts ammunition & belt boxes and general cleaning and polishing up of the person and camp	
"	5.12.16		Cleaning parades, kit inspections and general inspections for cleanliness	
"	6.12.16		The usual routine and parades. Four classes of instruction for the men of the new draft and lectures by Officers.	
"	7.12.16		Usual parades and classes.	
"	8.12.16		Usual routine. Movement Orders received that the Company will move into billets at VILLE. The Company being clear of CARNOY camp by	

A. Mossman [?] Major
88th M. G. Coy

2449 Wt. W14957/M90 750,000 1/16 J.B.C. & A. Forms/C.2118/12.

Instructions regarding War Diaries and Intelligence Summaries are contained in F. S. Regs., Part II. and the Staff Manual respectively. Title Pages will be prepared in manuscript.

or

INTELLIGENCE SUMMARY

(Erase heading not required.)

Place	Date	Hour	Summary of Events and Information	Remarks and references to Appendices
CARNOY	8.12.16		12 noon on the 9th inst. Billeting Officer accordingly sent on in advance to arrange billets for the Company and Movement Orders issued by 6 pm (a copy attached)	Appendix A.
CARNOY VILLE	9.12.16		Company moved off by Sections at half an hour interval the first section leaving at 9 am, the Company clear of CARNOY CAMP at 11 am. Transport followed Company. arrived at VILLE 2 pm and men billeted	
VILLE	10.12.16		Cleaning of guns tripods & ammunition limbers &c Usual guards & parades	
VILLE	11.12.16		Usual parades.	
VILLE	12.11.16		Orders received that Company would move on the 14th inst. to MOLLIENS VIDAME transport preceding the Company on the 13th by road. Movement Orders (copy	Appendix B.

[signature] Major
88th [illegible]

2449 Wt. W14957/M90 750,000 1/16 J.B.C. & A. Forms/C.2118/12.

Instructions regarding War Diaries and Intelligence Summaries are contained in F. S. Regs., Part II. and the Staff Manual respectively. Title Pages will be prepared in manuscript.

WAR DIARY
or
INTELLIGENCE SUMMARY
(Erase heading not required.)

Place	Date	Hour	Summary of Events and Information	Remarks and references to Appendices
VILLE	12.12.16		attached) issued at 5 pm	
"	13.12.16		Transport loaded by 8.30 am & proceeded to DAOURS. Billeting Officer sent forward to MOLLIENS VIDAME and HANGEST to arrange billets for the Company	
VILLE CROUY	14.12.16		Company paraded at 11.30 am and marched to EDGE HILL where it entrained at 2 pm for HANGEST arriving at the latter place at 5.30 pm. No billets available in HANGEST the company marched to CROUY about 1½ miles where it was billeted for the night. Rations had been issued and were carried by the Company	
CROUY MOLLIENS VIDAME	15.12.16		Company paraded at 11.30 am and marched to MOLLIENS VIDAME arriving at 2 pm where billets were allotted to the men. Transport already here, arrived the previous evening.	

A. Morris Capt.
88th F. Coy

WAR DIARY

or

INTELLIGENCE SUMMARY

(Erase heading not required.)

Instructions regarding War Diaries and Intelligence Summaries are contained in F. S. Regs., Part II. and the Staff Manual respectively. Title Pages will be prepared in manuscript.

Place	Date	Hour	Summary of Events and Information	Remarks and references to Appendices
~~[illegible]~~ MOLLIENS VIDAME	16.12.16		Company in billets have at once proceeded to clean themselves guns etc paraded 11.30 for inspection. Weather fine. The making of beds for the men & improvement of billets making washhouses etc to be commenced on Monday.	
"	17.12.16		Parades. Church parades only.	
"	18.12.16		Training carried out as per syllabus of training attached for reference	Appendix
"	19.12.16		ROUTE MARCH via MOLLIENS VIDAME, BOUGAINVILLE, FLOXICOURT, DREUIL MOLLIENS. Board of examining Officers sitting examining the men of the company in mechanism stoppages and elementary training & standard test.	
"	20.12.16		Usual parades improvements to billets & horse stabling commenced the building of latrines etc	

A.H. Morris Major
88th M.G. Co

Instructions regarding War Diaries and Intelligence Summaries are contained in F. S. Regs., Part II. and the Staff Manual respectively. Title Pages will be prepared in manuscript.

WAR DIARY
or
INTELLIGENCE SUMMARY
(Erase heading not required.)

Place	Date	Hour	Summary of Events and Information	Remarks and references to Appendices
Molliens Vidame	21/12/16		Route march cancelled owing to rain, Parades. Gun cleaning. Lecture on Sanitation	
	22/12/16		Parades as per programme.	
	23/12/16		Parades as per programme, Board of Examining officers finished.	
	24/12/16		Church Parade.	
	25/12/16		General Holiday	
	26/12/16		Route March & Baths. Improvement of billets continued	
	27/12/16		Parades as per programme. No 4 Section on the ranges	
	28/12/16		Route March. No 1 Section on the ranges.	
	29/12/16		Parades as usual. No 2 Section on the ranges.	
	30/12/16		Parades as per programme. Guards as usual.	
	31/12/16		Church parade.	

[illegible signature]
88th M. G. Coy

[illegible] Orders
by
Major R Morris Commanding
88th [illegible] Company
In the Field 8th [illegible]ember 1916

I [illegible]ment	The 88th Company will move into [illegible] tomorrow at Ville Sections will move independently with half hour intervals.
II [illegible]ute	The Company will proceed by the [illegible]noy – Meaulte – Ville route.
III Discipline	Section Officers will hand in their marching out [illegible] and certificates that the [illegible] have been left clean by 10am tomorrow. to the Adjutant.
IV Order of March	No 4 Section and Headquarters " 3 " " New Draft " 2 " " 1 "
V Starting Point	No 4 Section will pass the water tanks at entrance to Camp at 9-5 am.
VI March Discipline	It is hoped that the strictest attention be paid to March discipline en route.
VII Forward Billeting Officer	The Billeting Officer will meet sections on their arrival and conduct them to their Billets.
VIII Transport	Orders already issued. Officers Chargers will be at [illegible] Headquarters one quarter of an hour before the re[illegible] times of march of the Sections.

R Morris Major
88th [illegible] Co

(2)

The Company Orderly Room will close at CARNOY Camp at 10-0 am and will reopen at VILLE at 12 noon.

Blankets will be rolled in bundles of 10 and legibly labelled. The name of the Section being marked on each bundle and franked by the Section Officer. All baggage will be stacked near the Orderly Room by 8 am.

2nd Lieut R.G. White will perform the duties of Baggage Officer and superintend the loading and the unloading of Blankets etc.

Each Section will take with them the unconsumed portion of the days ration. One Cook will accompany each Section on the line of march and prepare dinners for arrival.

A.Morris Major Commanding
88th Machine Gun Company

Movement Orders
By
Major R Morris Commanding
88th Machine Gun Company
In the Field "Tuesday" 12th December 1916

[illegible signature]

I
vement

The company will parad at 11-50 am outside their billets on Thursday the 14th inst. on proceed to Edgehill to entrain for Hangest, two bicycles will be taken by [illegible].
Dress:- Marching Order (less packs) one Blanket and Waterproof sheet will be carried. On arrival the Company will be billeted at Hangest for the night and proceed to Molliens Vidame the following day.

II
ansport

Transport will be loaded by 8-30 am on 13th inst. and will parade at 10 am for marching to Daours where they will spend the night and proceed to Hangest the following morning under arrangements to be made by Transport Officer.

III
ggage Officer

2nd Lieut White will perform the duties of Baggage Officer. He will see that all limbers are properly loaded by 8-30 am on 13th inst.

IV
icers Kits

Officers kits will be ready for loading and stacked o[illegible] the Billets by 8-15 am on that day. Packs to be carried by Transport they will be stacked outside billets by 7-45 am and Sec. Transport each mans number and name will be legibly marked on outside flap of packs.

V
acks

VI
ations

The unconsumed portion of the days rations will be carried by the men together with the ration for the following day which will be issued on afternoon of the 13th. Water bottles will be filled.

VII
Kettles

The following Camp Kettles will be carried:-
One per Section, one Adv. quarter party, Two New draft Section Officers and N.C.O.s in charge of these parties will ensure a man or two men being detailed to carry them

Sheet 8

Lieut Owen to be forward billeting Officer & Corpl Clarke will parade outside the Church at MERICOURT on the 13th inst at 10 am where a lorry will be provided. They will be at detraining point HANGEST to guide the Company to its destination and report to the Divisional Staff Officer there.

Issued at 1700
12 Decr 16

[signature] Lieut and Adjutant
88th Machine Gun Company

Copies		
	1 to 3	Headquarters
	4	O.C. No 1 Section
	5	O.C. " 2 "
	6	O.C. " 3 "
	7	O.C. " 4 "
	8	Transport Officer

Syllabus of Training

Machine Gun Corps — 88th Machine Gun Company

Day	7.15 am to 7.35 am	9 am to 9.30 am	9.30 to 10.30 am	11 to 11.30 am	11.30 am to 12.30 pm	12.30 to 1 pm
Monday	Swedish Drill	Close order drill	Bombing Inst.	Gas Helmet drill	Gun Mounting	Lecture by Lieut Stonehouse
Tuesday	— Route March —					
Wednesday	Swedish Drill	[illegible]	Lecture by O.C. Company	Lecture on the use of Enemy Bombs	Gas Helmet Drill	Ceremonial Drill
Thursday	— Route March —					
Friday	Swedish Drill	Indirect Fire	Kit Inspection	Lecture on Discipline	Close Order (Ceremonial)	Gas Helmet Drill
Saturday	Swedish Drill	Immediate Action	Indirect Fire	Stoppages	Lecture By Lieut Owen	Bombing Inst.

16th December 1916

A. Morris Major Commanding
88th Machine Gun Company

Instructions regarding War Diaries and Intelligence Summaries are contained in F. S. Regs., Part II. and the Staff Manual respectively. Title Pages will be prepared in manuscript.

WAR DIARY
or
INTELLIGENCE SUMMARY
(Erase heading not required.)

Army Form C. 2118.

Place	Date	Hour	Summary of Events and Information	Remarks and references to Appendices
Molliens Vidame	Jan 1.		Parades carried out as per attached programme.	A.
✓	Jan 2.		Route march Molliens Vidame, Flesselles, Bougainville, Molliens Vidame	
	Jan 3		Mk 1 Section Class on range, remainder on operations as per appendix B	B
	Jan 4		Route March Molliens Vidame, Oissy, Floxicourt Molliens Vidame	
	Jan 5		The Company went on operations as per Appendix C.	C
	Jan 6		Parades as per programme	
	Jan 7		Church parade.	
	Jan 8		Parades as per Appendix D	D
	Jan 9.		Parades as per appendix D	
	Jan 10		Company paraded for cleaning Billets. Transport left via AILLY-sur-Somme for Corbie.	
	Jan 11		Company marched to Airaines and entrained for Corbie. arrived at Corbie at 5 A.M. and went into Billets.	D I
Corbie	Jan 12.		The Company paraded for Cleaning guns Tripods & Spare parts	
	Jan 13		The Company paraded for cleaning Belts and ammunition, Limbers were loaded after Church Parade. Church Parade	

[signature] Major

2449 Wt. W14957/M90 750,000 1/16 J.B.C. & A. Forms/C.2118/12.

Army Form C. 2118.

88th MACHINE GUN COMPANY. No. Date.

WAR DIARY
or
INTELLIGENCE SUMMARY
(Erase heading not required.)

Instructions regarding War Diaries and Intelligence Summaries are contained in F. S. Regs., Part II. and the Staff Manual respectively. Title Pages will be prepared in manuscript.

Place	Date	Hour	Summary of Events and Information	Remarks and references to Appendices
CORBIE	14.1.17		Company in billets. Guns spare parts ammunition thoroughly overhauled, limbers &c and the usual parades.	
"	15.1.17		Movement orders received relative to our move tomorrow to MANSEL CAMP, usual parades.	
MANSEL CAMP CARNOY	16.1.17		Company paraded at 8 30 am and were conveyed to MANSEL CAMP by motor lorries the transport leaving at 8 am. Company arrived 12 noon and tents were allotted. Transport took over lines close to Company arriving half an hour after the Company	
"	17.1.17		Snow to depth of four inches fell early this morning. Chiropody parades and gun cleaning. General cleaning of the camp	

[signature] Lt Capt

2449 Wt. W14957/M90 750,000 1/16 J.B.C. & A. Forms/C.2118/12.

Army Form C. 2118.

WAR DIARY
or
INTELLIGENCE SUMMARY
(Erase heading not required.)

Instructions regarding War Diaries and Intelligence Summaries are contained in F. S. Regs., Part II. and the Staff Manual respectively. Title Pages will be prepared in manuscript.

88th MACHINE GUN COMPANY. No. .... Date ....

Place	Date	Hour	Summary of Events and Information	Remarks and references to Appendices
CARNOY	18.1.17		Parades & Guards as usual together with Chiropody parades	
MANSEL CAMP	19.1.17		Usual parades & cleaning. Officers reconnoitring New Sector	
	20.1.17		Camp routine weather conditions snow & frost.	
	21.1.17		Church parades Officers reconnaissance of new sector	
	22.1.17		Movement orders received relating to the relief of the 86th Machine Gun Company tomorrow. Arrangements made with O.C of that Company and movement orders issued a copy of same attached for reference.	Appendix E
GUILLEMONT MORVAL	23.1.17		Company arrived GUILLEMONT 1 pm where they rested for two hours and then marched off to their various positions, having five guns in the front system three in support four in Reserve & four	FRANCE 57c S.W. 1:10000

[illegible]

2449 Wt. W14957/M90 750,000 1/16 J.B.C. & A. Forms/C.2118/12.

Instructions regarding War Diaries and Intelligence Summaries are contained in F. S. Regs., Part II. and the Staff Manual respectively. Title Pages will be prepared in manuscript.

WAR DIARY
or
INTELLIGENCE SUMMARY
(Erase heading not required.)

88th MACHINE GUN COMPANY.
No. ....
Date. ....

Army Form C. 2118.

Place	Date	Hour	Summary of Events and Information	Remarks and references to Appendices
GUILLEMONT	23.1.17		Company Headquarters GUILLEMONT. The position of the guns were as follows (positions mentioned in last movement order Appendix E these were taken over) The weather conditions severe very hard frost during the night freezing most of the day. Relief complete by 10.30 pm. Two days rations were taken with the forward guns Transport remained at MANSEL CAMP,	Appendix E
"	24.1.17		Fire programme chiefly by night direct and indirect on enemy's dumps and communications. Hard frost by day and night necessitating fire action in order to keep the guns in working order notwithstanding the non freezing mixture of glycerine being used.	

[illegible signature]

2449 Wt. W14957/M90 750,000 1/16 J.B.C. & A. Forms/C.2118/12.

Instructions regarding War Diaries and Intelligence Summaries are contained in F. S. Regs., Part II. and the Staff Manual respectively. Title Pages will be prepared in manuscript.

WAR DIARY
or
INTELLIGENCE SUMMARY
(Erase heading not required.)

Army Form C. 2118.

Place	Date	Hour	Summary of Events and Information	Remarks and references to Appendices
GUILLEMONT MORVAL	25.1.16		The weather still continues frosty. Shelling in this Sector is normal. Operation Orders received of an attack on the enemy's trenches by the 87th Brigade at present occupying the left Brigade frontage including instructions for the co-operation of our guns in assisting the attack with covering and barrage fire. Instructions were also received for taking up 4 positions in the 87th Brigade area. Accordingly No 2 Section being the Reserve Section relieved two guns of the 87th M.G.C and took up two other positions (vide Operation Orders) in that area. Operation Orders were issued at 15 15 and sent by Orderly to Sections Officers. The Company Reliefs being provided for by relieving by half teams instead of Sections as heretofore.	APPENDIX E F
GUILLEMONT	26.1.16		Weather still remaining cold and fine. Information received that zero was fixed for 5.30 am tomorrow morning. Section Officers were accordingly notified. Atmospheric conditions being good aerial activity increased resulting in increased enemy shelling slightly above the average for the few preceding days. Rations by pack mule and hand.	

A. Morris [signature]

Instructions regarding War Diaries and Intelligence Summaries are contained in F. S. Regs., Part II. and the Staff Manual respectively. Title Pages will be prepared in manuscript.

WAR DIARY
or
INTELLIGENCE SUMMARY
(Erase heading not required.)

88th MACHINE GUN COMPANY. No. .... Date ....

Army Form C. 2118.

Place	Date	Hour	Summary of Events and Information	Remarks and references to Appendices
GUILLEMONT MORVAL	27.1.17		At 5.30 am the artillery opened a perfect barrage on the enemy's line, support trenches and strong Points. There was no [illegible]. Guns of the mobile section took up positions in "NO MANS LAND" half an hour previous to the commencement of the barrage, these were ready to engage any hostile machine Guns that opened fire. The remaining guns of the Company carried out barrage fire as per Operation Orders. The objectives were gained and the new positions consolidated. The Germans were sending up S.O.S signals during the attack but their artillery did not respond with alacrity. ~~All positions [illegible]~~ During the day the enemy opened a heavy bombardment chiefly on support trenches and DURK WALKS this he kept up throughout the night	APPENDIX F.

[illegible signature] Major

2449 Wt. W14957/M90 750,000 1/16 J.B.C. & A. Forms/C.2118/12.

Instructions regarding War Diaries and Intelligence Summaries are contained in F. S. Regs., Part II. and the Staff Manual respectively. Title Pages will be prepared in manuscript.

WAR DIARY
or
INTELLIGENCE SUMMARY
(Erase heading not required.)

Army Form C. 2118.

88th MACHINE GUN COMPANY.
No. ....
Date ....

Place	Date	Hour	Summary of Events and Information	Remarks and references to Appendices
GUILLEMONT MORVAL	28.1.17		Enemy shelling vigorously. Notification received that we were extending our newly captured positions about 200 yards West. Operation Orders issued accordingly so far as regards our machine gun fire. Weather still dry & cold. Heavy shelling in front of MORVAL.	Appendix G
"	29.1.17		Zero fixed for 5.30 am (This extension of our front line did not materialise until a later date. Enemy shelling our support lines & communications. Fire programme carried out every evening on enemy's lines and roads. The temperature decreasing it is found necessary to increase the 1/8th part of glycerine (non freezing mixture) to 25% and also to keep up fire during the night in order to keep all the guns in working order. Our casualties were due chiefly to the shelling after the attack. Rations & water by pack animal [illegible].	
"	30.1.17		Guns [illegible] in Right Sector ie 12 guns relieved by teams of the 86th M.G.C. and sections returning to Coy HQ GUILLEMONT bring guns tripods and belt boxes out of line with them. Last teams arriving P.T.O. [illegible signature]	

2149 Wt. W14957/M90 750,000 1/16 J.B.C. & A. Forms/C.2118/12.

Instructions regarding War Diaries and Intelligence Summaries are contained in F. S. Regs., Part II. and the Staff Manual respectively. Title Pages will be prepared in manuscript.

WAR DIARY
or
INTELLIGENCE SUMMARY
(Erase heading not required.)

Army Form C. 2118.

88th MACHINE GUN COMPANY. No. .... Date ....

Place	Date	Hour	Summary of Events and Information	Remarks and references to Appendices
GUILLEMONT	31.1.17		Last teams arrived Coy Hq at 5.30 am, tea provided for them. at 3.30 pm teams left Headquarters to relieve the 87th M.G. Coy in the left sector, guides & having been previously arranged for, and the following positions taken up. N35c.8 2. T5b 6.6. T6a 5.7. T6b 7.7. 4 guns in ANTELOPE TRENCH. T5d 1.7. T10a 8.6 T9b 7.5 T9b 5.7. T5d 3.3. The four guns of No 2 Section already in this area being relieved. On relief they returned to Headquarters at 3.30 am 1st Feby. Disposition of guns 4 front 4 support 4 Reserve 4 Company Headquarters.	FRANCE 57c S.W. 1:10000

[signature]

2449 Wt. W14957/M90 750,000 1/16 J.B.C. & A. Forms/C.2118/12.

A

88th Machine Gun Company
No. ......
Date ......

88th Machine Gun Company

Programme of Training for week ending 6th January 1917

Monday — No I & II Section Range; 7.15-7.35 am Swedish Drill; 9-9.30 am Gas Helmet Drill; 9.30-10.30 am Combined Drill; 11 am-12 noon Elevating & Traversing Dials and Rapid Laying; 12-1 pm Cleaning Guns etc

Tuesday — Route March —

Wednesday — No IV Section and Class Range; 7.15-7.35 am Swedish Drill; 9-10 am Close Order Drill; 10-10.30 am Bombing; 11-11.30 am Lecture; 11.30 am-12.30 pm Immediate Action; 12.30-1 pm Cleaning Guns etc

Thursday — Route March —

Friday — No I & II Sections Range; 7.15-7.35 am Swedish Drill; 9-10 am Immediate Action; 10-10.30 am Gas Helmet Drill; 11-11.30 am Lecture; 11.30-12.30 pm Close Order Drill; 12.30-1 pm Cleaning Guns etc

Saturday — 7.15-7.35 am Swedish Drill; 9-10 am Immediate Action; 10-10.30 am Bombing; 11 am-12 noon Kit Inspection; 12 noon-1 pm Lecture by O.C. Coy

31st December 1916

H Leighton 2nd Lieut. for Major Commanding
88th Machine Gun Company

Operation Orders
By
Lieut. Jeff-Reveley Commanding
88th Company Machine Gun Corps

B

Ref :- 29th Div! Trench Diagram 1/10000 No. 5 a.

[illegible] Brigade will attack and capture the two German lines of trench opposite [illegible] front occupied by the right Brigade of the 29th Division on January 3rd at 10-00 which hour will be zero.

II The attack will be carried out by the Worcestershire on the right and the Hampshire on the left.

III At zero an Artillery Barrage will be placed about 150 yards in front of [illegible] trench in no mans land.

At 00-03 the Artillery barrage creeps forward, pace of Barrage 50 yards per minute until it reaches first objective.

At 00-07 Barrage moves forward to 2nd Objective. On reaching 2nd objective the barrage will continue creeping forward till it reaches a line 300 yards in front of final objective when it will remain until the position has been consolidated and strong points made.

IV 4 Guns under 2nd Lieut. H. Leighton will prior to zero take up a position in no mans land or otherwise, where they can take on any target which may present itself, these guns will move forward at 00-10 to the captured position two guns with the Worcesters and two Guns with the Hampshire.

V The 4 Guns in support will form a barrage of interlaced cones of fire 300 yards behind the final objective, these guns will hold themselves in readiness to move up into the captured position if necessary.

VI 4 Guns in Reserve will bring direct overhead fire onto beat all enemy communication and indirect fire anywhere the hostile forces might mass for a counter attack.

VII The 4 Guns remaining will be in Brigade Reserve.

VIII Every man will carry 2 sandbags and 2 Mills bombs, 1 pick & 1 shovel will be carried by each team.

IX As much Ammunition as possible will be carried by the guns moving forward.

X Forward Reserve Ammunition dump will be on the German Road 300 yards behind our original firing line. The Reserve Ammunition will be with the 4 guns in Brigade Reserve.

M. Jeff-Reveley. Lieut. Commanding
88th Company Machine Gun Company

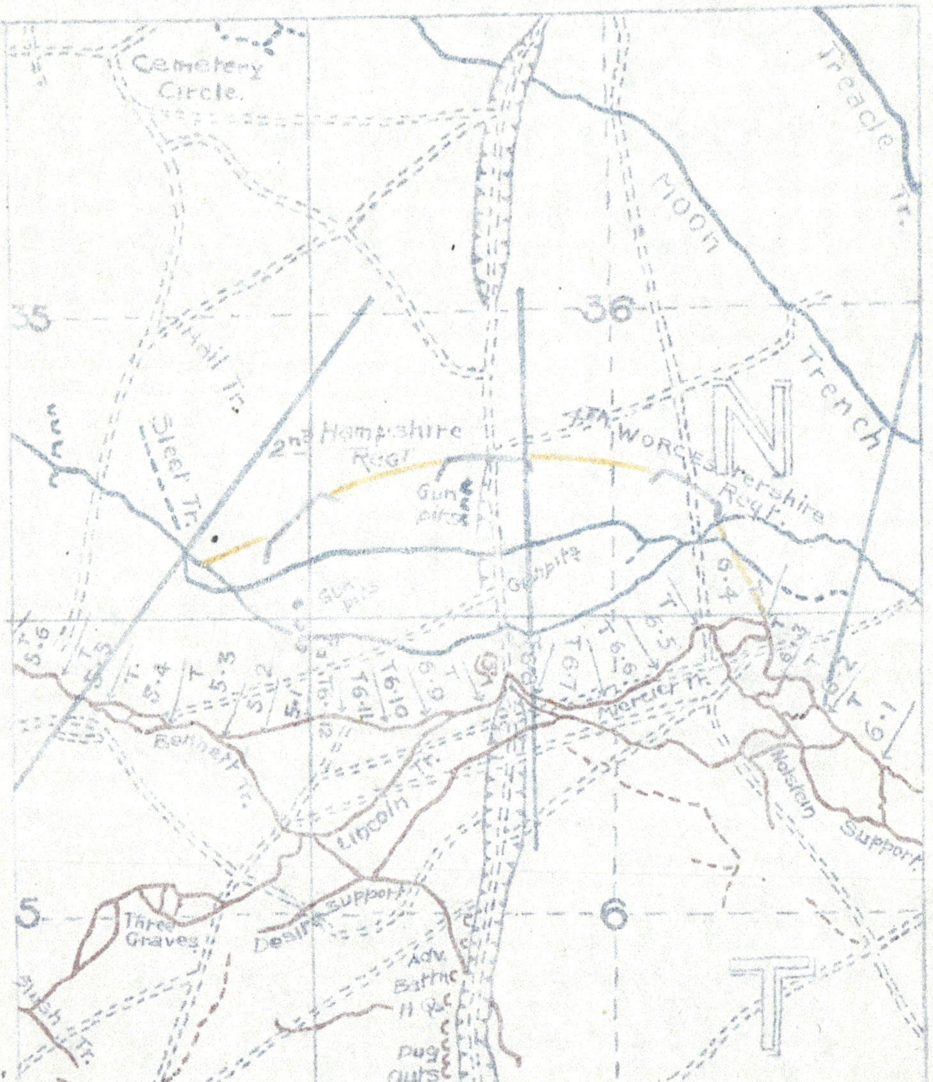

Cemetery Circle.
Treacle Tr.
Moon
Trench
35
36
Hall Tr.
Steel Tr.
2nd Hampshire Regt
4th Worcestershire Regt.
Gun pits
N
Bonnet Tr.
Mercier Tr.
Lincoln Tr.
Holstein Support
5
6
Three Graves
Desire Support
Adv. Battn H.Q.
Dug outs
T
Bush Tr.
Boyau Michel.

SCALE 1:10,000. SECRET

88th MACHINE GUN COMPANY.
No. ....
Date ....

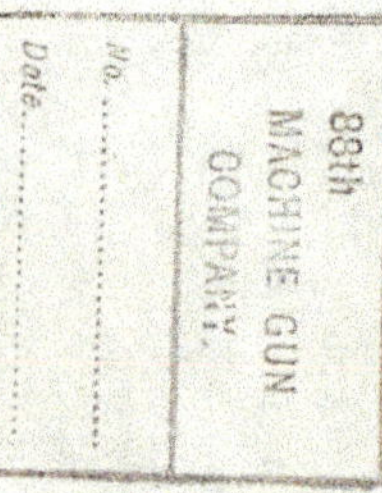

C

Operation Orders
By
Lieut Goff Keeley, Commanding 88th M.G.C. (1).

REFERENCE 29th Divnl TRENCH map SCALE 1:10000

1. The 88th Brigade will attack & capture the 2 German lines of trenches opposite the front occupied by the right Brigade of the 29th Division on Jan. 6th at a time Zero, which will be notified [illegible].

2. The Attack will be carried out by the Essex Regt on the right & the Newfoundland Regt on the left.

3. At Zero an Artillery Barrage will be placed about 100 yards in front of forming up trench, in No Mans land.
At 00.03, the Artillery Barrage creeps forward (pace of barrage 50 yds per minute) until it reaches first objective. At 00.07 Barrage moves forward to second objective. On reaching second objective the barrage will continue creeping forward until it reaches a line 200 yds in front of final objective, where it will remain until the position has been consolidated & strong Points made.

4. The Infantry are attacking in three waves with mopping up parties behind the 1st & 2nd waves.

5. Strong points are being constructed after the positions have been captured at
(1). Astride Road; N 36 D 25 · 4,
(2). " " ; N.36 C. 6 · 4,
(3) About point; N.36 D. 0 · 2.

6. 4 Guns under 2nd Lieut D. Stonehouse will prior to zero take up a position in No Mans Land or otherwise where they can take on any target which may present itself. These guns will move forward [illegible] yds behind the second wave of advancing infantry & take up positions in the 2nd line of captured trenches, where they can protect the flanks of the strong points;
Two Guns on the left & two guns on the right.

7. 4 Guns in support will form a barrage of interlaced cones of fire 200 yds behind the final objective. These guns will hold themselves in readiness to move up into the captured positions if necessary.

8. 4. Guns in reserve will bring overhead fire to bear on all enemy communications & indirect, ie to bear on any point where the hostile forces might mass for a counter attack.

Operation Orders. (2).

9. 7 guns will be in Brigade Reserve.
10. Every man will carry 2 sandbags & 2 Mills Bombs. 1 pick & shovel will be carried by each team.
11. As many S.A.A. boxes as possible will be carried by guns moving forward.
12. Forward Ammunition Dump is on the Sunken Rd. 300 yds behind our original firing line.
The Reserve Ammunition will be with the guns in Brigade Reserve.

Copies.
No 1. Brigade Staff.
No 2. O.C. Newfoundland Regt.
No 3. O.C. Essex Regt.
No 4. } Section Officers
No 5. }
No 6. } Diary
No 7. }

on the field

5th January 1917

[illegible] Lieut.
Commanding 88 Machine Gun Company

[illegible] of Training [illegible] Jan 8th to 10th

Monday 8th — No 3 Section [illegible] Range — Squad Drill — 9 to 10 am Elementary Drill — 10 to 10.30 am Mechanical Drill — 11 to 12 [illegible] — 12 to 1 pm Cleaning [illegible]

Tuesday 9th — [illegible]

Wednesday 10th — Firing Range — Squad Drill — 9 to 10 am Immediate Action — 10 to 10.30 am Mechanism — 11 to 12 noon Close order Drill — 12 to 1 pm Cleaning Guns

January 7th 1917

2nd Lieut [illegible]
88th Machine Gun Company

Appendix D I

Movement Orders
By
Captain C.H. Jelf-Reveley Commanding
88th Machine Gun Company
In the Field "Tuesday" 9th January 1917

I
Movement — The Company will [illegible] at [illegible] on Thursday 11th inst. [illegible] Company parade [illegible] proceed to [illegible] to entrain for Corbie where they will be billeted.
Dress [illegible] Marching Order [illegible] and blanket will be carried.

II
Transport — Transport will be loaded by [illegible] on the 10th inst. All arrangements for [illegible] of Transport will be made by [illegible] and Transport Officer.

III
Baggage Officer — 2nd Lieut White will perform the duties of Baggage Officer. He will see that all limbers are properly loaded [illegible] on the 10th inst.

IV
Officers Kits — All Officers kits will be at the [illegible] by 4 pm on the 10th inst. ready for loading. 2nd Lt. [illegible] will accompany these kits.

V
Rations — The unconsumed portion of the day's ration will be carried, also Rations for the following day.

VI
Camp Kettles — 6 Camp Kettles for the sections and one for H.Q. Party will be carried. N.C.O.s in charge of parties will ensure that men are detailed to carry them.

VII
Advance Party — 2nd Lieut Stonehouse will be forward billeting Officer. Corpl. [illegible] will accompany him. They will parade at B.H.Q. at 8 am on the 10th inst. and proceed by motor lorry. Two Bicycles will be taken. On arrival at Corbie they will report to the Staff Captain at the Town Majors Office.

VIII
Rear Party — The Rear Party will be Corpl. Riding and the two Sanitary men. They will clear all Latrines after the Company have left and see that all Billets are clean, all Latrines will be taken down and the material collected and stacked in a central place. Detailed instructions will be handed to the N.C.O. in charge of this party.

C.H. Jelf-Reveley. Captain Commanding
88th Machine Gun Company

APPENDIX E.

Movement Orders
by
Major A. Morris Commanding
88th Machine Gun Company

In the Field 22 January 1917

1. Information The 88th M.G.C. will relieve the 86th M.G.C. in the right sector of the Divisional Front on the afternoon & evening of the 23rd inst.

2. Movement Sections will move independently under section officers according to Time Table.

No 1 Sec		9.30 am
II	"	9.35 "
III	"	9.40 "
IV	"	9.45 "
H.Q	"	9.50 "

They will march to H.Q. 86th M.G.C. GUILLEMONT STATION where guides will await them.

3. Transport. One limbered G.S. Waggon is allotted to each section and one to H.Q. for the purpose of carrying guns ammunition &c. These will be loaded by 9 am tomorrow morning under the personal supervision of Section Officers & accompany their sections on the line of march.

4. Rations & Cakes The unconsumed portion of the days ration will be carried on the men in addition those forward guns hereafter detailed will take into the line 2 days rations.

5. Ammunition 8 Belt boxes per gun will be taken to H.Q. 86th M.G.C. & there handed over if not required for the line.

6. Sectors No I Section will relieve the following guns of the 86 Coy T6b 95.45. U1a 85.10. U1d 40.60 U2a 215.10.

6. Sector — No IV Section will relieve the support positions U 1d 80.05. T6c 55.50 T6d. 70.30. U 7a 30.65.
No III Section will relieve the Reserve guns at T10b 90.45. T11a 80.35. T11 central T11d 90.05.
No II Section will be in Reserve at Coy Hq.

7 Inter Coy Reliefs. — One N.C.O. & two men will be the personnel of a gun team for the four forward guns only, the third man will accompany his teams to the gun positions and then return immediately to Company Headquarters as guides for ration & other parties. One man will be detailed as section runner the remainder will stay at Coy Hq. All other teams will have their full complement of men. The period for relief for the forward guns will be every 48 hours if possible.

8. Extra blankets & packs — These will be handed in to the Quartermasters Stores by 9 am tomorrow. One blanket per man will be taken to the trenches.

9. Non freezing mixture Whale Oil — Section Officers will ensure that all guns are filled with ⅓ part glycerine & that Whale Oil is taken into the trenches with the men. Both are obtainable from the Quartermaster Sergeant.

10. Trench Waders Waterproof Capes — Section Officers when issued with these will ensure that careful check is kept & it is hoped there will be no deficiencies during this tour in the trenches.

11. Maps. — Section Officers may obtain these on application to the Orderly Room.

12. Reports — Early morning reports must reach Coy Hq 8 am

13. Handing over Certificates — The usual handing over Certificates will be rendered

14. Office — Orderly Room closes 9.30 am Mansel Camp tomorrow morning & opens at GUILLEMONT at 2 pm.

Copies 1 & 2 Hq
3 O.C. No 1 Section
4 " 2 "
5 " 3 "
6 " 4 "
7 " Transport.
(3–7) By Orderly

Issued at 1800

[signature]
Lieut & Adjt
88th M.G.C.

Copy. No:

Appendix ~~III~~ F

Operation Order No: 5.
By
Major. A. Morris Commanding
88th Machine Gun Company

In the Field

January 25th 1917.

Map reference
Trench map. Scale 1: 10,000.

1. Information

A. Enemy – The enemy is entrenched on line. LANDWEHR – LANDSTURN. PRUSSIAN TRENCH. Opposite the 29th Division.
His morale is weak

a. Border Reg:
b. Royal Inniskilling Fusiliers

B. Own Troops – The 87th Brigade will form the assaulting troops. The number of battalions to be employed as per margin

2. Intentions

It is the intention of the G. O. C to assault the German line on the frontage N.36.d.4.2 to N.35.d.8.0. and ERSATZ POINT in rear in N.36.c. and to consolidate and hold the ground gained.

3. Distribution

The 88th Machine Gun Company will participate in the attack.

NO. I SECTION (Commander as per margin.) Will remain in its present position during the operation and will be responsible for the 88th Brigade frontage.

NO: I. SECTION under Lieut: Stonehouse

They will remain where they are at present in their permanent battle emplacements and will watch for enemy movements in the enemy sector paying particular attention to BOSNIA TRENCH.

NO II SECTION under Lieut Wilson

NO II SECTION will be employed as follows
2 guns at T.6.a.7.7. for defensive purposes

Linear Targets from O.31.c.4.4. to N.36.d.7.0

of the present front line.

2 guns at T.6.b.5.7. whose linear targets will be as per margin.

NO III SECTION under Lieut: Warre.

NO: III SECTION will remain in its position in the intermediate line for defensive purpose. This is subject to relief which if takes place NO I will read NO III.

NO IV SECTION under Fire Control Commander

NO: IV SECTION will form the mobile section and will be responsible for the right flank of the assaulting troops.
Its approximate position will be N.36.d.4.2.
The particular duty of this section will be to adopt a counter offensive against any hostile offensive machine gun, rifle or trench engine which may impede the attack.

4. Fire Control Commander Lieut: R.F.L. Owen.

Fire Control Commander as per margin will be responsible for the direction control and maintenance of fire as per programme.
The 8 guns operating in the 87th Brigade area will be under the Fire Control Command marginly named.

5. Location of Hostile Machine Guns

Machine Guns are suspected in the following places.
N.36.d.6.1 N.36.c.6.0. N36.c.6.4. T.5.b.90.85.
Special observers will be posted in order to detect immediate opening of hostile fire. The area from which the fire comes will be heavily barraged by the counter offensive guns.

6. Preliminary and Protective measures.

Each Officer will ensure that the barrel casing contains 1/8th part glycerine previous to the operation.
That the oil is not coagulated a

that there is sufficient supply of water for replenishment.

7 Preliminary Reconnaisance and Fire Registration — Reconnaisance reports will reach this office by 9am on the 26th inst: also a certificate to the effect that all guns have been carefully registered, and fire observation obtained.

8. Forward Ammunition Dumps — Each gun will have a local reserve of 5,000 rounds S.A.A. Independent of the main reserve.

9. Explanatory — Every man must know the duty assigned to him and his part in the operation.

10. Disposition Reports — Disposition reports will be rendered 15 minutes after the operation.

Issued at 1500.

Copy No 1 Operation Order File
" " 2 87th Brigade
" " 3 88th Brigade
" " 4 O. C. No 1. Section
" " 5 O. C. No 2 Section
" " 6 O. C. No 3 Section
" " 7 O. C. No 4 Section

Major Commanding
88th Machine Gun Company

By Orderly 1515

APPENDIX G.

88th MACHINE GUN COMPANY.
No. ....
Date ....

Operation Order No 6
by
Major A. Morris Commanding
88th Machine Gun Coy

Copy 9

In the Field
28.1.17

Reference
29th Div Map 1:10,000.

1. Information (a) A further advance will be carried out tomorrow as an extension of our present frontage in enemy territory

(b) Own troops The 88th M.G. Coy will participate in the operations ✗.

2. Intentions It is the intention of the G.O.C. to extend this 200 yards in order to improve our observation and establish superiority by this means.

3. Distribution
2Lt Warre
Four guns
The four guns in the right forward area Commanded as per margin, will engage STAR and BOSNIA TRENCH a sharp look out being kept for enemy machine guns which must be engaged

✗
Lt R.F.L. Owen
The four guns commanded as per margin will engage PRUSSIAN TRENCH and the junction of SAXON and MARS particular look out being kept for hostile machine guns.

4. Fire action Boundaries There will be no fire West of O.31 C.O.O. and

EAST of U2 C.25.90. the area between these two points forming the barrage zone

5. **Special Observers** A special observer will be posted on each gun to look out for and locate any hostile machine guns which will be immediately engaged

6. **Zero** Will be at the moment the barrage falls

7. **Glycerine Spare Parts** The usual precautionary measures as regards Glycerine and Spare Parts will be observed The ratio of glycerine must now be increased owing the decrease of temperature to 25%

8. **Ammunition Supply** The ammunition supply will be maintained as heretofore. The usual gun complement of 3,500 and the usual 5,000 rounds per gun

9. **Range** The normal sight used will be battle sight range

10. **Disposition** Will be as before

Report ISSUED at 1930

Copy No 1 Operation Order file
" " 2 87th Brigade
" " 3 88th Brigade
" " 4-8 O's C Sections
" " 9+10 War Diary

By orderly 2000

A. Morris Major
Commd 88th M.G.C.

CONFIDENTIAL

WAR DIARY

OF

88th Company Machine Gun Corps

PERIOD

1st February 1917 to 28th February 1917

(VOLUME 9)

Instructions regarding War Diaries and Intelligence Summaries are contained in F. S. Regs., Part II. and the Staff Manual respectively. Title Pages will be prepared in manuscript.

WAR DIARY
or
INTELLIGENCE SUMMARY
(Erase heading not required.)

Army Form C. 2118.

88th MACHINE GUN COMPANY
No. ....
Date ....

Place	Date	Hour	Summary of Events and Information	Remarks and references to Appendices
GUILLEMONT	1.2.17		Enemy shelling heavily around the area of our two right front guns, otherwise normal. Sections being relieved every four days. Firing on enemy's tracks and roads.	FRANCE 57c S.W. 1:10,000
"	2.2.17		The cold dry spell ~~[illegible]~~ still continues. The guns in the forward area can only be visited by night.	
"	3.2.17		New enemy work observed in front of our newly established line, this we pay particular attention to, ~~firing~~ with continuous fire throughout the night and also ~~of~~ MOON TRENCH	
"	4.2.17		No II Section (Reserve Coy HQ) relieved No IV Section (Front system) in turn relieving those in support. 48 hours rations are taken into the forward area by night. Careful attention is being paid to the men's feet for prevention of frostbite. French powder is now being used instead of Whale oil and is well rubbed into the feet every day under supervision of an officer. Shelling normal.	[illegible signature]

2449 Wt. W14957/M90 750,000 1/16 J.B.C. & A. Forms/C.2118/12.

Instructions regarding War Diaries and Intelligence Summaries are contained in F. S. Regs., Part II. and the Staff Manual respectively. Title Pages will be prepared in manuscript.

WAR DIARY
or
INTELLIGENCE SUMMARY
(Erase heading not required.)

Army Form C. 2118.

Place	Date	Hour	Summary of Events and Information	Remarks and references to Appendices
GUILLEMONT	5.2.17		a Copy of Movement Orders received as to our being relieved by the 59th M.G.C. on the 7th instant and that we were to be billeted at COISSY One officer and a N.C.O. accordingly sent forward as an advance party	
"	6.2.17		Movement orders issued at with reference to relief by the 59th M.G.C. (copy attached) and forwarded to persons therein named. Enemy artillery normal. Our own guns firing on New enemy work + communications	
"	7.2.17		The 59th M.G.C arrived Coy Headquarters at 2 pm where guides were waiting for them to take them to their positions. Gun teams for Reserve area moved off at 4.30 pm and those for Intermediate + Forward Sectors at 5 pm Relief complete at 11 pm and Company entrained at GUILLEMONT detraining at CARNOY whence they marched to MANSEL CAMP where hot soup	[signature]

2449 Wt. W14957/M90 750,000 1/16 J.B.C. & A. Forms/C.2118/12.

Instructions regarding War Diaries and Intelligence Summaries are contained in F. S. Regs., Part II. and the Staff Manual respectively. Title Pages will be prepared in manuscript.

WAR DIARY
or
INTELLIGENCE SUMMARY
(Erase heading not required.)

Army Form C. 2118.

Place	Date	Hour	Summary of Events and Information	Remarks and references to Appendices
MANSEL CAMP	7.2.17	23.55	was issued to the men. The men remained under canvas for the night.	
COISY	8.2.17		The Company embussed for COISY at 3 pm arriving there at 7.30 pm and were allotted billets. Transport units marched arriving COISY about the same time	
COISY	9.2.17		Cleaning of guns equipment etc. all ammunition thoroughly overhauled, limbers etc oiled & polished	
"	10.2.17		In billets. weather remaining cold hard & dry usual morning parades and instructional classes.	
"	11.2.17		Church Parades.	
"	12.2.17		~~[illegible]~~ Usual Parades and Guards.	[signature]

2449 Wt. W14957/M90 750,000 1/16 J.B.C. & A. Forms/C.2118/12.

Instructions regarding War Diaries and Intelligence Summaries are contained in F. S. Regs., Part II. and the Staff Manual respectively. Title Pages will be prepared in manuscript.

WAR DIARY
or
INTELLIGENCE SUMMARY
(Erase heading not required.)

88th MACHINE GUN COMPANY.
No. ....
Date..........

Army Form C. 2118.

Place	Date	Hour	Summary of Events and Information	Remarks and references to Appendices
COISY	13.2.17		ROUTE MARCH. ROUTE:- COISY CARDONNETTE POULAINVILLE	
			COISY Instructional classes attended this parade	
"	14.2.17		Usual morning parades and inspections.	
"	15.2.17		Usual parades and inspections	
"	16.2.17		Instructional classes and parades	
"	17.2.17		~~The~~ Group Orders received with reference to our move forward into the sector of SAILLY SAILLISEL movement orders issued accordingly, limbers packed and loaded.	
"	18.2.17		Stood by for final orders to move, thoroughly cleaned all billets and surroundings	
LA NEUVILLE	19.2.17		Orders received Company marched to LA NEUVILLE via ALLONVILLE and QUERRIEU where Company billeted for the night. Transport marched with Company.	

[signature]

Instructions regarding War Diaries and Intelligence Summaries are contained in F. S. Regs., Part II. and the Staff Manual respectively. Title pages will be prepared in manuscript.

WAR DIARY
or
INTELLIGENCE SUMMARY.
(Erase heading not required.)

88th MACHINE GUN COMPANY.

Army Form C. 2118.

Place	Date	Hour	Summary of Events and Information	Remarks and references to Appendices
LA NEUVILLE	20.2.17		Company entrained at 11am at LA NEUVILLE transport left by road at 9am and proceeded to MANSEL CAMP CARNOY where they stayed the night in huts. Officers left 8am and proceeded to Headquarters 52nd Company at HAIE WOOD near COMBLES and reconnoitred the new sector we were taking over. It was arranged to have teams to relieve rear guns (which could be relieved in daylight) at headquarters 2.30pm and remaining teams at 5.30pm.	MAP FRANCE AMIENS 17
MANSEL CAMP COMBLES HAIE WOOD SECTOR:- SAILLY-SAILLISEL	21.2.17		Eight teams left MANSEL CAMP 11am remainder of Company at 2pm marched to H.Q. 52nd M.G. Coy where guides were waiting them. Relief completed 10.30pm and we occupied the following positions No I Section (N1) U 14 d 7.1 (N2) U 14d 75.20 (N3) U 14d 40.75. (Posts) ~~[illegible]~~ No IV Section (N4) U 14b 30 35 (R3) U 14a 8 3. (O1) U 20 a 95.90 (O2) U 14c 95.25 No III Section (P1) U14c15.80. (P2) U 14c 2.3. (P4) U 13a 70 25. (Q3) U 13d 25.70. Transport at MARICOURT 2 days rations taken with the ~~two forward teams~~ three sections in the line. Weather conditions the thaw has now set in making roads and trenches once again in their normal muddy condition	FRANCE COMBLES 57c SW 4

A5834 Wt. W4973/M687 750,000 8/16 D. D. & L. Ltd. Forms/C.2118/13.

Instructions regarding War Diaries and Intelligence Summaries are contained in F. S. Regs., Part II. and the Staff Manual respectively. Title pages will be prepared in manuscript.

WAR DIARY
or
INTELLIGENCE SUMMARY.
(Erase heading not required.)

88th MACHINE GUN COMPANY.
No. ....
Date ....

Army Form C. 2118.

Place	Date	Hour	Summary of Events and Information	Remarks and references to Appendices
COMBLES			Mule lines established at COMBLES to facilitate getting rations and S.A.A forward.	
SAILLY SAILLISEL	22.2.17			
"	23.2.17		Enemy shelling normal weather misty making observation difficult. Water rations taken forward by pack animals also S.A.A. average 16000 rounds per night. Posts gun position changed to O III as shown on annexed map.	Appendix A.
"	24.2.17		Conditions normal enemy shelling chiefly confined to SAILLY SAILLISEL and BAPAUME ROAD. shells 5.9 + gas shells.	
"	25.2.17		Section III Coy Reserve relieves No 1 Section front guns taking with them 2 days rations relief complete 10 pm. Enemy shelling heavily, barrage with 5.9 cms + gas shells along BAPAUME - PERONNE Road about 9 pm which slightly delayed relief, casualties 4 O.Rs enemy shelling SAILLY SAILLISEL. Transport lines Bloc to MARICOURT	
"	26.2.17		Enemy shelling normal weather. misty making observation difficult	[signature]

A5834 Wt. W4973/M687 750,000 8/16 D. D. & L. Ltd. Forms/C.2118/13.

Instructions regarding War Diaries and Intelligence Summaries are contained in F. S. Regs., Part II. and the Staff Manual respectively. Title pages will be prepared in manuscript.

WAR DIARY
or
INTELLIGENCE SUMMARY.

(Erase heading not required.)

Army Form C. 2118.

88th MACHINE GUN COMPANY.
No. ....
Date............

Place	Date	Hour	Summary of Events and Information	Remarks and references to Appendices
COMBLES SECTOR:- SAILLY SAILLISEL	27.2.17		Operation Orders received that the 86th Brigade were attacking a sector of the enemy's line at a time to be notified later and that this Company should give covering fire for the assaulting troops and assist in the barrage. Operation Orders issued accordingly (Copy annexed)	Appendix B.
"	28.2.17		Zero fixed for 5.20 am roughly half an hour before dawn and our guns participated in the attack as per Operation Orders. The attack was successful and objectives gained. Enemy put a heavy barrage on our front line and SAILLY SAILLISEL immediately after our own guns had opened fire and also barraged the roads leading to the village. Throughout the day he shelled our roads and batteries intermittently	

[illegible signature]

A5834 Wt. W4973/M687 750,000 8/16 D. D. & L. Ltd. Forms/C.2118/13.

APPENDIX A.

WAR DIARY

88 M.G.C.

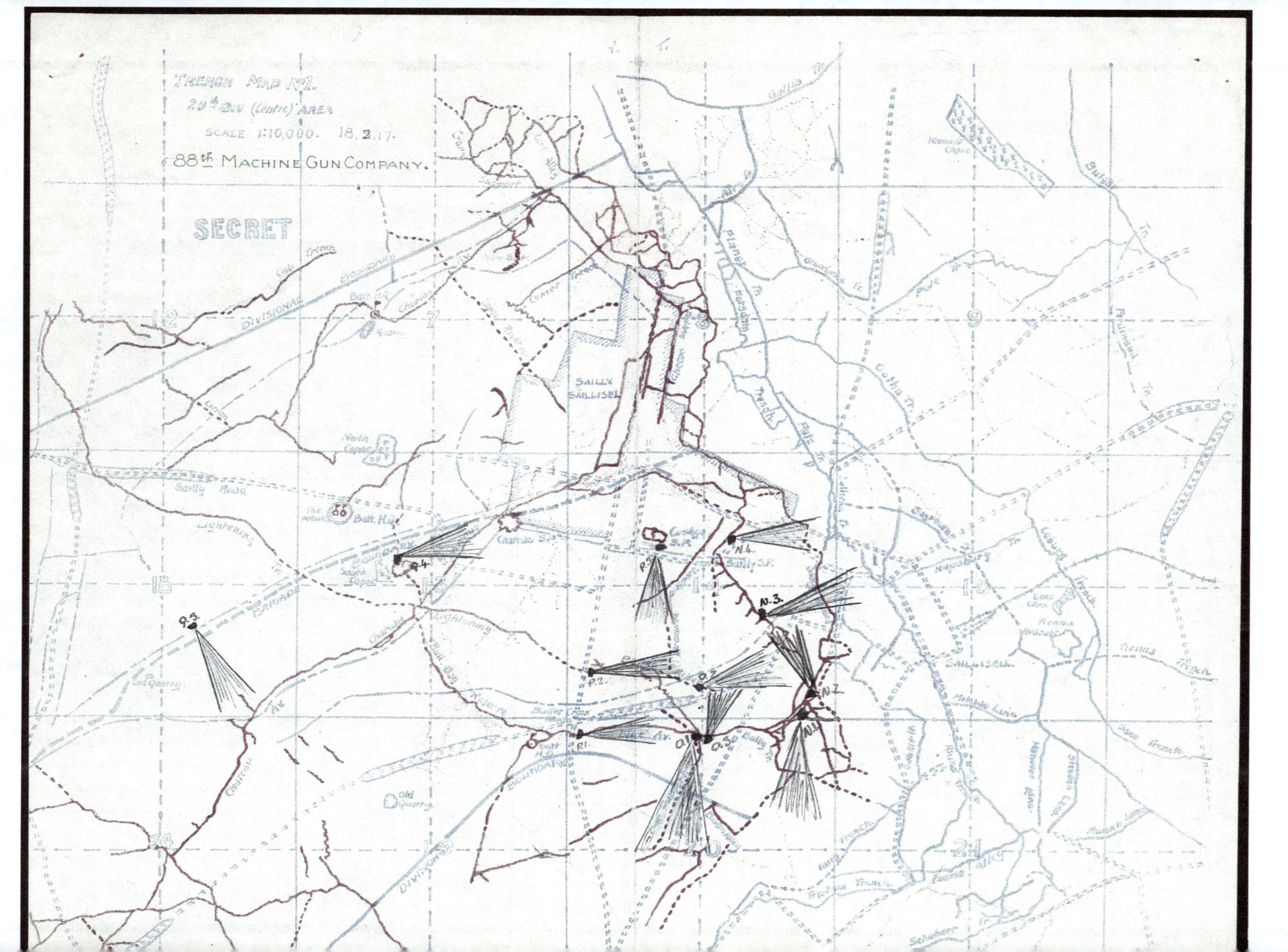

TRENCH MAP NO1.
29th DIV (Centre) AREA
SCALE 1:10,000. 18.2.17.
88th MACHINE GUN COMPANY.
SECRET
SAILLY SAILLISEL
SAILLISEL
Planet Tr.
Potsdam Trench.
Pfalz Tr.
Gotha Tr.
Coburg Trench.
Sailly Road
Lightening Tr.
DIVISIONAL BOUNDARY
BRIGADE BOUNDARY
Chateau S.P.
Old Quarry
North Copse
South Copse
Batt. H.Q.
N.1.
N.2.
N.3.
N.4.
O.1.
O.2.
O.3.
P.1.
P.2.
P.5.
Q.3.
Q.4.
Mihiel Lane
Schubert Tr.
Fritsch Trench.
Kenna Trench.

Copy No: 9

Operation Order No: 8.

By Major A. Morris Commanding
88th Machine Gun Company

In the Field February 25th 1917.

Appendix "B"

Reference. 29th Div: Area 1 : 10,000.

1. Information — (A) Enemy. The enemy holding the front opposite the 29th Divisional area are composed of reserve troops of the 94th and 87th regiments. Their morale is doubtful.

Frontage U.14 b. 85.25. to U. 8. d 45. 90. — (B) Own Troops. The 86th Brigade will form the assaulting troops and will attack on a frontage as marginally defined. Date and time will be notified later.

2. Intentions — It is the intention of the G.O.C. to capture and consolidate the frontage as detailed in 1.(B)

3. Distribution — No: 3. Section under 2nd Lieut: Warre. — The five guns in the forward area (Commander as per margin) will barrage Bayreuth Trench and prevent movement in this area. They must also screen observation and form the right impenetrable shield of the defiladed zone through which the assaulting troops will advance.

No: 1 Section under 2nd Lieut Stonehouse (5 Support Guns) — Will barrage Hapsburg Avenue for 3/4 hours after zero, then intermittent bursts throughout the period of consolidation.

No: 4. Section under Lieut: Leighton — No: 4 Section will form the mobile section and will pay particular attention to Gilbert Trench. Their chief duty will be to neutralise any enemy machine gun or rifle fire.

4. Reserve Ammunition and Water — Each gun will have 6,000 rounds S.A.A. reserve independent of the main reserve. A water dump is established at U.19.a. 6.3. Each N.C.O. will take a 2 gallon petrol tin of water in his pack which has been treated with 25% non freezing mixture.

Sheet. 2.

5. Transport. Transport will immediately draw 72 boxes of ammunition which must be available.

6. Reports. Reports will be sent to Company Headquarters.

7. Communications. Communications will be established as heretofore.

8. Medical. The nearest aid post is on the FREGICOURT ROAD.

A.M. Morris Major Commanding
88th Machine Gun Company

Issued at 1515

Copy No: 1. Operation Order File
" " 2. 88th Brigade
" " 3. O.C. No: 1. Section
" " 4. O.C. No II Section
" " 5. O.C. No III Section
" " 6. O.C. No IV Section
" " 7. O.C. 87th Company

By Orderly 1530

Copies Nos 8-10 War Diary

CONFIDENTIAL

War Diary
of
88th Company M.G. Corps

PERIOD

1st March 1917 to 31st March 1917

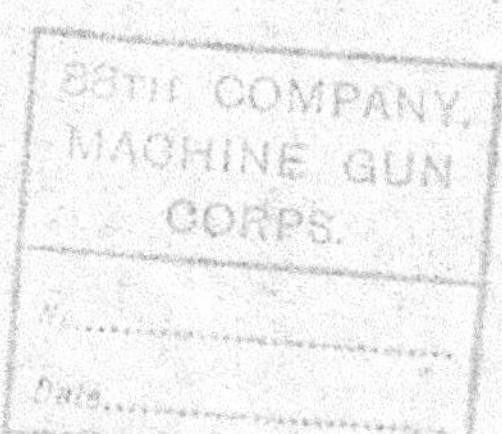

WO 1/2

(VOLUME 10)

Army Form C. 2118.

WAR DIARY
or
INTELLIGENCE SUMMARY.
(Erase heading not required.)

Instructions regarding War Diaries and Intelligence Summaries are contained in F. S. Regs., Part II. and the Staff Manual respectively. Title pages will be prepared in manuscript.

Place	Date	Hour	Summary of Events and Information	Remarks and references to Appendices
HAIE WOOD SAILLY SAILLISEL	1.3.17		Enemy using a considerable number of gas shells, counter battery work and shelling of communications. Weather misty. No II Section relieved the four forward guns of No III Sec that section relieving No I [illegible]	
"	2.3.17		Enemy [illegible] front line and enemy artillery fairly active 4 teams of 87th M.G.C. relieved No II Section. Orders Re Relief by 3rd Guards Brigade received ~~[illegible]~~ Movement Orders issued accordingly (Copy attached)	Appendix A.
"	3.3.17		Relief by 3rd Guards Brigade M.G.C. as per Movement Orders Relief complete 8pm and Company marched to MEAULTE and encamped in huts last section arriving 2am	
MEAULTE camp	4.3.17		Last section arrived 2am. Transport in same camp as Company. Foot inspection and cleaning parades	
"	5.3.17		Classes of instruction in Range Taking, Machine Gun and Signalling. Guns and ammunition thoroughly cleaned. Kit inspection Bathing Parade and Pay.	

[illegible signature]

A5834 Wt. W4973/M687 750,000 8/16 D. D. & L. Ltd. Forms/C.2118/13.

Instructions regarding War Diaries and Intelligence Summaries are contained in F. S. Regs., Part II. and the Staff Manual respectively. Title pages will be prepared in manuscript.

WAR DIARY
or
INTELLIGENCE SUMMARY.
(Erase heading not required.)

Army Form C. 2118.

Place	Date	Hour	Summary of Events and Information	Remarks and references to Appendices
MEAULTE.	6/3/17		Usual Parades and inspections	
"	7/3/17		Ordinary Routine and Range practices Re-equipping the Company	
"	8/3/17		Close Order Drill, Gas Helmet drill daily and ordinary inspections	
"	9/3/17		Range practice and ordinary parades	
"	10/3/17		Route march MEAULTE, ALBERT foot inspections &c	
"	11/3/17		Church Parades	
"	12/3/17		Training as per syllabus of training annexed	Appendix B
"	13/3/17			
"	14/3/17			
"	15/3/17			
"	16/3/17			

[illegible signature]

A5834 Wt. W4973/M687 750,000 8/16 D. D. & L. Ltd. Forms/C.2118/13.

Instructions regarding War Diaries and Intelligence Summaries are contained in F. S. Regs., Part II. and the Staff Manual respectively. Title Pages will be prepared in manuscript.

WAR DIARY
or
INTELLIGENCE SUMMARY
(Erase heading not required.)

Army Form C. 2118.

Place	Date	Hour	Summary of Events and Information	Remarks and references to Appendices
MEAULTE	17/3/17		Training as per syllabus annexed. Transport loaded.	
"	18/3/17		Transport left for CAVILLON AREA at 2 pm halting at DAOURS for the night.	
"	19/3/17		Company paraded 5.45 am and marched to EDGE HILL entrained at 7 am for ARRAINES arrived ARRAINES 1 pm and marched to our old billets in MOLLIENS VIDAME arriving 3 pm Transport halted at ARGOEUVES for the night.	
MOLLIENS VIDAME				
"	20/3/17		Transport arrived at 2 pm, limbers unloaded guns etc cleaned.	
"	21/3/17		Company on the range.	
"	21/3/17		Route march BOUGAINVILLE BRIQUEMESNIL FLOXICOURT MOLLIENS VIDAME N.C.O. instruction in Road Reconnaissance	

Williams Major

2449 Wt. W14957/M90 750,000 1/16 J.B.C. & A. Forms/C.2118/12.

Army Form C. 2118.

WAR DIARY
or
INTELLIGENCE SUMMARY
(Erase heading not required.)

Instructions regarding War Diaries and Intelligence Summaries are contained in F. S. Regs., Part II. and the Staff Manual respectively. Title Pages will be prepared in manuscript.

[illegible] COMPANY, MACHINE GUN CORPS.

Place	Date	Hour	Summary of Events and Information	Remarks and references to Appendices
MOLLIENS VIDAME	23/3/17		Company on Range inspections	
"	24/3/17		Route march route LINCEUX HALLIVILLERS CHAMPS AMIENOIS. Foot inspection	
"	25/3/17		Church parades	
"	26/3/17		Brigade training	
"	27/3/17		Range work instruction digging of gun emplacements	
"	28/3/17		Range, instruction digging & loading of limbers	
LA CHAUSSEE	29/3/17		Company marched to LA CHAUSSEE as per Movement Order attached	Appendix C.
LA CHAUSSEE VIGNACOURT	30/3/17		Company continued march arriving VIGNACOURT noon.	

[illegible] Major

Army Form C. 2118.

WAR DIARY
or
INTELLIGENCE SUMMARY
(Erase heading not required.)

Instructions regarding War Diaries and Intelligence Summaries are contained in F. S. Regs., Part II. and the Staff Manual respectively. Title Pages will be prepared in manuscript.

Place	Date	Hour	Summary of Events and Information	Remarks and references to Appendices
VIGNACOURT	21.3.17		Company halted for the day, orders received for continuing the march tomorrow. Close Order Drill Ammunition Guns etc cleaned Inspections.	MAP REFERENCE 1/100000 sheet 11.4.17 FRANCE

2449 Wt. W14957/M90 750,000 1/16 J.B.C. & A. Forms/C.2118/12.

1.

APPENDIX. A.

Movement Orders. No. 18.

By

Major A. Morris, Commanding.

88th. Company M. G. Corps.

In the Field.

2nd. March 1917.

1. Movement. The 88th. Company M. G. Corps will be relieved by the 2nd. and 3rd. Guards Brigades on the afternoon of the 3rd instant; on relief the 88th. Company will march to MEAULTE where billets will be provided.

2. Advance party. 2nd. Lt. Leighton is detailed as forward billeting officer, he will leave Coy Hqr. at 10 a.m. on 3rd. inst. and arrange for billeting the Company at MEAULTE.

3. Guides. The following guides will be provided.–

No. III Section 2. guides to report Coy. Hqr. at 12 noon to-morrow for O.2. and P.3. positions (relief by 3rd Guards Brigade.)

1. Guide for O.3. position to be at BULLET CROSS ROADS 5.30 p.m. (relief by 2nd. Guards.)

O.1. position will not be relieved but will vacate position as soon as O.3. is relieved.

No. I Section, 4. guides; to report Coy Hqr. at 9 a.m. for P.1. P.2, Q3, and Q.4. positions.

1 guide to be at BULLET CROSS ROADS 5.30 p.m. for N.1. position (relief by 2nd. Guards Bde.)

2. guides. to report Coy Hqr. at 12 noon for N.3. and N.4. positions (relief by 3rd. Guards Bde.).

4. Relief. No II Section. O.C. No II Section will ensure that all tripods and belt boxes handed over by him to the 87th. Coy are brought to Coy. Hqr. and properly loaded on limber. At 10 a.m. will parade and march to MEAULTE.

No IV Section. will have guns, spare parts, tripods and belt boxes loaded by 10 a.m. and on relief will parade and march to MEAULTE with the Hqr. party.

A Morris

Headquarters. will load Headquarter equipment by 10 a.m. and on relief parade and march to MEAULTE with

No IV Section.

No. I Section. on relief will load at BULLET CROSS ROADS, except from positions Q.3: Guns etc. from this position will be carried to Coy Hq. Teams will report at Coy. Hq., parade under O.C. Section and march to MEAULTE. O.C. Section will ensure guns etc. are properly loaded.

No. III Section. on relief will load at BULLET CROSS ROADS, proceed to Coy Hq. parade and march to MEAULTE. O.C. Section will ensure limber properly loaded and provide brakesman, instruct driver to proceed to destination with Section.

V. Handing Over. No. Guns, tripods, spare parts or belt boxes will be handed over, or any equipment belonging to the Company.

VI Transport. Officers chargers as follows:— Coy Hq.

Lieut Owen,	10 a.m.
2nd. Lieut. Leighton	10 a.m.
2nd. Lieut. Stonehouse	12 noon.
2nd Lieut. Warre.	4 p.m.
C.O's and Adjutant	4 p.m.

1 limber	9-30 a.m.	Coy Hq.	(Headquarters).
1 "	10 a.m.	Coy. Hq.	(for Bullet Cross Roads 12 noon No. 1. Section).
1 "	noon.	Coy. Hq.	(for Bullet Cross Roads 5-30 p.m.)
1 "	noon.	Coy. Hq.	(for Guns and Soyers Stove).
2. "	noon.	Coy. Hq.	(Belt. Boxes.)
1 Mess Cart	11 a.m.	Coy. Hq.	

7. Blankets and Packs. If there is no available room on limbers packs will be brought to Coy Hq. by 9 a.m., and will be carried on the men. Blankets will be carried on the limber.

Transport not required for moving the Company from the line, will proceed under arrangement to be made by Transport Officer.

8. Rations. A hot meal will be supplied on arrival at destination.

Water. 20 tins of water will be at Cemetery Corner COMBLES at 5 p.m. for the relieving unit.

Cooks. One cook will proceed with 1st limber and take with him necessaries for providing a meal at destination. Dinners at 11.45 a.m. to-morrow.

P.T.O.

Officers will please take necessary extracts, initial against their names and return per orderly.

L. A. Fry Lieut. & Adjutant
88th Coy. M. G. Corps.

Issued at 20.30.

O.C. No 1. Section.
O.C. No 2. Section.
O.C. No. 3. Section.
O.C. No 4 Section.
Transport Officer.

88TH COMPANY
MACHINE GUN
CORPS
No.
Date.

88TH MACHINE GUN COMPANY.

PROGRAMME OF TRAINING FOR WEEKENDING MARCH. 18th

	7·15 am.–7·45	9 am – 10 a.m.	10·5 a.m. –10·35 am	10·45 –11·30 a.m	11·35 – 12·30 p.m.	2 p.m – 4 p.m.
MONDAY.	Physical Training.	Gun & Ammunit Cleaning.	Gas Helmet Drill.	Visual Training	Discipline. Lecture By O.C. Company.	Stoppages.
TUESDAY.	Swedish Drill.	Close Order Drill.	Gun & Ammunit Cleaning.	Indication and Recognition.	Interior Economy.	Route March.
WEDNESDAY.	Physical Training.	Guard Duties.	Judging Distance 1st Stage.	Gun & Ammunitn Cleaning	Close Order Drill.	Range Practice.
THURSDAY.	Swedish Drill.	—— Route March. ——				
FRIDAY.	Swedish Drill.	Judging Distance 2nd Stage.	Test of Elements Training.	Laying & Holding.	Interior Economy.	Belt Filling. (By hand)
SATURDAY.	Swedish Drill.	Fire Orders Elementary.	Fire Drill.	Indirect Fire.	Range Finding, Barr & Stroud.	Belt Filling Practice.
SUNDAY.	—— Divine Service. ——					

11/3/1917.

Copy No. 3

88th Coy Movement Order
By
Major A. Morris Commanding
88th Coy. Machine Gun Corps.
In the Field 26th March 1917.

I.

Movement. The Coy. will parade at 9.45 on the morning of the 29th inst. and march to LA CHAUSSEE Route: Oissy, Cavillon, Picquigny, billet there for the night and the following day march to VIGNACOURT.

II.

Billeting Party. 2nd Lt. Wilson, Sgt. Ayres and Sgt. [illegible] will leave MOLLIENS VIDAME at 7am. and arrange billets for the Coy. in LA CHAUSSEE on the morning of the 29th. They will take with them A.Bs.163 and cartoon sheets. They will also precede the Coy and arrange billets at VIGNACOURT.

III.

Transport. The following transport is allotted and will march behind units to which attached.

No 1 Section	2 limbers, the second limber carrying belt boxes (80)	
No 2 "	" " " " "	S. A. A.
No 3 "	" " " " "	S. A. A.
No 4 "	" " " " "	S. A. A.
Headquarters	1 limber	
Cooks	1 " carrying rations etc.	
Officers Kits	1	
Mess Stores	1	
Transport	1	

IV.

Area & Q.M. Stores. All Area Stores will be handed in to Batts.

One N.C.O. (Sgt. Shannon) to report to Brigade Headquarters at [illegible] on morning of 29th to conduct lorry to No 30 billet for Q.M. Stores and any other baggage (1 lorry).

V

Officers Kits — To be loaded on limber by 8 A.M. Mess Stores under arrangement with the Transport Officer.

VI

Marching out States to be handed in to Orderly Room by 9 A.M.

Marching out States certifs. — Section Officers will make a tour of their billets and ensure that they are left clean. The Orderly Officer will deal with all other billets latrines etc.

L. H. Fry Lieutenant and Adjutant,
88th Coy. Machine Gun Corps.

Issued at 1825

Copy No. 1 File
" 2 & 3 War Diary
" 4 O.C. No 1 Sect.
" 5 " " 2 "
" 6 " " 3 "
" 7 " " 4 "
" 8 O. i/c Transport.

} By Orderly.

Confidential

WAR DIARY

OF

88th Company M. G. Corps

PERIOD

From 1st April to 30th April 1917

(Volume No 11.)

Confidential.

From O.C. 88 Coy M.G.C

To Bde Major 88th Bde

Herewith War Diary for the month of April 19[illegible]

A Morris Major

Commanding 88 Coy M.G.C

30.4.17.

Army Form C. 2118.

Instructions regarding War Diaries and Intelligence Summaries are contained in F. S. Regs., Part II. and the Staff Manual respectively. Title Pages will be prepared in manuscript.

WAR DIARY
or
INTELLIGENCE SUMMARY
(Erase heading not required.)

Place	Date	Hour	Summary of Events and Information	Remarks and references to Appendices
VIGNACOURT BEAUVAL	1 Apl 17		Company marched with 1st line Transport to BEAUVAL arriving at 2 pm and billeted there for the night resuming the march on the following day weather conditions fair	Edition II
BEAUVAL MONDICOURT	2/4/17		Company marched with transport to MONDICOURT arriving 1 pm and encamped in hutments. Officers billeted in the village	France 1:10000 LENS 11.
MONDICOURT	3/4/17		Cleaning parades & inspections, halted for the day.	
MONDICOURT	4/4/17		Cleaning & inspection parades transport with the Company	
BREVILLIERS	5/4/17		Company marched with transport to BREVILLIERS where they were billeted	
"	6/4/17		Company training.	
COULLEMONT	7/4/17		Company marched to COULLEMONT and billeted.	

[illegible signature]

2149 Wt. W14957/M90 750,000 1/16 J.B.C. & A. Forms/C.2118/12.

Instructions regarding War Diaries and Intelligence Summaries are contained in F. S. Regs., Part II. and the Staff Manual respectively. Title Pages will be prepared in manuscript.

WAR DIARY
or
INTELLIGENCE SUMMARY
(Erase heading not required.)

Army Form C. 2118.

Place	Date	Hour	Summary of Events and Information	Remarks and references to Appendices
COLLEMONT	8/4/17		Cleaning parades + company training intensive digging	
COULLEMINT	9/4/17		Company training	
GOUY EN ARTOIS	10/4/17		Company marched to village in margin + encamped in hutments transport with company. Weather conditions snow + sleet	
"	11/4/17		Cleaning parades and training	

[illegible signature] Major

Army Form C. 2118.

WAR DIARY
or
INTELLIGENCE SUMMARY
(Erase heading not required.)

Instructions regarding War Diaries and Intelligence Summaries are contained in F. S. Regs., Part II. and the Staff Manual respectively. Title Pages will be prepared in manuscript.

Place	Date	Hour	Summary of Events and Information	Remarks and references to Appendices
ARRAS	12.4.17		The Company paraded at 8.30 and marched to ARRAS where we halted for two hours. Orders received from 88th Brigade for an attack by the Brigade the following morning. Objective being the 100 metre hill in front of MONCHY LE PREUX. Preliminary reconnaissance of the ground to be attacked made accordingly and arrangements made for relieving the 36th Machine Gun Company the same evening at 11 pm. Company arrived and relieved the 36th Company by 1 am, taking up Battle positions for giving covering fire to our own troops and controlling the following Woods Bois des Aubepines and Bois du Vert, the positions we took up were as follows. Four guns in MONCHY LE PREUX (Two in cellars Two at O1d 2.8 O1b 3.7.) Eight guns grouped (Four Les Fossés Farm reference N11b.8.4. Four guns La Bergère reference N12d 4.9) Four guns in reserve at	Reference 1:2000 Sheet 51B S.W.

[illegible signature]

2449 Wt. W14957/M90 750,000 1/16 J.B.C. & A. Forms/C.2118/12.

Instructions regarding War Diaries and Intelligence Summaries are contained in F. S. Regs., Part II. and the Staff Manual respectively. Title Pages will be prepared in manuscript.

WAR DIARY
or
INTELLIGENCE SUMMARY
(Erase heading not required.)

Army Form C. 2118.

Place	Date	Hour	Summary of Events and Information	Remarks and references to Appendices
ARRAS MONCHY	12.4.17		Coy Hq Orange Hill which took up positions in trench N4C 9.2. Orders were issued for the attack No I Section under 2Lt Stonehouse forming the mobile Section already in position in MONCHY No II Section under Lieut R.F.L. Owen near Les FOSSES FARM protecting the right flank 2Lt Leighton in command of No IV Section in LA BERGERIE and 2Lt Wane commanding No III Section who were in position on Orange Hill. Snowstorms at intervals with rain.	
"	13.4.17		The attack postponed until 5.30 am tomorrow morning, the day spent in improving emplacements. On first arrival to this part of the line what struck one most was the village of MONCHY although being in the firing line was still intact & the ground unbroken with shell holes so common on the SOMME Enemy shelling CAMBRAI Road. An attack made by a Brigade on our right caused the enemy to put barrages on our sector. From 10 pm till early morning the enemy sent over gas shells necessitating wearing of Respirators for most of the night.	[signature]

2449 Wt. W14957/M90 750,000 1/16 J.B.C. & A. Forms/C.2118/12.

Army Form C. 2118.

Instructions regarding War Diaries and Intelligence Summaries are contained in F. S. Regs., Part II. and the Staff Manual respectively. Title Pages will be prepared in manuscript.

WAR DIARY
or
INTELLIGENCE SUMMARY
(Erase heading not required.)

Place	Date	Hour	Summary of Events and Information	Remarks and references to Appendices
MONCHY LE PREUX	14.4.17		At 5.30 am we attacked the Essex on the ~~left~~ + Newfoundland on the right. The Hampshire Regt having dug a stepping off trench 500 yards in front of MONCHY. Two of our guns occupied this with the attacking Regts. and went forward on consolidation to the new position. It was here 2Lt Stonehouse was wounded in the right thigh he carried on & saw the other gun in position + was hit again, when he retired. This was the last heard of the two gun teams in charge of Sgt Shegold + Cpl Mackay. The enemy heavily counter attacked between the hours of 10.30 and 11 am with artillery support necessitating the retirement of the two Regiments. It is presumed that the two guns remained to cover their retirement. The stepping off trench was reoccupied + held. During the counter attack the two remaining guns of No. 1 Section accounted for many of the enemy as they were advancing.	

2449 Wt. W14957/M90 750,000 1/16 J.B.C. & A. Forms/C.2118/12.

Instructions regarding War Diaries and Intelligence Summaries are contained in F. S. Regs., Part II. and the Staff Manual respectively. Title Pages will be prepared in manuscript.

WAR DIARY
or
INTELLIGENCE SUMMARY
(Erase heading not required.)

Army Form C. 2118.

Place	Date	Hour	Summary of Events and Information	Remarks and references to Appendices
MONCHY LEPREUX	14.4.17		No II Section during the afternoon reinforced the two remaining guns of No I Section in MONCHY. Heavy barrage in & around the village. In the evening the six gun teams were relieved by the 87th Company. On relief returned to ARRAS arriving about 3 am	
"	15.4.17		No III Section relieved No IV in LA BERGERE and LES FOSSES FARM. Relief complete by 9 pm. Rain & snowstorms. Enemy shelling Roads & batteries heavily	
"	16.4.17		No III Section relieved by the 87th Company on relief proceeding to ARRAS. Heavy hostile shelling around FEUCHY CHAPEL	
"	17.4.17		No IV Section in position N4c9.2. proceeded to ARRAS with Coy Hq on instructions received through Brigade, heavy shelling by enemy	
ARRAS	18.4.17		Company in billets & cellars at ARRAS. cleaning of guns & S.A.A. inspections	
"	19.4.17		Intensive digging two teams of No I Section proceeded to LA BERGÈRE and relieved two teams of the 87th M.G. Coy. Enemy shelling Arras during the day & night.	

2449 Wt. W14957/M90 750,000 1/16 J.B.C. & A. Forms/C.2118/12.

Instructions regarding War Diaries and Intelligence Summaries are contained in F. S. Regs., Part II. and the Staff Manual respectively. Title pages will be prepared in manuscript.

WAR DIARY
or
INTELLIGENCE SUMMARY.
(Erase heading not required.)

Army Form C. 2118.

Place	Date	Hour	Summary of Events and Information	Remarks and references to Appendices
MONCHY LE PREUX			a very gallant officer Lieut Owen was killed. He had previously made a reconnaissance for his gun positions returned to lead his teams. These two teams suffered heavily. The other two teams took up positions in O 8 a central to protect the right flank of the Brigade as the troops on our left had not succeeded in gaining their objective. The enemy counter attacked at 11 am and was met with heavy fire from these guns. Of the twelve guns in N 12 b four of these went forward to SHOVEL TRENCH O 8 a under 2Lt Wilson for additional protection of the right flank. These guns (N12 b) suffered very heavy casualties from enemy shell fire four guns were put out of action and many of the personnel. Enemy shelling exceedingly heavy ~~throughout~~ the day with heavy counter attacks in which the enemy lost large numbers through our machine gun & artillery fire. Hand to hand fighting ensued	[illegible signature]

A5834 Wt. W4973/M687 750,000 8/16 D. D. & L. Ltd. Forms/C.2118/13.

Instructions regarding War Diaries and Intelligence Summaries are contained in F. S. Regs., Part II. and the Staff Manual respectively. Title pages will be prepared in manuscript.

WAR DIARY
or
INTELLIGENCE SUMMARY.
(Erase heading not required.)

Army Form C. 2118.

Place	Date	Hour	Summary of Events and Information	Remarks and references to Appendices
ARRAS	20.4.17		Intensive digging and usual parades, enemy shelling CAMBRAI ROAD heavily. Dump of 120,000 rounds S.A.A. established at N 12 b. for impending operation	
"	21.4.17		Intensive digging and preparing guns etc for action. Operation Orders issued (Copy attached)	Appendix A.
MONCHY LE PREUX LES FOSSES FARM	22.4.17		Company headquarters moved into Farm as stated in margin and the gun teams moved into battle positions for tomorrows offensive. Zero notified as 4.45 am, water dump established at N.12 b with the S.A.A. each man now carries on him 2 days Iron Rations & one days ordinary rations.	
"	23.4.17		At 4.45 am the barrage fell. The infantry assaulted & gained their objective No 2 Section the mobile section went forward and were met with very severe machine gun fire from O.14 A. CAVALRY FARM these hostile guns were engaged and after a time silenced The two guns engaging this target were in position in SHOVEL TRENCH They then pushed forward It was here that their Commander	Map.

[signature]

A5834 Wt. W4973/M687 750,000 8/16 D. D. & L. Ltd. Forms/C.2118/13.

Army Form C. 2118.

Instructions regarding War Diaries and Intelligence Summaries are contained in F. S. Regs., Part II. and the Staff Manual respectively. Title pages will be prepared in manuscript.

WAR DIARY
or
INTELLIGENCE SUMMARY.
(Erase heading not required.)

Place	Date	Hour	Summary of Events and Information	Remarks and references to Appendices
MONCHY LE PREUX	23.4.17.		in the BOIS DU VERT and BOIS DU SART woods. One of our ammunition Dumps was blown up early in the morning 60,000 rounds. but 60 boxes remained which 2Lt Lys got forward by means of ammunition carriers. The forward guns obtained a plentiful supply of ammunition from the ammunition carriers and few casualties. The first objective was consolidated.	
"	24.4.17		Heavy hostile artillery activity. During the afternoon the 86th Brigade attacked the Second objective and our forward guns gave covering fire. At 5 pm orders were received to vacate our positions & return to ARRAS that afternoon. Orders were issued accordingly teams collected & marched independently to our old billets it was here, on the main CAMBRAI ROAD that 2Lt Wane was killed by the bursting of an enemy shell. He was taken to the Dressing Station where he succumbed after doing excellent work during the period the Company was in the line as Fire Control Commander. Our casualties for	[illegible signature]

A5834 Wt. W4973/M687 750,000 8/16 D. D. & L. Ltd. Forms/C.2118/13.

Instructions regarding War Diaries and Intelligence Summaries are contained in F. S. Regs., Part II. and the Staff Manual respectively. Title pages will be prepared in manuscript.

WAR DIARY
or
INTELLIGENCE SUMMARY.

(*Erase heading not required.*)

Army Form C. 2118.

Place	Date	Hour	Summary of Events and Information	Remarks and references to Appendices
MONCHY LE PREUX 24.4.17			the two attacks were 1 officer wounded 2 killed 5 Other Ranks killed 31 wounded [illegible] many men were wounded & remained at Duty of these Sgt Rust was the most conspicuous for his devotion to duty. Throughout the attacks communication was very satisfactory and reports from each Officer were good and delivered quickly. The Company's transport did excellent work in getting S.A.A. &c up under Lieut Reveley. Guns destroyed & damaged 9. Animals [illegible]	
ARRAS	25.4.17		The Company paraded at 12 noon and marched to the station where it entrained for SIMENCOURT arriving at 2 pm where they were billeted, the remainder of the day spent in cleaning guns &c repairs.	
~~[illegible]~~ SIMENCOURT				
" GOUY EN ARTOIS +	26.4.17		The Company paraded at 9 am and marched to GOUY EN ARTOIS Headquarters were established in our old quarters & the Company billeted in the town repairing of guns & inspections Reorganisation generally.	
" COUIN COIGNEUX +	27.4.17		The Company paraded at 8.30 and marched to COIN via	[signature]

A5834 Wt. W4973/M687 750,000 8/16 D. D. & L. Ltd. Forms/C.2118/13.

Instructions regarding War Diaries and Intelligence Summaries are contained in F. S. Regs., Part II. and the Staff Manual respectively. Title pages will be prepared in manuscript.

WAR DIARY
or
INTELLIGENCE SUMMARY.
(Erase heading not required.)

Army Form C. 2118.

Place	Date	Hour	Summary of Events and Information	Remarks and references to Appendices
			BAILLEULMONT LA CAUCHIE HUMBERCAMP ST AMAND	
COUIN	27.4.17		SOUASTRE and were billeted in ROSSIGNOL FM arriving at 1 pm.	
COUIN	28.4.17		Company in billets ROSSIGNOL FARM parades inspections for reorganisation repairing of guns &c. A new draft of one Officer + 42 other ranks reported today and the training of them taken immediately in hand	
"	29.4.17		Church parades and tests of elementary training	
"	30.4.17		Usual parades. Company training	
				A.Wornith

A5834 Wt. W4973/M687 750,000 8/16 D. D. & L. Ltd. Forms/C.2118/13.

Appendix A.

Copy No. 8

Operation Order No. 10

– By –

Major A. Morris Commanding

88th Coy Machine Gun Corps

In the Field
21st April 1917

Reference special map Monchy le Preux 1:10,000

I.

(a) Information of own troops

The 29th Division will attack the German System of defence on the Divisions present frontage in conjunction with other Divisions by simultaneous action. Date & time to be notified later

(b) Enemy

The enemy at this phase of operations is considerably disorganised and is incapable of concerted action on a large scale. The enemy's morale has been considerably weakened by recent defeats.

II

Intentions

The attack will be carried out in two phases designated as the 1st & 2nd objectives

1st Objective (Blue Line) O.8 central – Infantry O.8 b.1.2. (exclusive) A line running up the spur through O.8 b.3.4. – O.8 a.45.95 – O.2 central – I.32. 6.7.3

2nd Objective (Red Line) O.9 b.5.0 – O.9 b.5.5 – O.3 d.5.0. – O.3 d.2.3. Eastern edge of Bois du Sart – I.33 b.8.1.

It is the intention of the G.O.C. to attack and consolidate both objectives

BOUNDARIES The boundaries between the 88th Brigade & 15th Div. on their right

A East West line from N.2 central to O.9 central thence to O.10 a.2.4

III

Distribution

4 guns

No II Sect. under Lieut. Owens. Mobile

No II Section (Commander as per margin) will form the mobile section at zero they will be in position on the Southern end of the jumping off trench about ~~O.1.b.2.2~~ N.2.b.6.2 and will go forward in the wake of the assaulting troops and take up a position about O.8 central and control by direct fire the road and houses in O.14 a when not masked by our infantry at zero plus seven hours will advance to 2nd Objective in rear of the infantry. The chief duty of this section will be to deal with any hostile offensive action such as machine guns, Rifle fire & Trench Mortars.

12 guns

No III Section under Lieut.

No IV Section under Lieut. McFeely

No I Section under Lieut Wilson

A Group of 12 guns Commanders and sections as per margin will be in position N.2.b.8.6 & will carry out barrage A for the 1st objective. Guns will open fire at zero on a N. & S. line from O.8 central to O.2 central remaining on this line until zero plus 8 minutes. at 0+8 minutes 0+16 minutes 0+24 minutes 0+32 minutes they will lift 200 yds. until the barrage line for the 1st objective is reached viz a N. & S. line from O.9 a.6.0. to O.3 a.0.4. where a standing barrage until zero plus 7 hours will be maintained

2 guns No III Section

2 – No IV

under Lieut.

At zero plus 6 hours six guns as per margin on orders received from the fire Control Commander will take up positions on sunken Road O.8 a to O.7 b and carry out barrage for the final objective on a North & South line

6 Sunken Rd. at 0+6 hours — from O. 10 central to O. 4. d. 0.6. (Barrage B)

remaining guns under — The six other guns at O. fl. in 7 hours will cease fire and move up to

1st Objective at 0+7 — positions on the first objective and be prepared to open on to Barrage B. should they be required.

IV

Preliminary Reconnaissance

The ground will be reconnoitred by each individual Section Commander

(a) Avenues of approach

(b) Tactical sites, both for direct and indirect fire

(c) Advanced positions

(d) Possibilities points for the disability of Sector

(e) Backward and lateral communication.

(f) Positions for fighting limbers in the event of the continuation of the advance

(g) Belt Filling Stations

(h) Forward S.A.A. Dumps and Water Dumps

(i) Assembly Points

(j) Establishment of visual stations

Each Section Officer will render a special preliminary reconnaissance certificate in addition to the usual early morning reports

V

Fire Control Comd. 2 Lt. Warre

Fire control commander as per margin he will be responsible for controlling the fire of the 12 guns at N.26. 8 6. and will give orders when the 1st Objective has been consolidated & the attack on the second is to take place for the 6 guns to move forward under 2 Lt. Wilson to the Sunken Road and will be responsible for obtaining disposition situation and intelligence reports from Sections and forwarding them to Company Headquarters.

VI

DUMPS

N.26.6.2. before O. 8 central O.9 a 7.4

S.A.A. Water

a S.A.A. and water dump have been established at N. 26. 6. 2. of 120,000 rounds, and petrol cans of water. Forward dumps to be established at before O. 8 central and O. 9 a 7. 4.

VII

Ammunition Supply. Officer:- 2 Lt. [illegible] — Water

(1) 4 belts per gun

(2) Belt filling stations

(3) Advanced Dumps

Carriers

7 No. 1. 8 No. 2. 7 No. 3 7 No. 4

Will be sub divided as per margin. The greatest amount of ammunition possible will be taken forward by means of bandoliers on the men in addition to the guns compliments. Ammunition carriers are detailed 8 to Lieut. [illegible] No. I. Section 7 to 2 Lieut. Warre No. III Section 7 to 2 Lt. McFeeley No. IV Section 7 to 2 Lt. Wilson No. I. Section the remainder 21 under the Ammunition Supply Officer as per margin will be responsible for establishing forward and advanced dumps. After the 1st Objective has been taken the A.S.O. will be responsible for establishing an advanced dump at before O. 8 central and a further advanced dump after the 2nd Objective has been attained at O.9.a.7.4. Each N.C.O going into action will carry a two gallon petrol tin in his pack. Replenishment of ammunition is one of the most elementary necessary factors which form the basis of fire effect.

VIII

Spare Parts Etc. — Special gun numbers to be detailed

IX

Artificers Shop — Will be established at Company Headquarters

X

Company Headquarters. — Les Fosses Farm. N.11.b.95.40

XI

Disposition Reports — Should reach Company Headquarters half an hour after the objective has been attained

XII

Fire Registration — Fire Registration must be obtained where possible each gun will range independently so as not to arouse the suspicion of the enemy of an impending attack. Not more than 20 rounds per gun should be expended for this purpose. Range on shell craters where possible to facilitate observation

XIII

a) Range Cards & Key Ranges — Range cards will be made from the assembly positions & Key Ranges to mark the progressive stages of the attack

b) Barrage Range Cards — Will be made from the map as from the enemy position. Due allowance must be made for the error of the day.

XIV

Special Observers — Each section will have its special observer to report the result of fire observation he should have a knowledge of his sector and an elementary knowledge of indication & recognition. His position should be in close proximity to the Fire Control Commander.

XV

Acknowledge

Issued at 1825

L. H. Fry Lieut & Adjutant for O.C. 88th Coy. M.G. Corps.

Copy No 1 Operation Order File
Nos 2 & 3 War Diary
" 4 O.C. No 1 Section
" 5 " No 2 Section
" 6 " No 3 Section
" 7 " No 4 Section
8 Ammunition Supply Officer
9. Fire Control Commander
10. Transport Officer

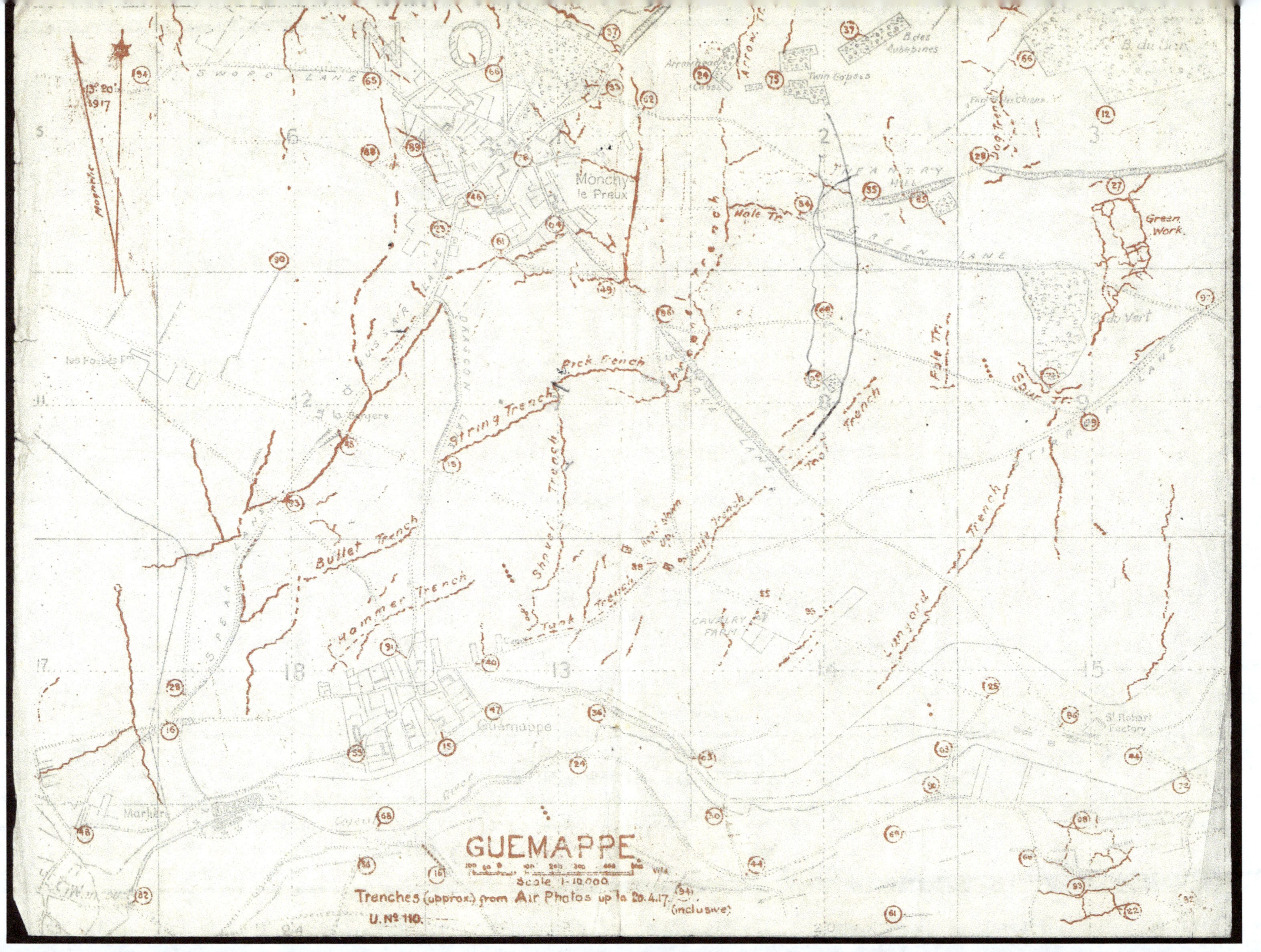

GUEMAPPE
Scale 1:10,000
Trenches (approx.) from Air Photos up to 20.4.17. (inclusive)
U. Nº 110.
Monchy le Preux
Guemappe
Cavalry Farm
St Rohart Factory
Green Work
Bois du Vert
Twin Copses
B. des Aubepines
Arrowhead Copse
Infantry Hill
Sword Lane
Green Lane
Dragoon Lane
Spear Lane
Pick Trench
String Trench
Bullet Trench
Hammer Trench
Shovel Trench
Tool Trench
Tank Trench
Lanyard Trench
Spur Tr.
Hole Tr.
Arrow Tr.
Dog Trench
Pole Tr.
Les Fosses Fm
la Bergere
Marliere
13°20' 1917
Magnetic

Instructions regarding War Diaries and Intelligence Summaries are contained in F. S. Regs., Part II. and the Staff Manual respectively. Title pages will be prepared in manuscript.

WAR DIARY
or
INTELLIGENCE SUMMARY.
(Erase heading not required.)

Army Form C. 2118.

Vol 14

Place	Date	Hour	Summary of Events and Information	Remarks and references to Appendices
ROSIGNOL FARM to ST AMAND	1.5.17		Company paraded at 6.45 am and marched to ST AMAND with 1st Line Transport arriving at 8 am Company encamped in hutments officers billeted in village Inspection parades.	MAP LENS 11.
ARRAS	2.5.17		Company paraded at 3 pm and marched via HUMBERCAMP LAHERLIERE where we entrained for ARRAS arriving 6.30 pm and were billeted for the night. Transport followed by road arriving at 8 pm. Fighting limbers packed and Company standing to ready to move at 45 minutes notice. Coy at this period is in Corps Reserve and ready to proceed to Brown line.	
ARRAS	3.5.17		Cleaning up of billets another draft of 6 men received thus making the strength of the Company up to 10 officers 190 other ranks 16 of these being at Divisional Depot Coy. Enemy shelling the Town	

A5834 Wt. W4973/M687 750,000 8/16 D. D. & L. Ltd. Forms/C.2118/13.

Instructions regarding War Diaries and Intelligence Summaries are contained in F. S. Regs., Part II. and the Staff Manual respectively. Title pages will be prepared in manuscript.

WAR DIARY
or
INTELLIGENCE SUMMARY.
(Erase heading not required.)

88TH COMPANY, MACHINE GUN CORPS.

Army Form C. 2118.

Place	Date	Hour	Summary of Events and Information	Remarks and references to Appendices
ARRAS	3.5.17		with High Velocity shrapnel. Transport lines outside Town. Reconnaissance of track by 2 officers for moving to Brown line.	
"	4.5.17		Cleaning of guns & ammunition ordinary parades. Training of the new Drafts.	
"	5.5.17		Usual Routine Parades. The Town shelled during the day & throughout the night.	
"	6.5.17		Church Parades. Weather conditions good.	
"	7.5.17		Company marched with transport to DAINVILLE in the afternoon where they were billeted	
DAINVILLE	8.5.17		Usual parades	

[signature]

A5834 Wt. W4973/M687 750,000 8/16 D. D. & L. Ltd. Forms/C.2118/13.

Instructions regarding War Diaries and Intelligence Summaries are contained in F. S. Regs., Part II. and the Staff Manual respectively. Title pages will be prepared in manuscript.

WAR DIARY
or
INTELLIGENCE SUMMARY.
(Erase heading not required.)

88TH COMPANY, MACHINE GUN CORPS.
No. .... Date ....

Army Form C. 2118.

Place	Date	Hour	Summary of Events and Information	Remarks and references to Appendices
DAINVILLE	9.5.17		Usual Routine Parades & Instructional Classes	
ARRAS	10.5.17		Usual parades during the morning Company paraded at 4.45 pm & marched with 1st line transport to ARRAS returning to our old billets. Cleaning of guns & overhauling of ammunition. The Company is now complete with 16 guns 3 Tripods Mark IV deficient. Strength of Personnel 10 Off 196 OR. The Commanding Officer & Adjutant made a Reconnaissance of the sector likely to be occupied by us.	
"	11.5.17		Usual Parades. Transport Lines on Racecourse outside ARRAS.	
"	12.5.17		Usual Parades	
"	13.5.17		Church Parades and Reconnaissance by section officers	
"	14.5.17		Morning Parades as usual, Company paraded at 7 pm & took up positions as follows. Coy Hq HOLT WORK H 25 d 3.4 No 3 Section Strong Points in rear MINCHY LE PREUX N 36 d 3.4. N 6 b 2.9. N 6 d 2.3 & N 6 b 8.7. Nos 2 & 4 Sections BROWN LINE from H 28 c 2.3 to the CAMBRAI ROAD No 1 Section in Reserve Coy Hq.	
"	15.5.17		Reconnaissance of the forward area by section Officers & arrangements made for Relief of 36th & 37th Companies M.G. Corps the same evening. After Relief the Coy occupied the following positions No IV Section I 25 c 9.6. I 25 b 75.40 I 31 b 25.25 I 31 b 30.85 No II Section I 31 b 50.00 I 31 d 70.25. I 31 d 75.10 H 36 b 95.35 No 3 Section in Strong Points as previously mentioned. On again coming into the same sect	

A5834 Wt. W4973/M687 750,000 8/16 D. D. & L. Ltd. Forms/C.2118/13.

Instructions regarding War Diaries and Intelligence Summaries are contained in F. S. Regs., Part II. and the Staff Manual respectively. Title pages will be prepared in manuscript.

WAR DIARY
or
INTELLIGENCE SUMMARY.
(Erase heading not required.)

88TH COMPANY. MACHINE GUN CORPS.
No. ....
Date ....

Army Form C. 2118.

Place	Date	Hour	Summary of Events and Information	Remarks and references to Appendices
[illegible] to MONCHY LE PREUX	15/5/17		occupied a few weeks ago the absence of heavy Enemy Artillery Action was noticed more especially the Range at which the guns were firing. This with other information ... from prisoners and other sources lead us to believe that the Enemy is withdrawing. There is great Aerial activity on the part of our own Planes very few of the Enemy's being seen.	Map Reference FRANCE 51 B NW.
Do.	16/5/17		Early on this morning the Section occupying Strong Points were relieved by the 86th Coy Machine Gun Corps. This Section returning to Coy Headquarters which were established on old German Gun Pits on H25b Central. No 1 Section going forward and occupying Strong Points at H23d87, H30b28, H29b Central & H36d29. The Enemy to-day is chiefly expending his ammunition on the Front Line with Counter Battery work.	
Do.	16/5/17		Positions on Rear Crest H19b were reconnoitred with a view to placing Guns for the protection of our Front by enfilading No Man's Land & German Trenches running through I32a. Enemy Artillery Activity below normal.	
Do.	16/5/17		~~Our positions remain unchanged~~. Rations are conveyed to Coy Headquarters by pack & limber as far as ORANGE HILL, from where they are man handled forward. Water for guns & Personnel conveyed in Petrol tins.	

A5834 Wt. W4973/M687 750,000 8/16 D. D. & L. Ltd. Forms/C.2118/13.

[signature]

Instructions regarding War Diaries and Intelligence Summaries are contained in F. S. Regs., Part II. and the Staff Manual respectively. Title pages will be prepared in manuscript.

WAR DIARY
or
INTELLIGENCE SUMMARY.
(Erase heading not required.)

88TH COMPANY, MACHINE GUN CORPS.
No.........
Date.........

Army Form C. 2118.

Place	Date	Hour	Summary of Events and Information	Remarks and references to Appendices
[illegible] to MONCHY LE PREUX	17/5/17		A sub section of No 3 Section took up position in REUX WOOD during the afternoon we have now 14 guns in action and 2 in reserve at Coy H.Qrs. Weather remains fine Enemy Artillery fire below normal. ~~Orders received~~	
	18/5/17		During the afternoon orders were received that the 87th Infantry Brigade were attacking Infantry HILL in the BOIS-DES-AUBPINES on the evening of the 19th and that we should support the attack by giving covering fire. Suitable positions were immediately reconnoitred. Operation Orders issued (copy attached for reference) Emplacements dug and ammunition and water taken forward this was completed by 3.30 a.m. 19th inst.	Appendix A.
"	19/5/17		Rations for the 20th were taken forward to all Gun Teams by 9 a.m. The barrage fell at 9 pm but Infantry were unable to advance owing to hostile machine gun fire. Our own guns were working well + the barrage was maintained with an ammunition expenditure of 40000 rounds. The enemy put his barrage down one minute after our own fell in answer to signals from his front line. ~~At~~ a quarter of an hour after zero a party of enemy were observed in I 33 c these were engaged by us with good results.	
"	~~[illegible]~~			

[illegible signature]

A5834 Wt. W4973/M687 750,000 8/16 D. D. & L. Ltd. Forms/C.2118/13.

Instructions regarding War Diaries and Intelligence Summaries are contained in F. S. Regs., Part II. and the Staff Manual respectively. Title pages will be prepared in manuscript.

WAR DIARY
or
INTELLIGENCE SUMMARY.
(Erase heading not required.)

88TH COMPANY, MACHINE GUN CORPS. No. .... Date ....

Army Form C. 2118.

Place	Date	Hour	Summary of Events and Information	Remarks and references to Appendices

Operation Order No 79
By
Major A Morris Commanding,
88 Company Machine Gun Corps
In the Field 18 May 1917.

Reference Special Maps Monchy le Preux
51 B NW + SW or French Maps 1-10,000

I

Information as own troops — The 87th Infantry Brigade will attack INFANTRY HILL + the BOIS-DES-AUBPINES in conjunction with the 167th Brigade (56th Division) on their light. The attack will take place under an artillery Barrage which will open at zero and a Machine Gun Barrage which will open at the same time along a line O9a71, O3d27, O3B12, O3a66, I33b56, I32d89, + I32a85.

Disposition 2/Lt Lyon M.C. / Lt Wilson MC / 2/Lt Gregson — The 88 Coy will employ 6 guns for defensive + 10 guns for Barrage purposes. 2 guns commanded as per margin in position at I27b93 will Barrage from I32d89 to I32a85. 4 guns commanded per margin in position at I27b93 will take up position about I0[?]a47 and Barrage from O3B12 to O3a66. [sic] as per margin will take up position about I25b20 near BAYONET TRENCH + Barrage from I33b central to I32d89. These 4 guns will be taken from positions H33d87, 429B central H36 O9535 + I26b7540. The latter 2 guns being of No 4 Section.

Gun Emplacs. — The ground has already been reconnoitred by officers concerned + emplacements are to be dug to night.

SAA (Reserve) — A reserve of 15,000 rounds per gun must be established. The detachment in Ricoux Wood will arrange to obtain his reserve supply from O.C. 154 M G Coy.

Rations Water — Rations for the 20th will be available at Coy H.Qrs at 7am tomorrow morning. Sections will arrange to draw these together with water for personnel + guns before 2 PM that day. Guns will be got into position immediately.

Issued at 2100

W. H. Fry
Lieut for O.C.
88 M.G.C.

A Morris

Copies to
Section Officers

A5834 Wt. W4973/M687 750,000 8/16 D. D. & L. Ltd. Forms/C.2118/13.

Instructions regarding War Diaries and Intelligence Summaries are contained in F. S. Regs., Part II. and the Staff Manual respectively. Title pages will be prepared in manuscript.

WAR DIARY
or
INTELLIGENCE SUMMARY.
(Erase heading not required.)

88TH COMPANY, MACHINE GUN CORPS.
No.............
Date...........

Army Form C. 2118.

Place	Date	Hour	Summary of Events and Information	Remarks and references to Appendices
SOUTH OF THE SCARPE TO MONCHY LE PREUX	20.5.17		about 6.45 am four hostile machine guns opened fire from the portion of BOIS DU SART in I 33 c these were engaged by four of our guns firing one belt each, no firing was seen from this direction since. During the evening the teams returned to their ordinary battle emplacements. Two guns in Reserve No III Section relieved 2 guns of No 4 Section.	
"	21.5.17		This evening Section in Strong Points No I relieved No II Section in front line, two anti aircraft positions were constructed and two Reserve Teams carried on with that work. Enemy planes flying low over our own front system were driven off during the evening. Weather continues fine. Enemy shelling front system of trenches and generally searching valleys.	
"	22.5.17		Enemy shelling normal. During the day five hostile planes were driven off by our Reserve guns. Our Company headquarters are in an old German 8" gun emplacement. Rations are brought to rear of ORANGE HILL by limbers thence man handled. Enemy motor lorries + trains observed at J 8 d also a number of men on foot. Enemy at night signals "Flash Light" from this direction at night usually about 10 pm.	MAP SCARPE VALLEY

[signature]

A5834 Wt. W4973/M687 750,000 8/16 D. D. & L. Ltd. Forms/C.2118/13.

Instructions regarding War Diaries and Intelligence Summaries are contained in F. S. Regs., Part II. and the Staff Manual respectively. Title pages will be prepared in manuscript.

WAR DIARY
or
INTELLIGENCE SUMMARY.
(*Erase heading not required.*)

88TH COMPANY. MACHINE GUN CORPS.
No. ....
Date ....

Army Form C. 2118.

Place	Date	Hour	Summary of Events and Information	Remarks and references to Appendices
SOUTH OF SCARPE TO MONCHY LE PREUX			we have sixteen guns in this area, four of these are in strong Points.	
	23.5.17		Shelling normal – Enemy aircraft fairly active. we are able to obtain good observation as we hold the high ground in this neighbourhood.	
	24.5.17		Considerable aerial activity. In the afternoon Major Morris and 2Lieut. Wilson started to go to Bde. H.Q. unfortunately they ran into heavy enemy shelling and 2Lieut. Wilson was killed.	
	25.5.17		Also Extract from 29th Div Intelligence Summary 6 a.m. 25th to 6 a.m. 26th reads as follows:- an enemy aeroplane was brought down very low indeed by the 88th Machine Gun Coy at H.35 b.3.5 but a shell burst amongst them as they were firing, causing several casualties including 4 Officers, and the plane righted itself and flew away. The officers killed were Lieuts H. Leighton and W. H. Fry, 2Lieut. Hutchinson of the 88th M.G. Coy and 2Lieut. N. Grant R.F.A. Enemy artillery was active throughout the day.	
	26.5.17		Lieut White rejoined the Company and during the night 26/27 relieved 2Lieut. McFeely who returned to gun pits at H.Q. H.35.a. Central. 2Lieut. Mantle joined the Company and took over No 2 Section. Considerable enemy shelling in neighbourhood of SCABBARD and BAYONET Trenches and also on the reverse slope of ORANGE HILL.	
	27.5.17		at 8 A.M. today the bodies of 2Lieuts Hutchinson and Grant, Cpl Walls, Pte Grieve were buried at Div. Burial ground at H.36.c.5.3 Ref. Special Map. MONCHY-LE-PREUX. Scale 1:10,000.	W Morris

A5834. Wt. W4973 M687 750,000 8/16 D. D. & L. Ltd. Forms/C.2118/13.

Instructions regarding War Diaries and Intelligence Summaries are contained in F. S. Regs., Part II. and the Staff Manual respectively. Title pages will be prepared in manuscript.

WAR DIARY
or
INTELLIGENCE SUMMARY.
(Erase heading not required.)

88TH COMPANY, MACHINE GUN CORPS.
No.......
Date.......

Army Form C. 2118.

Place	Date	Hour	Summary of Events and Information	Remarks and references to Appendices
South of Scarpe to MONCHY-LE-PREUX	27.5.17		At 8.30 p.m. six enemy aircraft flew over our lines but were driven off by our Anti-Aircraft guns in H.35.6.	
	28.5.17		Enemy artillery active – from 8 - 9 p.m. HARNES Trench and ORANGE Lane were shelled. Out of the shells fired at HARNES Trench nine failed to explode (8.30 p.m.) but 50 % of shells failed to explode. No. 2. Section (4 guns) moved into positions in O.1.a in preparation for operations on night of 29/30th. Copy attached of Company operation orders re attack by 86th Bde on HOOK Trench on night of 29th/30th.	
	29.5.17		Operations postponed. Enemy shelling normal in morning, in the afternoon there was practically no shelling. One of our aeroplanes was shot down towards dusk.	
	30.5.17		Operation orders attached re operations by the 86th and 88th Bdes. ELBOW Trench and north end of SCABBARD Trench were shelled in the morning. Enemy artillery unusually quiet in afternoon – aerial activity normal.	
	31.5.17		During operation enemy at first put up a barrage along the [?] line but his fire was not very intense – throughout operation he frequently sent up flares bursting into two and sometimes more red stars whilst in the air. Orders for relief of Company on night 1/2 came in today we are being relieved by the 9th Coy. O.C. 9th Coy came to H.Q. this morning to make arrangements about the relief. Enemy artillery quiet today – aerial activity normal. Operation Orders No 82. Re relief is attached	[illegible signature]

A5834 Wt. W4973 M687 750,000 8/16 D. D. & L. Ltd. Forms/C.2118/13.

Instructions regarding War Diaries and Intelligence Summaries are contained in F. S. Regs., Part II. and the Staff Manual respectively. Title pages will be prepared in manuscript.

WAR DIARY
or
INTELLIGENCE SUMMARY.
(Erase heading not required.)

88TH COMPANY. MACHINE GUN CORPS.
No. ....
Date ....

Army Form C. 2118.

Place	Date	Hour	Summary of Events and Information	Remarks and references to Appendices
South of Scarpe to Monchy-le-Preux	31.5.17		In the attack last night [30th-31st] our Troops [reached] their objective at most points but owing to hostile bombing attacks were unable to maintain the ground won, we are now holding our original line. The attack at 11.25 pm. last night on O.25.b.3.0 by a Company of our left Brigade failed in the face of hostile artillery and machine gun fire. The enemy then attacked our posts B and C. but we remain in possession of them.	

A5834 Wt. W4973/M687 750,000 8/16 D. D. & L. Ltd. Forms/C.2118/13.

Operation Order No 80 — Copy No. . .

By

Major A. Morris, Commanding

88 Coy M. G. Corps.

In the Field 28th May 1917.

Ref. Special Map Monchy-le-Preux

I Information own troops	The 86th Infantry Brigade (H.Q. at H.5.a central) with the assistance of a Battalion of 112th Infantry Brigade will attack HOOK TRENCH from the block at O.8.b.2.1. to the northern end of the trench at O.2.b.4.0. on the night of 29/30 May at an hour Zero to be notified later.
II. Disposition	88th Machine Gun Company will furnish 10 guns for Barrage Fire. 6 guns will remain in their normal positions for the protection of the Brigade Frontage.
2/Lt Gregson	No 1 Section (4 guns) under commander as per margin will remain in their present positions for protective purposes. 1 gun (No 4 Section [illegible]) will remain in its present position. 1 gun (No 4 " [illegible] guns) will take up a position in a Shell Hole (if possible) near BAYONET TRENCH at I.25.c.00.40. 2 guns (No 4 Section) now in Anti-Aircraft positions will move up into positions in Shell Holes (if possible) N. of BAYONET TRENCH in I.25.c.
Lt White	The 4 guns (No 4 Sect) will have a Barrage Line from O.3.a.6.6. to I.33.c.5.6. All 6 guns will be under Comd. as per margin.
2/Lt Neale	No 3 Section Comd. as per margin will take up positions in Shell Holes (if poss.) in O.1.d. and their Barrage Line will be from O.3.b.1.2 to O.3.a.6.6.
2/Lt Lys MC	The 2 guns in ROEUX WOOD under Comd. as per margin will have a Barrage Line from I.33.c central to I.32.d.8.5.
Lt White	1 gun in ELBOW TRENCH (No 3 Sect) and 1 gun (No 3 Sect) in SCABBARD TRENCH will remain for protective purposes

Copy No. . . .

III Positions Time	I All Guns will be in position 24 hours before Zero 2 If possible guns should be placed in Shell Holes especially those doing Barrage Fire. 3 There will be no intensive M.G. Fire before Zero. Fire action during the day should be normal
IV Barrage Guns Others	The 10 Barrage Guns will only open fire on an S.O.S. Signal or heavy Hostile Machine Gun Fire. The Fire of other Guns will be reduced to a minimum no 2 guns firing at the same time unless Hostile Machine Guns open fire when normal night lines will be engaged
V Rations & Water	48 hours rations will be drawn on 28th for consumption on 29th & 30th. Two cans of water per Team will be drawn and more will be available if necessary.
VI SAA Reserve	All Guns in line are complete with 10,000 rounds per Gun Guns doing Barrage Fire will have a reserve of 4,000 rounds per Gun.

Please Acknowledge

(Sd) Jelf-Reveley
Lieut & Adjutant
88 Coy. M G C.

Copies No 1 & 2 War Diary
" 3 to 6 Sect Officers
Copy No 7 File

Issued at . . . .

Movement Orders No 2
By
Major W. Morris Commanding
88th Coy M G Corps
In the field 31st May 1917.

I
Relief — The 88 M G Coy will be relieved by the 9th Coy on the night of [illegible]

II
Indents — Indents, [illegible] Returns will be handed over. Indents must be complete with necessary [illegible]. All Bills must be full. Handing over certificates will be prepared in duplicate [illegible] will reach H.Qrs. with morning report tomorrow.

III
Guides — Sgt. [illegible] & men will be at junction of [illegible] road and track leading to [illegible] at 8 PM on the 1st and will guide relieving Coy. to Forward Headquarters.
Guides [illegible] will be at Coy. H.Qrs. at 8.30 to guide relieving teams to their positions

IV
Reports — On completion of relief sections will report at H.Qrs. and will be given instructions re [illegible]

V
No 2 Sect — No 2 Section will return at dusk this evening to their former Anti-Aircraft positions. Carrying party will assist on move

VI
[illegible] night [illegible] must be explained to relieving officers also any information that may be of value must be given them.

VII
4 — Sections now in Bayonet Trench will be reoccupy their former positions to-morrow morning (1st)

Confidential

War Diary

88th Machine Gun Coy

From 1st June 1917 to 30th June 1917

(Volume No 13)

Vol 13

Instructions regarding War Diaries and Intelligence Summaries are contained in F. S. Regs., Part II. and the Staff Manual respectively. Title pages will be prepared in manuscript.

WAR DIARY
or
INTELLIGENCE SUMMARY.
(Erase heading not required.)

88TH COMPANY MACHINE GUN CORPS. No. 1701 Date 1/7/17

Army Form C. 2118.

Place	Date	Hour	Summary of Events and Information	Remarks and references to Appendices
North of Scarpe to Monchy-le Preux.	1.6.17		artillery fire normal. at 10 pm relieving by (9th) arrived at Headquarters in Gun Pits, relief was then carried out by teams - guides from all teams were at H.Q. waiting for the relieving teams. Relieving teams going to right sector had one casualty otherwise relief went off quietly.	
ARRAS	2.6.17		Last section reached Arras at about 5 a.m. Company paraded for Baths at 9 am. Cleaning of guns, Tripods etc and clothing parade at 5 pm. all officers, N.C.O's & men were comfortably billeted.	
	3.6.17		Cleaning Parades were carried out and Company was paid out. all preparations were made for the move on the 4th inst. Transport was Brigaded and left at 4 pm. Movement orders attached.	
	4.6.17		Entrained at ARRAS at 10 a.m. and arrived at CANDAS at 3.30 pm we marched from detraining point to CANAPLES - it was very hot marching. arrived at destination at 5.30 pm. Billets good for officers and very fairly good for men.	
CANAPLES	5.6.17		Parades ~~at~~ as Appendix A. No Physical Training was done. Transport arrived at 2 pm.	

A5834 Wt. W4973 M687 750,000 8/16 D. D. & L. Ltd. Forms/C.2118/13.

Instructions regarding War Diaries and Intelligence Summaries are contained in F. S. Regs., Part II. and the Staff Manual respectively. Title pages will be prepared in manuscript.

WAR DIARY
or
INTELLIGENCE SUMMARY.
(Erase heading not required.)

Army Form C. 2118.

88TH COMPANY MACHINE GUN CORPS

Place	Date	Hour	Summary of Events and Information	Remarks and references to Appendices
~~6.6~~ CANAPLES	6.6.17		Nos. 3 & 4 Secs. Parades as per Appendix. A.	
			Nos 1 & 2 Secs. on Range.	
			Bathing in pool ~~was~~ allowed between hours of 2 pm & 7 pm.	
	7.6.17		Nos. 3 & 4 Secs on Range.	
			Nos. 1 & 2 Secs. Parades as per Appendix. A.	
			8 men from 4th Bn. Worcestershire Regt, 1st Newfoundland Regt, 1st Essex Regt (24 in all) reported last night for instruction in Vickers Gun.	
			Two Range Wardens also reported for duty on Range.	
			T/Lieut. G. F. Nichols, T/Lieut. A. D. C. Burrell, 2/Lieut. G. C. C. Byron, 2/Lieut. B. W. Shipworth reported for duty today.	
	8.6.17		The Company Paraded at 8 am. to march to training ground for Close order Drill. other Parades as per Appendix. A.	
	9.6.17		Church Parade. C of E at 11 A.M. and 5.30 pm. R.C. 11 A.M. and 7 pm. N.C. 5.30 pm.	
	10.6.17		1/2 Coy on Range 9 AM – 12 noon. Other Parades as per Appendix. B.	
	11.6.17		Parades as per Appendix. B. Signs being completed for Orderly Room, Cookhouse etc.	

A5834 Wt. W4973/M687 750,000 8/16 D. D. & L. Ltd. Forms/C.2118/13.

Instructions regarding War Diaries and Intelligence Summaries are contained in F. S. Regs., Part II. and the Staff Manual respectively. Title pages will be prepared in manuscript.

WAR DIARY
or
INTELLIGENCE SUMMARY.
(Erase heading not required.)

Army Form C. 2118.

Place	Date	Hour	Summary of Events and Information	Remarks and references to Appendices
CANAPLES	12.6.17		Parades as per appendix. B. ½ Coy on Range with German gun. One entry sent in for Div. Horse Show on 16th.	
	13.6.17		Parades as per appendix. B. Field Ambulance held their "Sports Day" today. Our Sergeants Team beat theirs but lost in open Competition.	
	14.6.17.		Parades as per appendix. B. The Company paraded at 9.30 pm for night operations. Scheme as appendix. C.	
	15.6.17		Parades as per appendix. B. Training of instructional Class is proceeding well. Company Drill on Training ground was fairly satisfactory but men need plenty of Drill.	
	16.6.17		R.A.M.C. Concert party gave a concert in the Orchard behind R.A.M.C. Bgde hors at 7 pm, it went off very well. Instructional Class went to the Range and did fairly well considering their short training. Remainder of parades as per appendix. B.	
	17.6.17		Divine Service.	
	18.6.17		Parades as per appendix. D. Intensive Digging was carried out by a special party as per Diagram attached, it was found that only the emplacement itself could be completed in the allotted Time	

A5834 Wt. W4973 M687 750,000 8/16 D. D. & L. Ltd. Forms/C.2118/13.

Instructions regarding War Diaries and Intelligence Summaries are contained in F. S. Regs., Part II. and the Staff Manual respectively. Title pages will be prepared in manuscript.

WAR DIARY
or
INTELLIGENCE SUMMARY.
(Erase heading not required.)

Army Form C. 2118.

Place	Date	Hour	Summary of Events and Information	Remarks and references to Appendices
CANAPLES	19.6.17		Parades as per appendix D. Half the Company on Range "A" this is a six hundred yard Range and is very suitable for machine gun work, it is situated near the Bois de Bellevel. Company Sports were held today and went off well, the entries were good for most events. a Company dinner was held in the evening and the men appeared well satisfied.	
	20.6.17		Prizes for Sports were distributed at 9 am. Special digging party on "Spanner emplacement" are improving.	
	21.6.17		Half the company on Range - Automatic aiming, overhead Fire, Fire discipline Training, others parades as per appendix D.	
	22.6.17		Parades as per appendix D.	
	23.6.17		Demonstration on Range before Divisional Commander. (a) Intensive digging (Spanner emplacement) (b) overhead Fire (c) Barrage practice (d) Fire discipline Training. Parades as per appendix D.	
	24.6.17		Divine Service.	
	25.6.17		Cleaning of Guns, Tripods & spare parts. loading of limbers in preparation for move.	

A5834 Wt. W4973 M687 750,000 8/16 D. D. & L. Ltd. Forms/C.2118/13.

Instructions regarding War Diaries and Intelligence Summaries are contained in F. S. Regs., Part II. and the Staff Manual respectively. Title pages will be prepared in manuscript.

WAR DIARY
or
INTELLIGENCE SUMMARY.
(Erase heading not required.)

Army Form C. 2118.

Place	Date	Hour	Summary of Events and Information	Remarks and references to Appendices
CANAPLES, to DOULLENS	26.6.17		The Company paraded at 9.45 a.m. to march to DOULLENS, arrived at DOULLENS at 1 p.m. and went into billets. movement orders attached.	
	27.6.17		The Company paraded at 1.30 am and march to DOULLENS station NORTH and train left at 5.19 a.m. arrived at PROVEN at marched to camp at F.15.b.5.5 ref. Belgium sheet 28 N.W. 5A. the men are accomodated in tents.	
PROVEN AREA.			2 officers and 100 men were on detraining duties at PROVEN station all night.	
	28.6.17		at 12.45 noon nos 2, 3 & 4 Sections paraded to march to ~~relief~~ relief of 176th Coy. no 4 Section is relieving anti-aircraft guns in A.15.b. nos 2 and 3 Sections are relieving guns in B.15.a ~~and~~, B.16.d. and B.23.a Headquarters of 176th Coy are at A.16.a.9.8. accomodation tents. Transport lines are at H.Q.	
	29.6.17		no. 1 Section and the attached party paraded at 9.30 am to march to H.Q at A.16.a.9.8. Headquarters party and orderly Room are not moving at present as C.O. is too unwell to move. Reports received this morning to the effect that relief was completed alright.	
	30.6.17		accomodation in Z Defences is very good - all emplacements covered and all men in good dug-outs. no 2. Section engaged a hostile aeroplane at 8.30 pm on 29th but no result was observed. Heavy rain all day. enemy counter battery shelling rather heavy. Camp at A.16.a.9.8 required considerable cleaning up.	

A5834 Wt. W4973/M687 750,000 8/16 D. D. & L. Ltd. Forms/C.2118/13.

Movement Order No. 84.
By
Major. A. Morris. D.S.O. Commanding
88th Company Machine Gun Corps
In the field "Monday" 25th June 1917.

I Parade	The Company will parade at 10.30am to march to. Doullens. Dress. Marching Order.
II Entraining Point	The Company will proceed by No 12 Train leaving "Doullens" South Station at 05.19 on the 27th. The Company will arrive at the station at 02.19. Entrainment must be complete half an hour before the time of departure of train.
III Detraining Point	The detraining station is "Proven". Lieut. Burrell and 2nd Lieut. Gregson. and 100 men will relieve a party of similar strength of 87th Bgde who will be on detraining duties at. Proven.
IV Rations	Rations for day of entrainment will be carried on the man. The supply wagon will carry one days rations & will accompany the Transport.
V Transport	The Transport will parade outside Company Headquarters at 10.15 am. and will march with Company to "Doullens". Breast Ropes for Horse Trucks must be carried by Transport. Ropes for lashing vehicles on the flat trucks will be provided by the railway. The Transport Officer will render a certificate to the effect that his lines are in a clean and sanitary condition, to reach Company Orderly Room by 9-30 am.
VI Picquet	Serg^t^ Buck & 3 men will be on picquet duty for front end of train " Wright & 3 men " " " " " " Rear " " " These picquets will be on duty at all stops and will prevent troops leaving the train.
VII March discipline	All ranks are reminded that the strictest march discipline must be maintained throughout the march to Doullens.
VIII Marching out State	The Transport Officer will obtain from Orderly Room a Complete Marching Out State. Showing number of men, Horses, G.S. Limbered Wagons. & bicycles. and will hand this state to R.T.O. on arrival at point of Entrainment.
IX Certificates	Section Officers will render certificates to reach Orderly Room. by 9.30 am to the effect that the billets occupied by their sections are in a thoroughly clean & sanitary condition.

Company Orders
By

IX Certificates

Lieut Nichols will render a certificate to the effect that the Cookhouse, Ablution places & Latrines are in a clean & sanitary condition.

2nd Lieut Bryan will remain in "Canaples" for one hour after departure of Company and will obtain from the Maire a certificate to the effect that any claims against the Company have been rendered. This certificate must be handed into Orderly Room at the earliest opportunity.

C.D. Jeff. Reveley Lieutenant & Adjutant
88th Company Machine Gun Corps

Issued at

Copies No I Office File
" " 2-5 Section Officers
" " 6 Transport Officer
" " 7,8 War Diary

Appendix A.

PROGRAMME OF TRAINING

FOR WEEK ENDING – SATURDAY 9TH JUNE, 1917.

		9–10 A.M.	10–11 A.M.	11–12 A.M.	2–3 P.M.		
SUN	PHYSICAL TRAINING 7–7.30 A.M.						
MON							
TUE		GAS DRILL & INSPECTION	LAYING & HOLDING	STOPPAGES	CLEANING BELTS & AMM.		
WED		ROUTE MARCH					
THU		STANDARD TESTS	VISUAL TRAINING	LECTURE	CLEANING GUNS ETC.		
FRI		INTENSIVE DIGGING	GAS DRILL WITH FIRE ACTION	STANDARD TESTS	BELT FILLING		
SAT		COMPANY INSPECTION	INDIRECT FIRE	INTERIOR ECONOMY			

HALF THE COMPANY ON RANGE DAILY.
CLASS OF INSTRUCTION DAILY.

RIFLES & AMMU INSPECTION
DAILY AT 9. A.M PARADE

88TH COMPANY MACHINE GUN CORPS.

SIGNED

Appendix B.

PROGRAMME OF TRAINING

FOR WEEK ENDING - SATURDAY 16TH JUNE 1917.

	7-7-30.A.M.	9-9-30.A.M.	9-30-10-15.A.M.	10-30-11 A.M.	11-12 NOON	2-3. P.M.	9.30. P.M.
SUN							
MON							
TUE	P.T.	INSPECTION OF RIFLES, S.A.A. GAS HELMETS	CLOSE ORDER DRILL	STOPPAGES	INDIRECT FIRE	BELT-FILLING	
WED	"	GAS DRILL COMBINED WITH FIRE ACTION	INTENSIVE DIGGING	MECHANISM.	FIRE ORDERS	GUN CLEANING	
THU	"	STANDARD TESTS	HANDLING OF ARMS	LECTURE BY SECTION OFFR			NIGHT OPERATIONS
FRI						BELT FILLING	
SAT			INTERIOR	ECONOMY			

88TH COMPANY MACHINE GUN CORPS.

SIGNED

Spanner Machine Gun Emplacement.

TASK - 1 hr.

No. OF MEN - 4 MEN.

RATE - INTENSIVE DIGGING.

IMPLEMENTS - 2 PICKS & 2 SHOVELS.

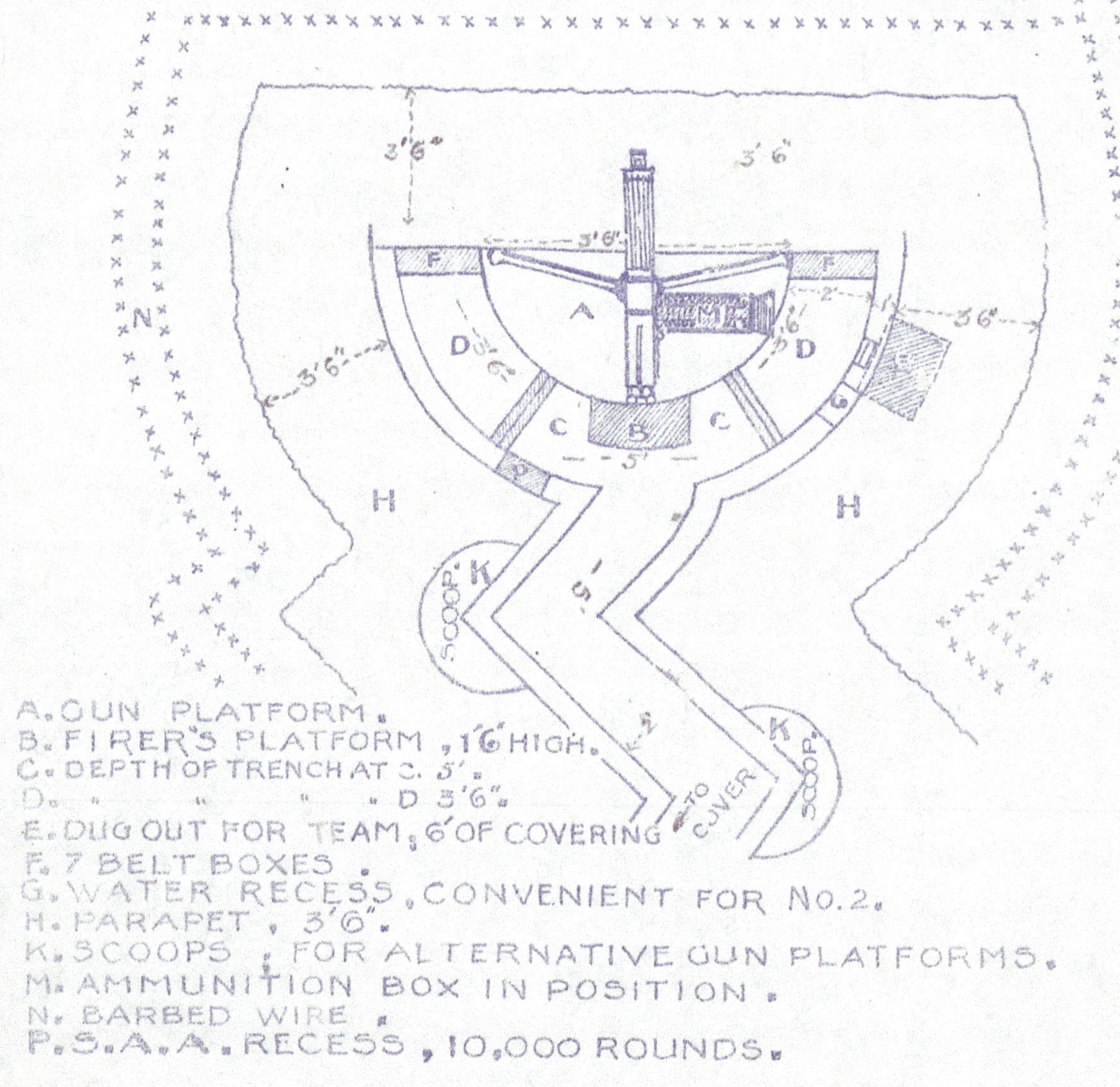

A. GUN PLATFORM.
B. FIRER'S PLATFORM, 1'6" HIGH.
C. DEPTH OF TRENCH AT C. 5'.
D. " " " D 3'6".
E. DUG OUT FOR TEAM, 6' OF COVERING.
F. 7 BELT BOXES.
G. WATER RECESS, CONVENIENT FOR No. 2.
H. PARAPET, 3'6".
K. SCOOPS, FOR ALTERNATIVE GUN PLATFORMS.
M. AMMUNITION BOX IN POSITION.
N. BARBED WIRE.
P. S.A.A. RECESS, 10,000 ROUNDS.

THE EMPLACEMENT HERE ILLUSTRATED IS FOR 1 GUN TEAM, ON AN ALLOTTED TASK OF ONE HOUR, THIS EMPLACEMENT SHOULD BE COMPLETED. IT IS ASSUMED THAT THE OFFICER WOULD BE MAKING A RECONNAISSANCE (II) THE N.C.O. MAKING A RANGE CARD (III) AND THE No 1. TUNING HIS GUN FOR FIRE ACTION & THEREFORE WOULD NOT BE AVAILABLE FOR DIGGING.

Appendix C

– 88th Company Machine Gun Corps –

Night Marching by Compass.

Section & time	Distance	Bearing	Points marked.
No I Section at Zero	250x	345°	Pile of Four Sand bags
	150x	304°	Pile of Sand bags near trench & 3 sticks
	270x	350°	Bush near Road
No II Section at Zero + 0015.	500x	81°	Two Petrol Tins
	300x	192°	X Point.

Points to be observed.

I Strict silence to be maintained

II No smoking after reaching point X.

III Sections to move in file, and care must be taken that they keep well closed up.

14th June 1917

[signature] Lieut & Act Adjt

– 88th Company Machine Gun Corps –

Appendix D.

— PROGRAMME OF TRAINING —

FOR WEEK ENDING - SATURDAY 23RD JUNE 1917.

	7-7-30.A.M	9. A.M.	9-15-10-15	10-30-11-30	11-30-12-30	2-3-30.P.M.	9-30.P.M.
SUN			DIVINE SERVICE				
MON	PHYSICAL TRAINING	INSPECTION OF RIFLES & S.A.A.	INTENSIVE DIGGING		GUARD DUTIES	CLOSE ORDER DRILL	
TUE		"	GAS DRILL WITH FIRE ACTION	TESTS OF ELEMENTARY TRAINING	KIT INSPECTION	SPORTS	
WED		"	DIGGING AGAINST TIME	BELT FILLING		CLOSE ORDER DRILL	
THU		"	DIGGING EMPLACEMENTS		LAYING & HOLDING	JUDGING DISTANCE	NIGHT OPERATIONS
FRI		"	ELEMENTARY TESTS	BELT FILLING		CLOSE ORDER DRILL	
SAT			COMPANY DRILL	LECTURE	GUN CLEANING		

HALF COMPANY ON RANGE DAILY

88TH COMPANY MACHINE GUN CORPS.

SIGNED.

Movement Order No. 83

By

Major A. Morris, Commanding.

88th Company, Machine Gun Corps

In the Field

I. The officer below named is detailed as entraining officer, to report to Brigade entraining officer 1 hour before arrival of Unit for entrainment. 2nd Lieut. [illegible], M.O.

II. Advanced Party. To leave Arras on the 3rd inst. 2nd Lieut. McFeeley, Sgt. Sharman, Private Olden, Sgt. Buck, must take three days rations with them. Will meet Staff Captain at the MAIRE CANAPLES [illegible] a.m. on the 4th. 2nd Lieut. McFeeley will assume the duties of Town Major.

III. Transport. (a) Will march under Brigade arrangements. Water Carts will accompany the 1st Line Transport. The Master Cook will make arrangements cooking and carrying water in dixies as the Transport leaves on the 3rd inst. Transport will be procured for these on the 4th. Officers kits should be reduced to a minimum any kit above regulation weight will not be accepted on the tactical train.

(B) Picket-ropes and pegs will be carried on each animal, to be used for picketing purposes at the Halting Stage.

(c) Each Limber will have a brakes-man.

(D) 60 Petrol tins will be carried. 16 on water cart crate and 44 on the 11 Limbers with crates. The Transport officer will render a certificate by 6. P.M. on the 2nd inst. That this establishment is complete.

(e) The Company shares a lorry with Brigade H.Qrs. This lorry on the 4th inst. will first take officers minimum kits to station. Pte. Blake and L/Cpl. Johnston are detailed for this purpose. On return they will load up with Officers Mess Stores, Dixies 20% of Blankets and Orderly Room Boxes. The Orderly Room clerk will be in charge of O.R. equipment. The guide reporting at Brigade H.Qrs. for lorry on morning of 4th inst. will receive written instructions from Staff Captain for the driver.

Movement Order (contd.)

IV
Rations

Rations for entrainment date will be carried with personnel by rail. the rations for consumption on the 5th will also be carried Rations for 6th inst. will be delivered by Supply Column to Q.M. Stores in new Area.

Billets. vacation of

Section Officers will be personally responsible that their billets are left in a perfectly clean state. The Orderly Officer will inspect billets each day and include it in his report.
Each Section Officer on vacating the Arras billets will certify that no damage has been done and that they are in a satisfactory state

C.H. Jelf-Reveley
Lieut. and Adjutant,
88th Coy. Machine Gun Corps

Confidential

War Diary

of

88th Machine Gun Coy

From 1st July 1917 To 31st July 1917

(Volume No. 14)

Instructions regarding War Diaries and Intelligence Summaries are contained in F. S. Regs., Part II. and the Staff Manual respectively. Title pages will be prepared in manuscript.

WAR DIARY
or
~~INTELLIGENCE SUMMARY.~~
(Erase heading not required.)

Army Form C. 2118.

Place	Date	Hour	Summary of Events and Information	Remarks and references to Appendices
			July 1st 1917. The Commanding Officer (Lieut. C.H. Jelf-Reveley) arrived with the Coy. H.Q. details from PROVEN and took over command of the Camp at A16 a 98 (BELGIUM NW28). This camp is situated in a small copse about 200x N. of the POPERINGHE RD to WOESTON, and about 1½ miles from the latter named place. The camp was prepared in readiness for the G.O.C.'s inspection, which, however, did not take place. One casualty was reported (Pte. Nightingale, shrapnel wound in hand) from No 2 Section which had 4 guns in the defences E of ELVERDINGHE. Throughout the day there was considerable Artillery counter-battery activity and, in consequence, shelling was fairly lively in the neighbourhood of all the Gun positions. A normal routine programme was carried out in the camp.	

A5834 Wt. W4973/M687 750,000 8/16 D. D. & L. Ltd. Forms/C.2118/13.

Army Form C. 2118.

Instructions regarding War Diaries and Intelligence Summaries are contained in F. S. Regs., Part II. and the Staff Manual respectively. Title pages will be prepared in manuscript.

WAR DIARY
or
INTELLIGENCE SUMMARY.
(Erase heading not required.)

Place	Date	Hour	Summary of Events and Information	Remarks and references to Appendices
			July 2nd 1917.	
	2-7-17	8.0AM.	The commanding officer and the second-in-command (LT. J.F. NICHOLS) rode to ELVERDINGHE and from there made a tour of the 8 gun positions in the L-retrenchment line. All these positions are strong with well concealed dug-outs, but firing could only be opened in the event of the front line defences being completely broken through. The two section officers in this line have, however, constructed anti-aircraft positions and from each of these enemy aeroplanes were engaged but no result was observed. In each case the hostile aeroplanes were at an altitude of from 3000-4000 feet.	
		7.0pm.	No 1 Section relieved No 4 Section on duty with four guns doing anti-aircraft work in the neighbourhood of the camp.	
	3-7-17	9.0AM.	Serjeant Elfes was wounded in the left side by a piece of the casing of a 5.9 shell fired at our heavy batteries while going up to ELVERDINGHE to reconnoitre gun positions in the Block-Houses, which would be occupied by the section in reserve here in the event of the enemy breaking through the front line.	
			The O.C. No 2 Section reported having opened fire, without result, on hostile aeroplanes coming over at night near ELVERDINGHE; the O.C. No 3 Sec. reported heavy shelling by the enemy in the neighbourhood of his gun positions at night.	

A5834 Wt. W4973/M687 750,000 8/16 D. D. & L. Ltd. Forms/C.2118/13.

Army Form C. 2118.

WAR DIARY
or
~~INTELLIGENCE SUMMARY.~~
(Erase heading not required.)

Instructions regarding War Diaries and Intelligence Summaries are contained in F. S. Regs., Part II. and the Staff Manual respectively. Title pages will be prepared in manuscript.

Place	Date	Hour	Summary of Events and Information	Remarks and references to Appendices
	4-7-17		The C.O. and Section Officers went up to the Coy. H.Q. of the 86th Coy. M.G.C. to reconnoitre the positions to be taken over by the Company in the relief of the 86th which is to be completed by dawn on the 7th inst. The Coy. H.Q. are situated on the bank of the YSER CANAL opposite the PILCKEM RIDGE. Operation orders for the relief were issued in the evening; a copy is attached as Appendix one.	I. Operation Orders for Relief of 86th M.G. Coy. 4-7-17.
			The four guns of No 2 Section were withdrawn (B.O. 1971 of 4-7-17) from the positions in ELVERDINGHE after 7.0 p.m.; but owing to heavy shelling in ELVERDINGHE and the roads leading therefrom, and to the heavy congestion of traffic on the roads, this section did not return to camp until after midnight.	

A5834 Wt. W4973 M687 750,000 8/16 D. D. & L. Ltd. Forms/C.2118/13.

Army Form C. 2118.

Instructions regarding War Diaries and Intelligence Summaries are contained in F. S. Regs., Part II. and the Staff Manual respectively. Title pages will be prepared in manuscript.

WAR DIARY
or
INTELLIGENCE SUMMARY.
(*Erase heading not required.*)

Place	Date	Hour	Summary of Events and Information	Remarks and references to Appendices
	4-7-17		The four guns in the ELVERDINGHE defences were withdrawn.	
	5-7-17		One section of the 86th M.G. Coy. came up to the camp at A16a 9.8. and took over from our No 1 Section engaged on Anti-Air-craft defensive work in the vicinity of the camp at 7.0 p.m. During the afternoon four enemy aeroplanes came over they were engaged by our A-A guns at the Camp but without effect, and afterwards attacked our observation balloons, driving two down, and setting fire to another one. M.G.s. were remarkably quick in engaging the hostile aircraft, and opened fire several minutes before the A-A Batteries.	
	6-7-17		Nos 1, 2 & 4 Sections left Camp at 6.45 A.M.; No 3 Section handed over its gun positions in the L- Defences to a section of the 86th Coy and the whole Coy then proceeded to the Canal Bank and took over from the 87th Coy. The relief was completed by noon. The Distribution of the Coy Officers at this time was as follows: Major A. Morris, D.S.O. Hospital. Lieut C.H. Telf. Rowley - Acting C.O. } Coy H.Q. " J.F. Nichol " 2/c } " R.G. White Transport. " A.D.C. Burnell O.C. No 4 Section 2nd Lt. B.W. Skipworth O.C. No 2 "	

Army Form C. 2118.

Instructions regarding War Diaries and Intelligence Summaries are contained in F. S. Regs., Part II. and the Staff Manual respectively. Title pages will be prepared in manuscript.

WAR DIARY
or
INTELLIGENCE SUMMARY.
(Erase heading not required.)

Place	Date	Hour	Summary of Events and Information	Remarks and references to Appendices
			Lt. C.D. Maule ... I/C No 3 Section. Lt. H Gregson ... I/C No 1 Section. Lt. E.A.M. Legg, M.C. On Course at S. Cecile Plage. Lt. S.C.C. Bryan } At Transport Lines. Lt. J.D.C. McFeely }	
			4 guns of No 1 Sec. were in the support and reserve lines of the Brigade Sector which is in front of the ZWANHOFF FARMS. 3 Guns of No 4 Sec. were also in the support and reserve lines. 2 guns of No 3 Section were in positions in the reserve line on the Canal Bank. The 4 guns of No 2 Section were in reserve for Night Firing. All Sections are engaged in trench works, Nos 1 & 4 making emplacements for a projected Corps M.G. barrage, No 3 improving overhead shelters at HQ on W. of Canal Bank and No 2 in improving emplacements in rear for night firing.	Appendix II Trench Map
			Throughout the day the whole of the sector was heavily shelled, and especially the Canal Bank. From 10.55 p.m to 12.30 the neighbourhood of Coy. H.Q. was bombarded with Gas Shells. No 2 Section fired 4000 rounds on the enemy support line. This seems to have been effective as the enemy's artillery searched constantly but unsuccessfully for these M.G.s. with Shrapnel. No 1 Section engaged an enemy aeroplane flying over our front line from S. to N and forced it to change direction eastwards.	

A5834 Wt. W4973/M687 750,000 8/16 D. D. & L. Ltd. Forms/C.2118/13.

Instructions regarding War Diaries and Intelligence Summaries are contained in F. S. Regs., Part II. and the Staff Manual respectively. Title pages will be prepared in manuscript.

WAR DIARY
or
INTELLIGENCE SUMMARY.
(*Erase heading not required.*)

*Army Form C. 2118.

Place	Date	Hour	Summary of Events and Information	Remarks and references to Appendices
			The R.F.C. reported enemy to be massing in his front line trenches. All gun teams were duly warned but no action developed.	
		7-7-17	The situation throughout the day remained generally normal. There was rather less shelling during the day but artillery activity was greater at night, when the enemy shelled the W. bank of the canal heavily and put over a barrage between our ALMA and BALACLAVA TRENCHES. This barrage damaged the emplacements we were constructing and one man was wounded in the hand but remained at duty. An enemy aeroplane was attacked and brought down by one of our aeroplanes behind the GERMAN lines. During the night No 2 Sec. fired 2500 rounds at the enemy's support line.	
		8-7-17	During the morning the enemy heavily shelled the whole sector. The acting D.M.G.O. Maj. Burrill of the 87th M.G. Coy visited the Coy and made arrangements for the establishing of Ammunition Dumps. There was a lull in the enemy's artillery activity from 6.0 to 10.0 P.M. but shelling was heavy in the neighbourhood of Coy H.Q. and all gun positions during the night. Our reserve team fired 17000 rounds at the enemy's support line. This provoked a lively artillery retaliation. Enemy artillery appeared to be searching for these guns for about 1½ hrs.	
			Satisfactory progress was made both by day and night with the company's programme of work.	

A5834 Wt. W4973/M687 750,000 8/16 D. D. & L. Ltd. Forms/C.2118/13.

Instructions regarding War Diaries and Intelligence Summaries are contained in F. S. Regs., Part II. and the Staff Manual respectively. Title pages will be prepared in manuscript.

WAR DIARY
or
INTELLIGENCE SUMMARY.
(Erase heading not required.)

Place	Date	Hour	Summary of Events and Information	Remarks and references to Appendices
			During the night the 1st Guards Brigade on our left front made a raid across the canal, but this did not affect the Company at all directly.	
	9-7-17		Very heavy shelling on both sides throughout the day. One shell which dropped near the Coy. H.Q. killed 3 men and wounded 5 others. These were No 21464 L/Cpl. Budden (the Coy. cook), No 54238 Pte Sherwood, and 10475 Pte Austin all killed; and, wounded, the following all privates: 14751 Barton, 20674 Erskine, 21485 Wake, 21501 Gardner 87675 Leach. 2nd Lt. B.W. Skipworth was wounded by shell-fire in the back while going out with the night firing party at night. Between 11.30 & 12.30 P.M. artillery activity reached its maximum intensity; the enemy put a barrage over the front and support lines and over the Canal Banks and Bridges and attempted a raid. Lieut. R.H. White left the Company to go as Second-in-Command to the 140th Coy. Lt. S.C.C. Bryan took over the duties of Transport Officer temporarily. Lt. J.A. Matheson reported for duty from the Base.	
	10-7-17		When the limber bringing up rations reached Coy. H.Q. at about 1.0 A.M. a shell killed the N.C.O. i/c and three men and destroyed 3 horses. The casualties were No. 57076 Pte Hill (Driver) killed, and, wounded: 20675 L/Cpl. Fairbairn, 72004 Pte Chant, 36262 Pte Chick. The four men killed were buried at 9.0 A.M. in the small field cemetery allotted to the division just behind the Canal Bank.	

A5834 Wt. W4973/M687 750,000 8/16 D. D. & L. Ltd. Forms/C.2118/13.

Instructions regarding War Diaries and Intelligence Summaries are contained in F. S. Regs., Part II. and the Staff Manual respectively. Title pages will be prepared in manuscript.

WAR DIARY
or
INTELLIGENCE SUMMARY.
(Erase heading not required.)

Army Form C. 2118.

Place	Date	Hour	Summary of Events and Information	Remarks and references to Appendices
			The remainder of the day was fairly quiet.	
			During the night the reserve section fired 7000 rounds at CACTUS JUNCTION a nodal point in the enemy's support line. Enemy machine guns searched for our night-firing positions but without success. Eight of the emplacements for the projected Corps M.G. Barrage were completed, and a reserve dump of 240,000 rounds S.A.A was established at Coy H.Q. This dump was made up of six small dumps each of 40,000 rounds.	
	11-7-17		Shelling during the day was noticeably below normal. One of our M.G. emplacements received a direct hit (C 13.5) and one man was wounded there.	
	12-7-17		Shelling was fairly heavy between 2.0 and 4.0 A.M., especially in the neighbourhood of the Canal Bank and Bridges.	
			Captain R. H. BRODIE arrived at 12.30 A.M. to take over command of the company. Between 2.0 and 6.0 A.M. he made a tour of the Gun positions and barrage emplacements with the DIV. M.G.O.	
	13-7-17		The Company was relieved in the line by the 86th Machine Gun Coy. and went into rest at a camp lying W. of the CROMBEKE-POPERINGHE RD. and N. of the S. Sixte Convent.	
	14-7-17		Lt. McFeeley with four guns and four teams of the attached men took over Anti-Aircraft duties, relieving the 87th Coy. at the Waterworks HARINGHE.	

A5834 Wt. W4973/M687 750,000 8/16 D. D. & L. Ltd. Forms/C.2118/13.

Instructions regarding War Diaries and Intelligence Summaries are contained in F. S. Regs., Part II. and the Staff Manual respectively. Title pages will be prepared in manuscript.

WAR DIARY
or
INTELLIGENCE SUMMARY.

(Erase heading not required.)

Army Form C. 2118.

Place	Date	Hour	Summary of Events and Information	Remarks and references to Appendices
18-7-17			The O.C. No 2 Section took his section to ELVERDINGHE where they were accommodated by the 2nd GUARDS BDE. This section is engaged in the preparation of emplacements for overhead firing in front of BOESINGHE with a view to coming operations.	
19-7-17			Lt. J.A. MATHESON went with an Advance Party to take over and prepare a new camp to be occupied by the Company at a point just W. of the PROVEN-ROUSBRUGGE RD. and N. of PROVEN.	
20-7-17			The Company moved into the new Camp, about 50 men being accommodated in a barn and the remainder in tents & canvas shelters. No 2 Sec. returned to camp about 3.0 P.M. This section suffered two casualties while working on the emplacements – Sjt. Wright & Pte Dickinson, both wounded.	
22-7-17			No 1 Section (S/O: Lt. Gregson) went into the line to complete certain carrying operations (water and ammunition) in connection with coming operations. This section returned about 8.0 AM on the 23rd. During the night 22/23 hostile aeroplanes attempted a small raid in the neighbourhood of the camp. There were probably about three. Six bombs were dropped near PROVEN but very little damage was done. Hostile planes also were over HARINGHE. These were possibly the same three. Some bombs were dropped	

Army Form C. 2118.

WAR DIARY
or
INTELLIGENCE SUMMARY.
(Erase heading not required.)

Instructions regarding War Diaries and Intelligence Summaries are contained in F. S. Regs., Part II. and the Staff Manual respectively. Title pages will be prepared in manuscript.

Place	Date	Hour	Summary of Events and Information	Remarks and references to Appendices
	22-7-17		close to the C.C.S. there but no serious damage was done. Two of our AA M.Gs with the detachment there opened fire and fired about 300 rounds but without any observed effect.	
	23-7-17		Field Scheme with 88th Inf. Bde. at HERZEEL; two sections of this Company took part with the O.C.	
	24-7-17		The Company moved at 10.0 A.M. to the Corps Staging Area, the old camp which had been occupied before at ST. SIXTE. 2Lt. McFEELEY was relieved at HARINGHE by a section of the 86th M.G. Coy.	
	25-7-17		Capt. R.H. Brodie was this day admitted to hospital sick; the command of the Company was taken over by Lieut. J. F. Nichols.	
	[struck out]		The fighting strength of the Company moved up to Battle quarters with the 4th Guards M.G. Coy. at the Forest Camp, near ONDBANK, in accordance with operation orders (Appendix III)	App. III. Operation Orders – Guards Div. M.G. Scheme
	26-7-17		The offensive planned originally to take place on the 28th was postponed and two of the four sections at Forest Camp were sent back to the Camp at ST. SIXTE. During the night a bomb was dropped by a hostile aeroplane over the Forest Camp and two men of the Company were wounded; the same bomb killed two men of the 227th Coy & wounded four, and wounded an officer of the 4th Guards M.G. Coy.	

Army Form C. 2118.

Instructions regarding War Diaries and Intelligence Summaries are contained in F. S. Regs., Part II. and the Staff Manual respectively. Title pages will be prepared in manuscript.

WAR DIARY
or
INTELLIGENCE SUMMARY.
(Erase heading not required.)

Place	Date	Hour	Summary of Events and Information	Remarks and references to Appendices
2	28-7-17		The offensive was fixed to open on the 31st and accordingly the other two sections moved up to the Forest Camp. On the night of the 28th two sections went forward to carry S.A.A. from a dump near TWIN COTTAGE to the emplacements. One section was gassed at the dump, the enemy's gas shells [illegible] before the men had time to adjust the Box Respirators. The [illegible] the [illegible] by R.E. and the work [illegible]	
	29-7-17		During the afternoon of the 29th the three sections forming the right group of the 2nd [illegible] under Capt. D.C. Burnell moved up [illegible] positions [illegible] prepared emplacements in front of the X-line [illegible]. The night 29/30th three of these emplacements had been damaged by direct hits. At the time [illegible] there was a certain amount of hostile shelling in the neighbourhood but the guns were [illegible] difficulty.	[illegible]
	30-7-17		During the same night 1000 [illegible] of S.A.A. were carried up and during the day [illegible] visibility made it an easy matter to [illegible] and lay the lines of fire.	

A5834 Wt. W4973/M687 750,000 8/16 D. D. & L. Ltd. Forms/C.2118/13.

Instructions regarding War Diaries and Intelligence Summaries are contained in F. S. Regs., Part II. and the Staff Manual respectively. Title pages will be prepared in manuscript.

WAR DIARY
or
INTELLIGENCE SUMMARY.
(Erase heading not required.)

Army Form C. 2118.

Place	Date	Hour	Summary of Events and Information	Remarks and references to Appendices
			Early on the morning of the 30th the remaining section moved up into positions near BOESINGHE. This section formed part of the left wing of the 2nd Echelon and came under the command of the O.C. 2nd Guards M.G. Coy.	
	31-7-17		On the night of the 30/31 the right sections moved from the X-line to occupy the emplacements. The area was again shelled with 5.9's and shrapnel but casualties were practically negligible. Barrage fire was opened in accordance with the orders of the D.M.G.O. Guards at 4.10 A.M. on the 31st on the ABRI WOOD LINE. At 5.10 AM the Barrage was lifted on to the MAJORS FM. LINE (Appendix IV). This barrage was stopped at 6.45 AM by order of the D.M.G.O. Guards, there being no further need for its continuance. Firing was at the rate of 1 belt in 4 minutes, about 100,000 rounds being fired by the 3 sections on the right & about 40,000 rounds by the section on the left. During operations 1 gun on the left and 1 gun on the right were put out of action by enemy shell-fire. The total casualties during the whole time the Company	Appendix IV Map of Gds. Div. Barrage Scheme

A5834 Wt. W4973/M687 750,000 8/16 D. D. & L. Ltd. Forms/C.2118/13.

Instructions regarding War Diaries and Intelligence Summaries are contained in F. S. Regs., Part II. and the Staff Manual respectively. Title pages will be prepared in manuscript.

WAR DIARY
or
INTELLIGENCE SUMMARY.
(*Erase heading not required.*)

Army Form C. 2118.

Place	Date	Hour	Summary of Events and Information	Remarks and references to Appendices
			was in the line were: 1 man killed, 1 officer and 16 O.R. wounded (including 12 admitted to hospital gassed). The C.O. brought to the notice of the G.O.C. the gallant conduct of 2/Lt. C.D. Mantle and No 41090 Pte. Thorpe R (attached 8th Battn Worcester Regt.) 2/Lt. Mantle although himself greatly weakened by the effects of the gas shell bombardment on the 28th brought his section safely back to Camp & refused to be relieved by another officer in the command of his section. Later at about 10.0 P.M. on the 30th he was wounded in the right shoulder, and although much weakened and in great pain refused to leave the trenches & returned twice during the progress of the barrage to control the fire of his section. It was not until he had brought his section back to the Rear Camp that he could be prevailed on to go to the Dressing Station. Pte Thorpe was put in charge of the work of carrying feed belts to the Guns of the Section in the left in front of BOESINGHE. This man showed admirable skill, courage, thoroughness, and devotion to duty in carrying	

Army Form C. 2118.

Instructions regarding War Diaries and Intelligence Summaries are contained in F. S. Regs., Part II. and the Staff Manual respectively. Title pages will be prepared in manuscript.

WAR DIARY
or
INTELLIGENCE SUMMARY.
(Erase heading not required.)

Place	Date	Hour	Summary of Events and Information	Remarks and references to Appendices
			at his task. The refilling point was about 75x from the guns & although the intervening ground was being heavily shelled he managed to keep the guns supplied.	
			The Barrage Scheme being completed the Company returned to the ST. SIXTE Camp and came once more under the orders of the G.O.C. 88th Inf Bde.	
			Thos Nisbet, Lieut. Cmdg. 88th M.G. Coy.	
			1/8/17.	

Appendix I

Operation Order
By
Lieut. G.H. Jelf-Reveley Commanding
88th Company Machine Gun Corps
In the Field. "Wednesday" 4/7/17.

I

The 88th Machine Gun Coy. will relieve 87th Machine Gun Coy. in the forward area on 6th July 1917

II

Relief of 88th M.G.C. By 86th M.G.C.

At 1900 on 5th July one Section of the 86th M.G. Coy. will relieve No1. Section of the 88th M.G.C. on anti-Aircraft duty.
On relief No1 Section will report at Coy. H.Qrs.
One Section of the 86th M.G. Coy. will relieve No3 Section 88th M.G. Coy. on the morning of the 6th July, on completion of No3 Section will move to new Coy. H.Qrs.
O.C. No3 Section will have guides at DAWSON'S CORNER at 9am

III

Tripods & Belt Boxes

Section Officers will obtain receipts for Tripods, Belt Boxes, etc. handed over to relieving Coy.
2/Lieut. Bryant will hand over Tripods & Belt Boxes belonging to Nos. 2 & 4 Sections and will obtain receipts

IV

Disposition
2/Lt. Gregson No1 Sect.
Lieut. Burrell No4 Sect.
2/Lt. Shipworth No2 "
2/Lt. Mould No3 "

Nos. 1 & 4 Sections commanders as per margin, will relieve the seven forward guns of the 87th M.G. Coy.
No2 Section, commander as per margin will relieve the four guns of the 87th M.G. Coy. on night firing duty.
Two guns of No3 Section commander as per margin, will relieve the two guns of the 87th M.G. Coy. on CANAL BANK. the other two guns will be on reserve at Coy. H.Qrs.

V

Guns & Spare Parts

Guns & spare parts of Nos. 1. 2 & 4 Sections will be loaded at 8 P.M. on evening of 5th and will be taken to new Coy. H.Qrs. under charge of Sgt. Sharman and one man per Section.

Operation Order (contd.)

VI
Parade
Nos 1, 2, + 4 Sections will parade at 6.45 am on 6th inst. will march to DAWSON'S CORNER where guides will meet and conduct them to Coy. H.Qrs.
The following will parade with No 4 Section under Lieut. Burrell and will be accomodated on arrival in the large dug-out in forward Sector:-
Sgt. Wright, L/Cpl. Weaver, 1 Sanitary man + 15 attached men
The H.Q. party under the C.S.M. composed as follows, will march with No 1 Section.
Ord. Room Staff, 4 Signallers, 4 Runners, + 1 Sanitary man.
Remainder of Coy. under Sgt. Buck will remain at Transport.
Coy. will march off by Sections at 100 yds. interval. On reaching DAWSON'S CORNER the Coy. will move by Teams at 110 yds. interval

VII
'hange[illegible]tif.
Each Section Officer will hand in, as early as possible, to Orderly Room, a copy of taking over certificate

VIII
'acks.
Packs will be left at Q.M. Stores.

IX
Transport
Transport and Q.M. Stores will move into lines occupied by 87th M.G. Coy. as soon as these lines are vacated.
Signaller's Stores, 2 days Rations, Cook's Stores (accompanied by 1 cook) Ord. Room Stores, + Officers Kits, will be conveyed to Coy. H.Qrs. on night of 6th July, under arrangements by Transport Officer

C.O. Jeff-Rowley Lieut
Officer Commanding
88th Coy. M.G. Corps

SECRET

Operation Orders No 2 — M.G./[illegible]

By

Lieutenant G. J. Nichols Commanding

88th Company Machine Gun Corps

I The 88th Machine Gun Company will support the Guards [illegible] in attack on a prescribed frontage with [illegible] fire on a [illegible] and at a zero hour to be communicated later.

II The 88th Machine Gun Company will come under the orders of the D.M.G.O. Guards Division at 6pm 25-7-1917.

III The fighting strength as laid down in Operation Orders I will move into FOREST AREA on "W" day. (Belgian 28.W. [illegible]) Fighting limbers of Sections will also move at the same time and remain in FOREST AREA.

The Transport Officer will take charge of the fighting [illegible] and will come under the orders of [illegible].

Sections of the Company will be distributed in [illegible] (D.M.G.O. Guards [illegible] No 2.)

[illegible]

The sections will [illegible] on X day [illegible] given in Operation Orders No 3. M.G./88/3.

At ZERO + 3 hours 2[illegible] minutes, Sections will pack up and go back to FOREST AREA under orders to be issued later by O.C. 88th M.G. Company.

On Z day O.C. 88th M.G. Company will move up [illegible] M.G. Company Headquarters until conclusion of the [illegible] 10 men will be with him as reinforcements.

Issued at ....

Copies No 1 to D.M.G.O. Guards Divn
" " 2 " Brigade Major 88th Bde
" " 3 " D.M.G.O. 29th Divn
" " 4–10 Officers 88th M.G. Coy
" " 11 Company File
" " 12 & 13 War Diary

G. J. Nichols, Lieutenant Commanding
88th Company Machine Gun Corps

2[illegible]th 7 1917.

SECRET.

Copy No. ....

Operation Orders [illegible]

By

Lieutenant A. D. C. Burrell Commanding

Advanced Headquarters 88th Company M.G.C.

I. The fighting strength as detailed in Operation Orders I. will come under command of Lieut. A. D. C. Burrell on "X" day.

II. On "X" day Nos 2. 3 and 4 Sections will move into their positions in the right wing 2nd Echelon. They will leave 4th Guards M. G. Coy. H.Q. at 3 pm. All sections will move by detachments at 150 yds interval, using Infantry Tracks 11 & 12. The right wing sections will use CLARGES ST. and HUNTER ST. No I Section will move at 4 pm and use Tracks 11 and 12 and BRIDGE ST. This section will then come under the command of Lieut. C. H. Hague Grenadier Gds.

III. Sections will have their guns in position by the night X/Y. No 2. 3 and 4 Sections will live in "X" line until Y/Z night, and will do any necessary work from there.

IV. Advanced Company Headquarters will be at the junction of X line and the railway (St Julien 28 N.W.2. B 18 a 28.85).

The D. M. G. O. Guards will be at the M. G. Dugout at CHASSEUR Farm until about Zero + 1 hour.

V. Any belt boxes which cannot be carried in by the sections will be brought by limber to the barrier ELVERDINGHE Rd together with 2 days rations, and water. The O.C. Sections will detail men to meet this limber, at 8 pm "X" night.

Issued at 10. am.

27-7-17

Copies No I to D. M. G. O. Guards
" II " Brigade Major 88th Bgde
" III " D. M. G. O. 29th Divn
" IV–X " Officers 88th Coy. M.G.C.
" XI Company File
" XII & XIII War Diary

(Sgd) A. D. C. Burrell Lieut
88th Coy M.G.C.

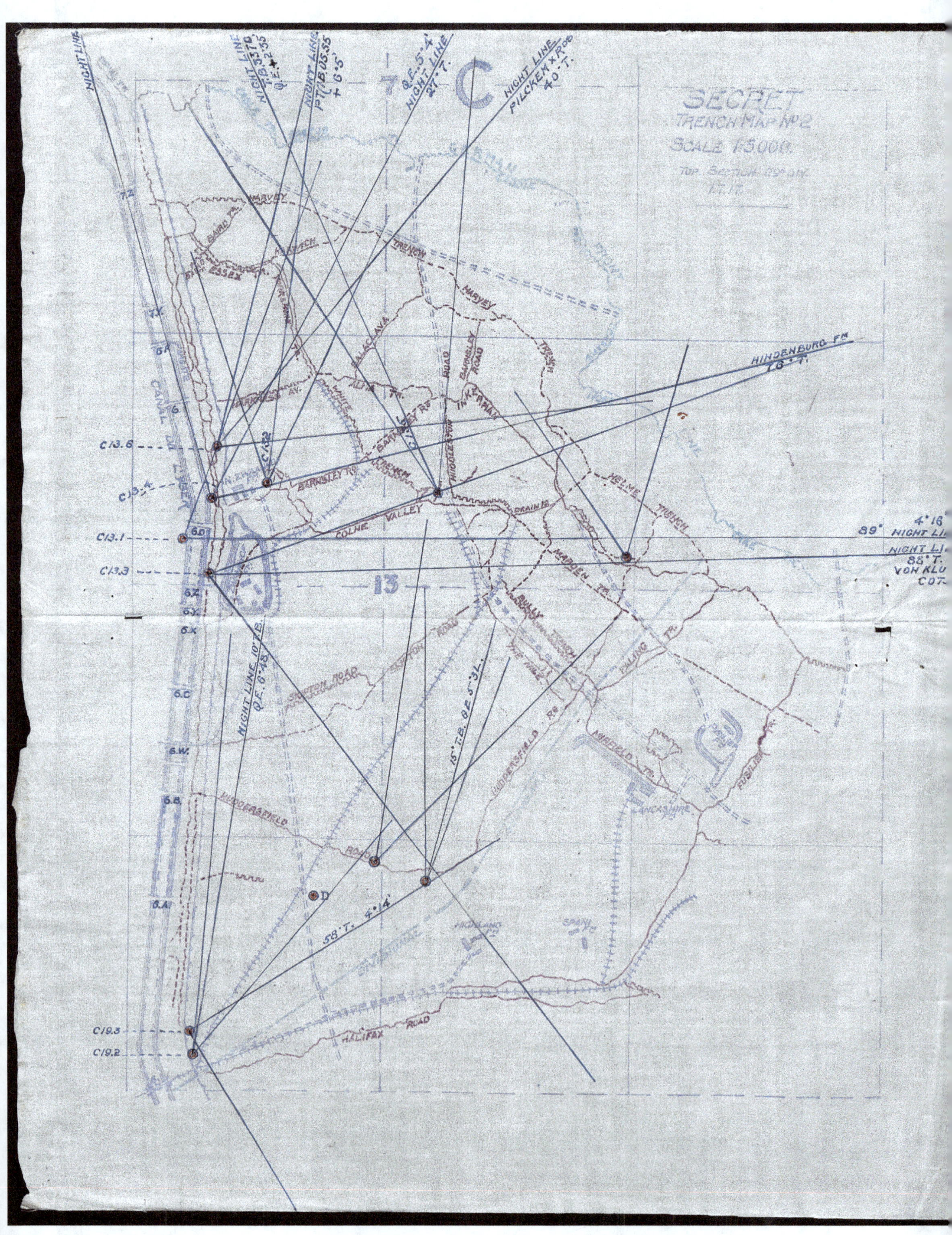

SECRET
TRENCH MAP No 2
SCALE 1:5000
NIGHT LINE
NIGHT LINE PILCKEM X ROS 40°T.
HINDENBURG Fm 76°T.
NIGHT LINE
C13.6
C13.4
C13.1
C13.3
C19.3
C19.2
13
HARVEY
TRENCH
HARVEY
BARNSLEY RD.
COLNE VALLEY
MELNE TRENCH
MADDEN TR.
BULLY TRENCH
HUDDERSFIELD ROAD
HALIFAX ROAD
NIGHT LINE 10°T.B. Q.E. 6°45'
15°T.B. Q.E. 5°3L.
58°T. 4°14'
CANAL DE L'YSER

SECRET

Copy No. 11. Appendix II

[illegible]

By

Lieut. G. F. Nichols Commanding

88th Company M.G. Corps

I In the ~~preliminary~~ forthcoming Operations details of which will be published later, all four sections of the Company will be engaged.
Sections will be under command of Officers as below:-

No. I Section 2nd Lieutenant A. Gregson.
" II " " J. A. Matheson.
" III " " C. D. Maule.
" IV " " G. J. C. McSeeley.

Sections 2, 3 & 4 will be grouped together under the Command of Lieut. A. O. C. Burrell.

II Each section will have two specially detailed N.C.O.s for Teams of four, and one Section Runner.
Lieut. Burrell will have three additional runners, and four additional runners will be detailed for communication between O.C. & forward [illegible]

III 16 men will be detailed for belt filling, 6 of these will be with No. I Section and 10 with 2, 3 and 4 Sections.

IV Ten men will be detailed in readiness to replace casualties and will go forward under orders from the O.C. Company.

V Every gun team will carry a red location screen which will be put up behind the gun when it is mounted for action. This applies more particularly to consolidating guns.
It will be erected in such a manner that runners are able to see the screen from distance away.

Issued at .....

Copy No. 1 B.G. 1st Gds Guards
" " 2 Brigade Major 88th Bde
" " 3 D.M.G.O. 29th Division
" " 4-10 Officers 88th Coy M.G.C.
" " 11 Company File
" " 12 & 13 War Diary

25-7-17.

D. Nichols, Lieut Commanding
88th Company M.G. Corps

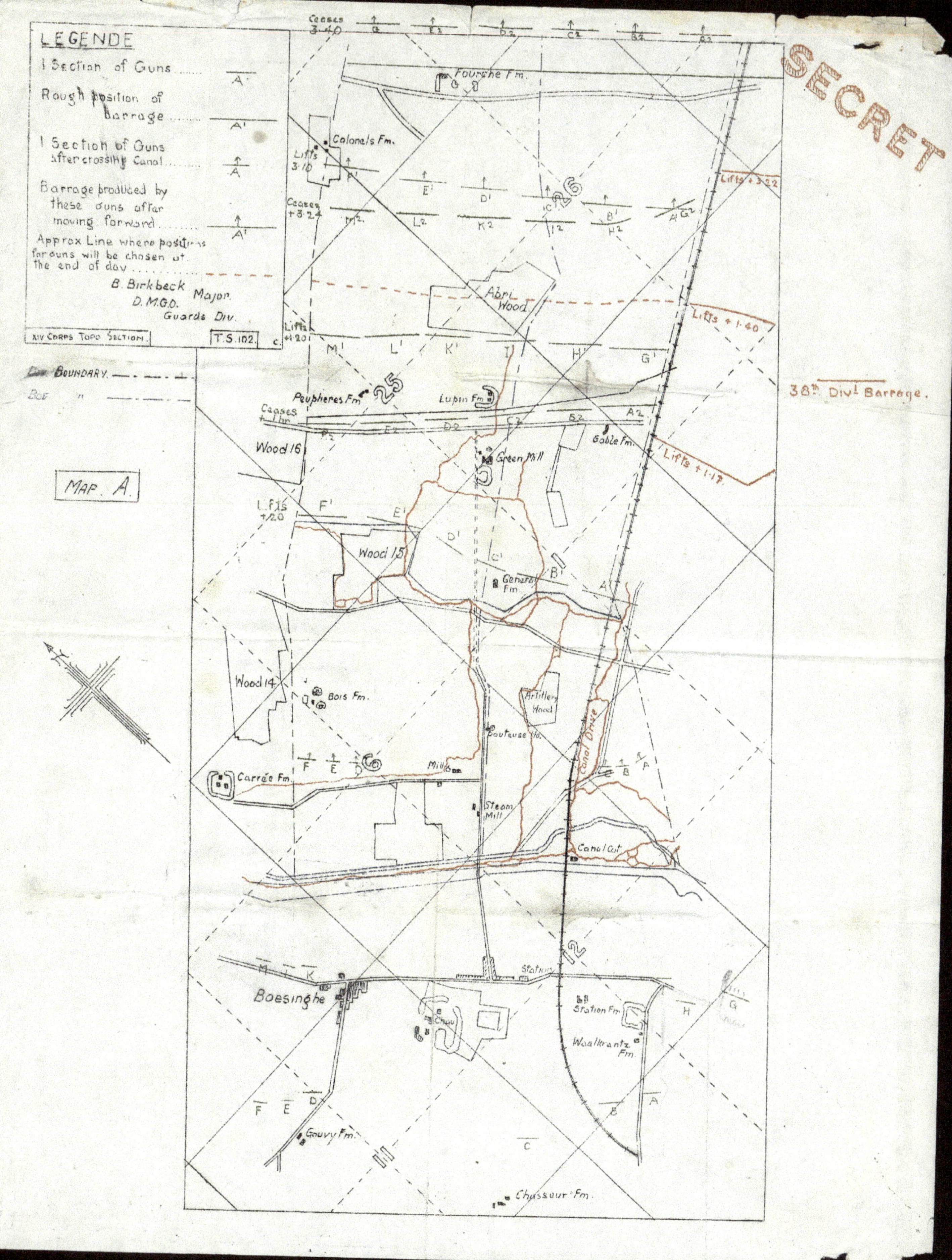
SECRET
LEGENDE
1 Section of Guns
Rough position of Barrage
1 Section of Guns after crossing Canal
Barrage produced by these guns after moving forward
Approx Line where positions for guns will be chosen at the end of day
B. Birkbeck Major.
D.M.G.O.
Guards Div.
XIV Corps Topo Section.
T.S.102.
BOUNDARY.
MAP. A.
38th. Divl Barrage.
Lifts + 3.22
Lifts + 1.40
Lifts + 1.17
Ceases 3.40
Ceases +3.24
Ceases +1hr
Lifts 3.10
Lifts +1.20
Lifts +1.20
Fourche Fm.
Calonels Fm.
Abri Wood
Peupheres Fm.
Lupin Fm.
Gable Fm.
Green Mill
Wood 16
Wood 15
Wood 14
Genard Fm
Bois Fm.
Artillery Wood
Carrée Fm.
Mill
Steam Mill
Canal Cut
Canal Drive
Boesinghe
Chau
Station
Station Fm.
Waalkrantz Fm.
Gouvy Fm.
Chasseur Fm.

appendix IV

Confidential

War Diary

of

88th Machine Gun Coy

FROM 1st Aug. 1917 To 31st Aug. 1917

(Volume No. 14)

Instructions regarding War Diaries and Intelligence Summaries are contained in F. S. Regs., Part II. and the Staff Manual respectively. Title pages will be prepared in manuscript.

WAR DIARY
or
~~INTELLIGENCE SUMMARY.~~
(Erase heading not required.)

Army Form C. 2118.

Place	Date	Hour	Summary of Events and Information	Remarks and references to Appendices
In the field	1/8/17		The company paraded at 9am to carry out the usual training programme. A party moved off at 11am & returned at 10pm, bringing all the remainder of [illegible] from the line, after the barrage scheme of 31/7/17.	
	2/8/17.	9am.	The usual training programme. At 10pm the company practised a night march of one mile along a track, wearing box respirators.	
	3/8/17.	9.30am.	The usual training programme was carried out. The weather during the past three days has been consistently bad, and has rather interfered with training.	
	4/8/17	9am.	The usual training programme. At 10am the company paraded for a packsaddlery demonstration. The O.C. Coy attended a Conference of Commanding Officers at Bde H.Q.	
	5/8/17	10am.	The usual Church Parades. The Commanding Officer & [illegible] went up to the line on a preliminary reconnaissance for forthcoming operations.	
	6-8-17		Training much impeded by inclemency of weather.	
	7-8-17		The Coy. moved up into battle quarters in the FOREST CAMP near WOESTON.	
	8-8-17		The Commanding Officer and Lt. Gregson made a further reconnaissance of the line E of the YSER CANAL and in front of LANGEMARCK. Lt. Gregson afterwards took up to a dump near ABRI WOOD, [illegible] rounds S.A.A. by pack mule – a successful operation. Lieut. J. J. Parkin reported for duty and took over Command of the	

A5834 Wt. W4973/M687 750,000 8/16 D. D. & L. Ltd. Forms/C.2118/13.

Instructions regarding War Diaries and Intelligence Summaries are contained in F. S. Regs., Part II. and the Staff Manual respectively. Title pages will be prepared in manuscript.

WAR DIARY
or
INTELLIGENCE SUMMARY.
(Erase heading not required.)

Army Form C. 2118.

Place	Date	Hour	Summary of Events and Information	Remarks and references to Appendices
	8-8-17		Company from Lt. J.F. Nichols who had held it temporarily since the admission to hospital of Capt. R.H. Brodie.	
			Pte Thorpe, Worcs. Regt. attd. 88 M.G.C. whose gallant conduct at BOESINGHE had been brought to the notice of the General Officer Commanding was awarded the Military Medal by the Corps Commander under authority delegated to him.	
	9-8-17		The Commanding Officer and Lieut J.F. Nichols carried out a further reconnaissance of the line. 2Lt. E.A. McKay, M.C. took charge of a party and moved 80,000 rounds S.A.A. from the dump at ABRI WOOD to a forward dump near proposed gun positions.	
	10-8-17		2Lt. S.C.C. Bryan took charge of a party and moved the remaining 20,000 rounds to forward dump. 2Lt. J.J.L. McFeeley [?] reconnoitred positions	
	11-8-17		with Lieut A.D.C. Burrell.	
	12-8-17		There was no Church Parade this day, no Chaplain being available.	
	13-8-17		The Commanding Officer inspected the fighting strength of the Company and afterwards with Lieut J.F. Nichols attended a Conference at Bde. HQ.	
	14-8-17		Nos 1 & 2 Sections went up to positions in rear of the front line in order to prepare barrage positions &c. These two sections were commanded by 2Lt. Hodgson [?] and 2Lt. S.C.C. Bryan respectively.	

Army Form C. 2118.

Instructions regarding War Diaries and Intelligence Summaries are contained in F. S. Regs., Part II. and the Staff Manual respectively. Title pages will be prepared in manuscript.

WAR DIARY
or
INTELLIGENCE SUMMARY.
(Erase heading not required.)

Place	Date	Hour	Summary of Events and Information	Remarks and references to Appendices
	15-8-17		Headquarters & Nos 3 & 4 Sections moved forward into Battle positions in accordance with Operation Orders (Appendix I) No 3 Sec. was commanded by 2/Lt. E. A. M. Hughes M.C. and No 4 Sec. by Lieut. A.D.C. Burrell. The Commanding Officer went forward (Lt. J.J. Parker) and with him 2/Lt. F.E.R. Foot. Lieut. J. F. Nichols remained behind at rear H.Q. 2/Lt. J.J.C. McFerlan had been admitted to hospital - sick on the 13th	Appendix I
	16-8-17		Operations continued as explained in detail in Report appended (Appendix II) Lieut. A.D.C. Burrell was killed in the morning just as his section was moving off from the starting point for the advance. 2nd Lieut. R. Williams was wounded at 4.0 pm after having got his sub-section of No 3 Sec. into position in the third objective. Lieut. J. F. Nichols left rear Headquarters at 1.30 pm and brought up a party with rations and water. As officer casualties had been serious he went to forward H.Q. and remained there to assist the C.O., sending the ration party back	Appendix II

A5834 Wt. W4973/M687 750,000 8/16 D. D. & L. Ltd. Forms/C.2118/13.

Instructions regarding War Diaries and Intelligence Summaries are contained in F. S. Regs., Part II. and the Staff Manual respectively. Title pages will be prepared in manuscript.

WAR DIARY
or
INTELLIGENCE SUMMARY.
(Erase heading not required.)

Army Form C. 2118.

Place	Date	Hour	Summary of Events and Information	Remarks and references to Appendices
	19-8-17		The Sections were relieved by No 227 Coy. They were then withdrawn and returned to the FOREST CAMP.	
	20-8-17		Camp routine.	
	21-8-17		Usual training programme carried out in Camp. The undermentioned were recommended by the Commanding Officer for gallant conduct and good work [redacted]	
			[redacted] Lt. E.A.M. Hopps M.C. --- [redacted]	
			Sgt. J. Pursglove --- [redacted]	
			Corpl. Aggcroft --- [redacted]	
			Pte Bennett --- [redacted]	
	22-8-17		Lts Beveridge, Morris & Barr joined for duty with the Coy from Mtd. Base Depot. Distribution of officers now with Company is now as follows—	
			C.O. Lieut. J.J. Parkin.	
			2/C – " J.F. Nicholls.	
			T.O. 2/Lt. H. Thompson. — At Corps Reinforcement Camp	
			No 1 Sec. " R. Beveridge. — Lt. W.H. Tulf Rowley	
			2 " { " S.C.C. Burgess — 2/Lt. L. Mathieson.	
			{ " H. Morris	
			3 " { " E.A.M. Hopps M.C.	
			{ " R. Barr	
			4 " " V.E.R. Ford.	

Instructions regarding War Diaries and Intelligence Summaries are contained in F. S. Regs., Part II. and the Staff Manual respectively. Title pages will be prepared in manuscript.

WAR DIARY
or
INTELLIGENCE SUMMARY.
(*Erase heading not required.*)

Army Form C. 2118.

Place	Date	Hour	Summary of Events and Information	Remarks and references to Appendices
	24-8-17		The Coy. moved up to forward area to take over BARRAGE positions from the 83rd Coy. The following names were submitted for the General Award list (New Years Honours) for good work in the field Sgt. Smith. A/Sgt. Kitchen. A/Cpl. Morris. L/Cpl. Fordham Pte. Dimmott.	

Instructions regarding War Diaries and Intelligence Summaries are contained in F. S. Regs., Part II. and the Staff Manual respectively. Title pages will be prepared in manuscript.

WAR DIARY
or
INTELLIGENCE SUMMARY.

(Erase heading not required.)

Army Form C. 2118.

Place	Date	Hour	Summary of Events and Information	Remarks and references to Appendices
	24-8-17		(4) A [illegible] S.O.S. [illegible] through the front [illegible] Brigade [illegible] point [illegible] (5) Direct fire [illegible] the [illegible] Right Sections were [illegible] with (4) and (5).	
	25-8-17		On the night of the 24th/25th [illegible] the enemy [illegible] All guns participated and 4,150 rounds were fired. [illegible] BEARS [illegible] point [illegible] During the [illegible]	[illegible]
	26-8-17		During the night of the 26-27 [illegible]	

Instructions regarding War Diaries and Intelligence Summaries are contained in F. S. Regs., Part II. and the Staff Manual respectively. Title pages will be prepared in manuscript.

WAR DIARY
or
INTELLIGENCE SUMMARY.

(Erase heading not required.)

Army Form C. 2118.

Place	Date	Hour	Summary of Events and Information	Remarks and references to Appendices
	[illegible]		During the night [illegible]	
	27.8.17		[illegible]	[illegible]
			of the Division on the right [illegible]	
			[illegible]	
	28.8.17		The Barrage Positions [illegible]	
			[illegible]	
	29.8.17		[illegible] FOREST AREA	[illegible]
	30.8.17		[illegible] Camp	[illegible]
			[illegible]	1:40,000
			[illegible]	
			[illegible]	
			[illegible]	
			J J Paskin [illegible]	

A5834 Wt. W4973/M687 750,000 8/16 D. D. & L. Ltd. Forms/C.2118/13.

Copy No 13

War Diary
Appendix I.

Preliminary Operation Orders By Lieutenant J.J. Paskin, Commanding 88th Company Machine Gun Corps

In the Field 11th August 1917.

I.

The 29th Division will attack on a prescribed frontage on a day and at an hour ZERO - to be notified later

II.

The assault will be made by the 88th Brigade on the RIGHT and the 87th Brigade on the LEFT. The 86th Brigade will be in Divisional Reserve. The 1st French Army will attack on the LEFT of the Division and the 20th Division on the RIGHT.

III.

88th M.G. Coy

Nos. 1 & 2 Sections will take part in the Divisional M.G. Barrage No1 will form I GROUP and No2 H GROUP. These two Sections together with a Section of the 86th M.G. Coy (K GROUP) will act under the direct orders of O.C. 88th M.G. Coy.
Nos 3 & 4 Sections will be at the disposal of the G.O.C. 88th Infantry Brigade for consolidation (Appendix II)

IV.

Communication

Communication within the Company will be by runners. Four runners will be kept at disposal of O.C. Coy at Forward H.Qrs. Four will be at Rear H.Qrs. and two will be detailed by each Section Officer for communication between himself and Company H.Qrs.

V.

Rations & Water

At ZERO each man will be in possession of the unexpended portion of the days rations, one complete days rations and the Iron Ration. These must be carried on the person by the individual. For succeeding days, rations will be drawn by Sections at Advanced H.Qrs.

At ZERO each gun team will be in possession of two filled petrol tins. Further supplies of water will be drawn from Advanced Coy. H. Qrs.

The C.O. wishes to impress on Section Officers the absolute necessity for returning all empty petrol tins. Unless this is done it will be impossible to maintain the supply of water. Every opportunity must be taken of salvaging petrol tins.

VI Extracts from "M.G. Instructions No 1"

When guns used either for Barrage or consolidation move forward to new positions, the First Aid box will always be attached to the rear cross-piece.

Every gun team will carry a red location screen which will be put up behind the gun when it is mounted for action. This applies more particularly to consolidating guns. It will be erected in such a manner that runners are able to see the screen some distance away.

VII Appendix I

Extracts from 29th Div. M.G. Barrage Instructions (amended)

J. Paskin Lieutenant Commanding
88th Coy M.G. Corps.

Copies to:

Copy No 1. 88th Inf. Bdge.
" " 2 D.M.G.O. 29th Div.
" " 3 O.C. 88th M.G. Coy.
" " 4 2/c " " "
" " 5 O/c. No 1 Sec. 88 M.G. Coy.
" " 6 " " 2 " " "
" " 7 " " 3 " " "
" " 8 " " 4 " " "
" " 9 Transport Officer " "
" " 10 O.C. No 3 Sect 88th M.G. Coy.
" " 11 O.C. 86th M.G. Coy.
" " 12 & 13 War Diary
" " 14 Files.

Issued at 10 am 11.8.17.

Appendix I

Extracts from 29th Divisional M.G. Barrage Instructions (Amended)

Emplacements — Pits may be dug or shell holes converted. In either case platforms must be sandbagged and made firm. Tripod must be bedded in sandbags to prevent sinking. 32 triangular boxes are available if required. Lower limit of traverse must be blocked. Aiming Posts giving all limits of traverse and zenith will be put up for each gun before "Y" day.

Amm.n — 35 Belts per gun will be the average amount fired. Each Barrage gun will be provided with 8 spare Belts in addition to existing 14 Belts per gun. These will be filled before ZERO. 400,000 rounds S.A.A. is being got up to ABRI WOOD and from this dumps of 40,000 rounds will be made by each group of 8 guns.

Rate of Fire — One Belt in 4 minutes during the advance and 1 belt in 10 minutes during a pause. Belt filling arrangements must be made to keep up with this rate as far as possible.

Water. — One petrol tin per gun and one for gun teams to be at each gun position before ZERO.

Barrels — Each gun will start with a new Barrel. A few rounds should be fired beforehand to remove grease packing. Barrels will be changed on completion of Barrage. Not more than 1 gun in each group to change Barrels at a time.

Bearings — All compasses should be tested and errors noted. Steel helmets and tripods should not be near enough to effect bearings. As there are few land marks each group should erect posts at suitable distances for Ref. Objects. Gun positions must be checked by measurements as well as the Section Range finding instrument can be used for this.

Danger Space — Each group commander will arrange to mark out the danger space immediately in front of the groups and will arrange to warn troops in the neighbourhood. The danger space must not include any regular track or duck walk that will be required for communication or reinforcements.

Appendix. II.

Extract from 88th Bde. Instruction No. 8.

2 Sections of 88th M. G. Coy. will be available for the attack, of which 1 Section will go forward to the 3rd objective where they will take up positions.

The remaining Section of 88th M. G. Coy will remain with the 2 reserve companies 1st ESSEX Regt. until the situation on our right is cleared up, and will be at the disposal of the O.C. 1st ESSEX Regt. 1 Section of 86th Bde M. G. Coy will also be available after ZERO.

This Section will go forward as soon as possible and will place 2 Guns at the disposal of O.C. HAMPSHIRE Regt, and 2 guns at the disposal of O.C. NEWFOUNDLAND Regt. in 1st objective.

No. 3 Section is alloted the task of consolidating the 3rd objective and No 4 Section is placed at the disposal of O.C. 1st ESSEX Regt.

Operation Orders Appendix III

By

Lieut. J. J. Paskin, Commanding

88th Company M. G. Corps.

In the Field 27/8/17.

I At 1.55 P.M. (ZERO) to-day 27th, the Division on our right are attacking a position.

2 88th M. G. Coy. will cooperate by means of Indirect Fire.

3 Targets are allotted as follows:-

No1. Section U10c80.15 – U10d02 No2 Section U10d00 – U16b19.

No3 Do. U16b43.95. No4 Section U10d2800.

4 Fire will be at the rate of 1 Belt in 6 minutes from ZERO till ZERO+20 minutes, and intermittent bursts of fire from ZERO+20 mins. till ZERO+3 hours

5 Section Officers will arrange that only two of their guns are firing at the same time.

6 As the operations will be carried out in daylight, arrangements must be made for concealment where necessary.

7 Belts will be filled as soon as fired so as to be ready for the usual S.O.S. if required.

8 Section Officers will take immediate steps to lay out the necessary lines.

9 As many men as possible will be kept under cover to lessen possible casualties.

10 Acknowledge

J. J. Paskin

Lieutenant Commanding

88th Company M. G. Corps

29th Divisional M.G. Barrage.

Group.	Position approx.	1st Barrage Z – +5.	2nd Barrage Z+5 – Z+40	3rd Barrage Z+40 – +1.40	4th Barrage + S.O.S. +1.40 – +2.15.
H. ?th M.G. Coy.	U26D14	not to be fired	U22A94 to U22B13	Move Forward	U17D.0.8. to U17D.35.70.
I. ?th M.G. Coy.	U26D33		U22B20.25 to Buildings U22B35.15.	Move Forward	U17D.0.8. to U17D.35.70.
K. ?th M.G. Coy.	U26D.86.		U22B35.05. to U22B.7.2.	Trench U17a.00.25 to U23.A45.90.	Becomes Divisional Reserve

Cancelled

Amendment to 88th Machine Gun Company
Preliminary Operation Order dated [illegible]

The Divisional Machine Gun Barrage Scheme has been amended. The Scheme as far as H. I. & K. Groups are concerned now stands as follows

	1st & 2nd Barrage	3rd Barrage	4th Barrage	S.O.S.
TIME	Z. to Z + 40	Z + 40 " + 1.40	+ 1.40 to + 4.20	Z + 4.20 onwards.
Rate of Fire	1 Belt in 4.	1 Belt in 10	Intermittent bursts of fire except Z + 2.40 to Z + 3.10 at 1 Belt in 4	4 Belts for first 4 mins then 1 Belt in 4.
Group				
H. [illegible]	U22 A 9 4 to U22 B 1.3	Move Forward	U17 A. 4.3. to U17 Central	Trench U17 A. 4.3 to U17 A. 75. 65. and U17 B. 3. 2 to U17. B. 4. 2.
I. [illegible]	U22 B 20 25 to Buildings U22 B 35. 15	Move Forward	U17 D 0.8 to U17 D. 35. 70	Trench in U17 A. 8. 5.
K [illegible]	U22 B 35. 05 to U22 B. 7 2	U17 C. 0. 0. to U23 A. 15. 90	Becomes Divisional Reserve	

J Parkin
Lieutenant [illegible]
88 [illegible]

Operation Orders No M G 88/5

By

Lieutenant J J Paskin Commanding,

88th Company Machine Gun Corps

In the Field 14th August 1917

No XIII

I.

The projected attack on the prescribed positions will be made on 16th inst

Zero hour will be notified later

II. 88th Machine Gun Company will cooperate in accordance with instructions issued

III. On X/Y night Nos. 1 & 2 Sections will move to their alloted positions to complete their preparations for M.G Barrage.

On Y Z night Nos. 3 & 4 Sections will move to assembly positions with the Battalions to which they are allotted, under arrangements to be issued to Section Officers.

Two guns of No 3 Section will report to C.O. 4th Worcestershire Regiment at RUISSEAN FARM. The remaining two guns will assemble in rear of the assaulting Companys 1st Essex Regiment. No 4 Section will assemble with the reserve Companys. 1st Essex Regiment.

Route to Assembly Position:- BOESINGHE PONTOON, HUNTER STREET, then taped track.

IV. Alterations in M.G Barrage Scheme have been communicated to Officers concerned

V.

Advanced Coy. H.Q. 1. Before Zero + 3 hours 10 minutes in Concrete Dugout U26 c 32

2. After Zero + 3 hours 10 minutes in Concrete Dugout U27 b 07

VI

Rations & Water See Preliminary Operation Orders.

VII

Oil Nos. 1 & 2 Sections will each take with them a petrol can full of oil. This will become a Company reserve of oil at U27 b 07.

VIII

S.A.A. dumps As soon as Nos. 1 & 2 Sections are in position near TUFF'S FARM they will send back men to carry up S.A.A. from existing dumps.

VIV
One runner from each sub group (H. & K.) will report at Advanced Company H.Q. (J.26.c.3.5) before 2 pm and remain.

Communication. Each group will send a representative to Advanced Company H.Q. at 1 am "Z" day.

XI
Reports. As soon as positions are consolidated Section Officers will send (on Message Form A) to Advanced Company H.Q. the map locations of their Section H.Q. and of their guns. These should be plotted on map and approximate direction of field of fire indicated.

XII
Medical. Sections will make use of R.A.P's established near Battalion H.Qs. Field Ambulance Relay Posts U.26.c.9.3 and U.27.[illegible]

XIII
Dugouts. All ranks are warned to be on their guard against booby traps laid in dugouts evacuated by the enemy.

J.J. Parkin Lieutenant Commanding,
88th Machine Gun Company.

Copy No. 1 88th Inf Bde.
2 D.M.G.O. 29th Division
3 O.C. 88th M.G. Coy.
4 2 i/c
5 Officer i/c Sect. 88 M.G. Coy.
6 " 2
7 " 3
8 " 4
9 Transport Officer
10 O.C. No. [illegible] Sect. [illegible] M.G. Coy.
11 O.C. [illegible] M.G. Coy.
12-13 War Diary
14 File

Issued at 7 pm

Report on Operations from 16/8/17 to 18/8/17.
88th Machine Gun Company.

To:- G.O.C.
88th Infantry Brigade.

Sir,

I have the honour to submit the following report on the part played by the 88th M.G. Coy. in the operations commencing 16/8/17:-

The tasks allotted to the guns of the company were as follows:-

(A) Two Sections to take part in the Divisional M.G. Barrage Scheme

(B) One Section to be at the disposal of O.C. 1st Bn Essex Regt. to cover the right flank of the Brigade in the event of that flank being exposed by the 20th Division being held up in the Village of LANGEMARCK.

(C) One Section to assist in the consolidation of the final objective of the Brigade (The "Red Line")

A. Barrage. In preparation for this a dump of 100,000 rounds of S.A.A. was formed near the 1st barrage positions. The two Sections were sent up on "X" day to dig emplacements put out aiming posts and generally complete their preparations. These two Sections formed "H + I" groups and together with "K" group (One Section 86th M.G. Coy.) acted under my orders. They occupied positions near U26d.14, U26d33, U26d68 respectively.

At Zero these groups opened fire on the line H, I, K, (see attached "A1 O")

At Zero+40 min. H. and I. groups moved forward and took up positions near TUFF'S FARM and opened fire on the line H2 I2. Firing was intermittent except during the periods Zero to Zero+40 min., Zero+2 hrs 40 mins. to Zero+3 hrs 10 mins. when rapid fire was used, these periods being the actual times of advance of the infantry to the 1st + 3rd objectives respectively.

At Zero+3 hrs. 10 mins. the guns ceased fire and were relaid on the "S.O.S." barrage line, with orders to fire if called for by "S.O.S." Signal.

B. The Section detailed for the right flank assembled with the ESSEX REGT. near TUFF'S FARM. While there it came under heavy artillery fire. The Officer Lt. A.D.G. Burrell, was killed and many men killed and wounded. Three guns with their equipment were lost. The Section Sergeant collected as many of the remaining men of the Section as he could and with his one remaining gun reported to 2nd Lt. C.W.M. Lys, M.C. who took him forward to the RED LINE with his Section.

Report on Operations (Contd.)

C. Consolidation One Sub-section was allotted to the 4th Bn The WORCESTERSHIRE REGT. These under 2nd Lt. Williams assembled at RUISSEAU FARM. They followed up the advance of the infantry and got into action about noon in the RED LINE in positions U16d68 and U16c93. 2nd Lt. C.A.M. Lys, M.C. with the other Sub-section of this Section and the remaining gun of the Section that was scattered at TUFF'S FARM followed up the advance of the ESSEX REGT. and eventually placed his guns in position in the RED LINE at U16d82, U17c41 and U17c30.15. The position soon after 12 noon on Z day was as shown on attached "A1 (2)". During the afternoon there was considerable movement of the enemy opposite the front held by the 4th WORCESTERSHIRE REGT. Large parties (estimated at 40-50 men) were seen to move by rushes from the direction of a blockhouse (U16d68 ?) towards our left flank. These were either reinforcing the enemy firing line or assembling for a counter attack. Fire was opened on these by the three left guns at close range and also by the extreme right gun. Each gun commander claims to have inflicted heavy casualties on the enemy. Many more could have been inflicted had more ammunition been available in the front line. It was necessary to keep several belt boxes in hand in case a determined counter attack should develop.
On the front of the ESSEX REGT. a German Officer on a white horse was seen across the BROENBEEK. Fire was opened but without effect. Intermittent fire was used against small parties of the enemy during the day and casualties inflicted. Between 6.30 P.M. and 7 P.M (roughly) an organised counter attack developed against the Brigade on our right, eventually forcing the line back for some distance. Our right gun opened fire as did also a Lewis Gun Post near it. Many casualties were inflicted on the enemy and later a Captain in the D.C.L.I. thanked the Sergeant i/c the gun and told him that our fire had helped to save the situation. This gun opened fire some considerable time before our Artillery barrage came down. About 3 P.M. on Z day I was told by D.M.G.O. that the 87th & 88th Infantry Brigades were being relieved by the 86th Infantry Brigade. He ordered me to take over the M.G. defence of the forward system (BLUE, GREEN, & RED LINES) of the whole divisional front, S.O.S. barrage lines being arranged by 227th M.G. Coy. In accordance with these orders I sent 2nd Lt. S.C.C. Bryant to relieve one Section 87th M.G. Coy in

Report on Operations (contd)

RED LINE in positions U16c17.45 – U17c16.40 (4 guns). About 9 p.m. I received a message from D.M.G.O. that the situation on our right was liable to become critical. I went to see him and arranged to take up defensive positions on the right flank of the Divisional front, the line of the railway being selected for consolidation. I sent 2nd Lt. H. Gregson to take up 4 positions along the railway, with his section which had been freed from the S.O.S. barrage duties, by these being taken over by 227th Coy. 2 Lt. E.A.N. Lys, M.C. also redistributed his guns in depth according to a scheme prepared by D.M.G.O. This reorganisation was complete at dawn on Z+1 day see attached maps A1.(3). It was a delicate operation, entailing much reconnaissance by Section Officers under very difficult conditions. At dusk on Z+1 day D.M.G.O. arranged for 20,000 rounds S.A.A. to be sent up on pack mules to TUFF'S FARM. This was then carried forward to the two right sections. I was relieved by 227th M.G. Coy. on night Z+2/Z+3 days.

Casualties My final casualty list stands as follows:-

	Officers	O.R.
Killed	1.	5.
Wounded	1.	26.
Missing	0.	3.

In addition to these several men reported sick in the line, and a number were missing for a time but were found when conditions became more normal. These were chiefly men belonging to the Section that suffered heavily near TUFF'S FARM on Y/Z night.

I have the honour to be,
Sir
Your obedient Servant.

J.J. Parkin Lieut.
Cmdg 88 M.G. Coy.

20-8-17.

A.1. ①
S.O.S.
H.2.
K.2
K.1
H.1
Scale - 1:20,000
YARDS 1,000 500 0 1,000 YARDS
9.7.17 No 2 Advanced Section A.P.& S.S.

Message Pad.

Your Message must be such as will enable the Addressee to know what the Situation is with You and your Neighbours.

NEGATIVE INFORMATION IS ALSO VALUABLE.

Strike out and alter sentences as necessary.

TO..

1. Am advancing to...
2. Am putting out (Have put out) protective parties.
3. Am sending out. Have sent out and am keeping out patrols to keep touch with the enemy.
4. Am (Have) consolidating (ed).
5. Our line now runs...
6. I require (give article or articles and No. required):

   Send the above to...
7. Troops on my right are (give situation)
8. Troops on my left are (give situation)
9. My strength now is.....................................
10. Am being shelled from..
11. Am held up by M.G., T.M., rifle, artillery fire from.................................
12. Am now ready to..
13. Enemy line runs..
14. Enemy (strength)..............................at......................................
    doing...
15. Have captured ....
16. Enemy prisoners belong to...
17. Enemy counter-attack forming up at...
18. Other remarks—

Time a.m. (p.m.)
Date...
Place...
(Map Ref. or mark on back of map).

Name...
Rank...
Platoon.................. Company.....................
Battalion..

5TH FIELD SURVEY Co R.E. (1176.)

A.1. ②
Scale – 1:20,000.
YARDS 1,000
500
0
1,000 YARDS.
9·7·17
Nº2 Advanced Section A.P.&S.S.

Message Pad.

Your Message must be such as will enable the Addressee to know what the Situation is with You and your Neighbours.

NEGATIVE INFORMATION IS ALSO VALUABLE.

Strike out and alter sentences as necessary.

TO..

1. Am advancing to..
2. Am putting out (Have put out) protective parties.
3. Am sending out. Have sent out and am keeping out patrols to keep touch with the enemy.
4. Am (Have) consolidating (ed).
5. Our line now runs..
6. I require (give article or articles and No. required):

Send the above to..

7. Troops on my right are (give situation)

8. Troops on my left are (give situation)

9. My strength now is......................................
10. Am being shelled from..
11. Am held up by M.G., T.M., rifle, artillery fire from..................................
12. Am now ready to..
13. Enemy line runs..
14. Enemy (strength)................................at...
    doing..
15. Have captured ....
16. Enemy prisoners belong to..
17. Enemy counter-attack forming up at...
18. Other remarks—

Time a.m. (p.m.)
Date..
Place..
(Map Ref. or mark on back of map).

Name...
Rank..
Platoon................. Company....................
Battalion...

5TH FIELD SURVEY CO R.E. (1,175)

Scale - 1:20,000

YARDS 1,000 500 0 1,000 YARDS

9-7-17 No 2 Advanced Section A.P.& S.S.

Message Pad.

Your Message must be such as will enable the Addressee to know what the Situation is with You and your Neighbours.

NEGATIVE INFORMATION IS ALSO VALUABLE.

Strike out and alter sentences as necessary.

TO..

1. Am advancing to..
2. Am putting out (Have put out) protective parties.
3. Am sending out. Have sent out and am keeping out patrols to keep touch with the enemy.
4. Am (Have) consolidating (ed).
5. Our line now runs..
6. I require (give article or articles and No. required):

Send the above to..

7. Troops on my right are (give situation)
8. Troops on my left are (give situation)
9. My strength now is......................................
10. Am being shelled from..
11. Am held up by M.G., T.M., rifle, artillery fire from:...............................
12. Am now ready to..
13. Enemy line runs..
14. Enemy (strength)...............................at..
    doing..
15. Have captured ....
16. Enemy prisoners belong to..
17. Enemy counter-attack forming up at...
18. Other remarks—

Time a.m. (p.m.)
Date..
Place...
(Map Ref. or mark on back of map).

Name..
Rank...
Platoon.................. Company.....................
Battalion..

5TH FIELD SURVEY Co R.E. (1176.)

CONFIDENTIAL

WAR DIARY

OF

88th MACHINE GUN COMPANY

FROM 1st September 1917 TO 30th September 1917

VOLUME No. 16

Vol 18

Instructions regarding War Diaries and Intelligence Summaries are contained in F. S. Regs., Part II. and the Staff Manual respectively. Title pages will be prepared in manuscript.

WAR DIARY
or
~~INTELLIGENCE SUMMARY.~~
(Erase heading not required.)

Army Form C. 2118.

Place	Date	Hour	Summary of Events and Information	Remarks and references to Appendices
In the Field	1-9-17		Training.	
	2-9-17		Church Parade in Morning.	
	3-9-17		Training as per Programme of training.	Appendix I Training Programme
	4-9-17		Rehearsal for Brigade Parade.	
	5-9-17		Inspection of 88th Inf. Bde. by G.O.C. 29th Divn. Bar to M.C. presented by G.O.C. Divn. to 2/Lt. E.A.M. LYS. M.C. and the M.M. to Cpl. ACQUROFF. C.S.M. PHILLIPS left for M.G. Base [illegible] for "interchange" for U.K. He was succeeded by C.Q.M.S. MAGGS from No 20 Coy.	
	6-9-17		Training.	
	7-9-17		Training. A very successful demonstration of the new "Barrage" Drill was carried out by Nos 1 & 3 Sections under Lt. L. Mathieson. This was attended by the D.M.G.O and a fair proportion of the officers of other Companies in the Divn.	
	8-9-17		88th Inf. Bde. Sports. These were held on the 8th September 1917 on the ground of the Essex Regiment: the proceedings lasted the whole day. There was a big turn out of all ranks including numerous [illegible] officers and at the finish the G.O.C. Division presented the prizes to the successful competitors.	Appendix II Programme 88th Inf Bde Sports

A5834 Wt. W4973/M687 750,000 8/16 D. D. & L. Ltd. Forms/C.2118/13.

Army Form C. 2118.

Instructions regarding War Diaries and Intelligence Summaries are contained in F. S. Regs., Part II. and the Staff Manual respectively. Title pages will be prepared in manuscript.

WAR DIARY
or
INTELLIGENCE SUMMARY.
(Erase heading not required.)

Place	Date	Hour	Summary of Events and Information	Remarks and references to Appendices
			The 88th M. G. Coy. was represented in all the events as per programme and were successful in gaining the following prizes: 3-legged race - - 1st Ptes. Winning [illegible] Slow Bicycle race - - 1st Pte Bygrave Obstacle race - - 2nd Cpl Sparks. In the tug of war the Company team was defeated in the first round by the Worcesters, the ultimate winners. Only after extra time did the M.G. team admit defeat in the football tournament and that was by the score of 1-2, the Worcesters winning both then and in the final round.	App.
	9-9-17		Church Parades	
	10-11-17 / 11-11-17		Training as per Training Programme	Appendix III Training Programme
	12-11-17		Move to Training Area at HERTZEELE.	
	13-11-17 / 14-11-17		Intensive training at Herzeele.	
	15-11-17		Brigade Operations. The Coy. participated in accordance with attached Operation Orders - Appendix	App. IV. Operation Orders MG88/7
	16-11-17		March to [illegible] Area - [illegible] Camp.	
	17-11-17		Training as per Training Programme	

A5834 Wt. W4973/M687 750,000 8/16 D. D. & L. Ltd. Forms/C.2118/13.

Instructions regarding War Diaries and Intelligence Summaries are contained in F. S. Regs., Part II. and the Staff Manual respectively. Title pages will be prepared in manuscript.

WAR DIARY
or
INTELLIGENCE SUMMARY.
(Erase heading not required.)

Army Form C. 2118.

Place	Date	Hour	Summary of Events and Information	Remarks and references to Appendices
	18-9-17		Training in accordance with Training Programme - Appendix attached	Appendix V: Training Programme
	19-9-17		"	
	20-9-17		Commanding Officer went forward to forward staging area and the line to make a preliminary reconnaissance for the Company.	
	21-9-17		Move to forward area. The Transport moved to BOX FARM, Sheet 28NW A11b and the Company went by train, leaving PROVEN SIDING at 11.0 PM and detraining at ELVERDINGHE RAILHEAD at 11.30 P.M. For the night 21-22 one section was accommodated at WELLINGTON FM (B8d) and remainder at EMILE FM. (B9d)	Map. Sheet 28NW B & F.
	22-9-17		The Company less 2 teams of No 4 Section and reserve gunners from each team moved into the line to relieve 2nd Guards M.G. Coy. Distribution of Coy at this time was as under;	Appendix VI Coy. orders. Map. BIXSCHOOTE 20 S.W. 2. 1:10,000
			A - Officers	
			I. Trenches. Capt. J.J. Parkin C.O.	
			Lt. L. Mathison No 1 Sec	
			Lt. S.C.C. Bryan " 2 Sec	
			Lt. W. Morris " 3 Sec	
			Lt. R. Brown 4 Sec	
			II. Rear HQ. EMILE FM.	
			Lt. J. L. Nichols 2/C	

A5834 Wt. W4973 M687 750,000 8/16 D. D. & L. Ltd. Forms/C.2118/13.

Instructions regarding War Diaries and Intelligence Summaries are contained in F. S. Regs., Part II. and the Staff Manual respectively. Title pages will be prepared in manuscript.

WAR DIARY
or
INTELLIGENCE SUMMARY.

(*Erase heading not required.*)

Army Form C. 2118.

Place	Date	Hour	Summary of Events and Information	Remarks and references to Appendices
	22-9-17 contd		Lt. C.D. Marsh - attd. H.Q. " T.E.R. Ford - Reserve Off. III. Transport - BOX FM. Lt. R. Brownridge. B. Company Strength (including 31 attached men)	

	I.O.	O.R.
Trenches	5	75
Rear H.Q.	3	63
10%		4
Transport	1	34
Extra Coy.	1	21
	10	197

Place	Date	Hour	Summary of Events and Information	Remarks and references to Appendices
			During the relief one other rank wounded	
	23/9/17		2/Lt. E.H. Singleton joined from base as transport officer. Strength increase 2. O.R	
	24/9/17		One other rank wounded. LANGEMARK Sta. and area behind shelled intermittently all day. Strength decrease 1. O.R. auth. AAQMG 283/3/11. U15c.2.0 During night 23/24 our gun position was heavily shelled with gas shells. The shells deposited a certain amount of phosphorescent substance over the gun numbers. This was removed with difficulty.	
	25/9/17		One O.R. (106463) Pte PROWSE, L) killed in action, buried at U15d 55, 60.	

A5834 Wt. W4973 M687 750,000 8/16 D. D. & L. Ltd. Forms/C.2118/13.

Army Form C. 2118.

Instructions regarding War Diaries and Intelligence Summaries are contained in F. S. Regs., Part II. and the Staff Manual respectively. Title pages will be prepared in manuscript.

WAR DIARY
or
INTELLIGENCE SUMMARY.
(Erase heading not required.)

Place	Date	Hour	Summary of Events and Information	Remarks and references to Appendices
In the field	25/9/17 Cont^d		One O.R. gassed at adv. Bde Hqrs. Our guns took part in an artillery shoot, object being to catch the enemy trying to escape from the artillery concentration. Guns used indirect fire except front line guns which used direct fire, no results observed owing to the smoke and the dusk.	20/11 25 b 2.2.
	27/9/17		One other rank reported missing,	
	28/9/17		One O.R. attached from 4th Worcester Reg wounded - shell-shock 31 Heavy enemy artillery shelling.	
	29/9/17		One O.R. wounded A heavy bombardment with gas shell took place & lasted for three hours from 12 midnight to 3 am. The front area received very little attention but the STEENBEEK and the area behind was kept under continuous fire. Enemy reported concentrating behind NEY WOOD. No attack followed Lieut NICHOLS J. F left company to proceed to the G.H.Q S.A. School The 87th M.G. Coy relieved us on the night 29/30th taking over 11 gun positions. Relief completed at 9.30. Company moved to FOREST CAMP. 28/A11a1.7	

J.J. Parkin Capt
Cmdg 88 M.G. Coy

A5834 Wt. W4973/M687 750,000 8/16 D. D. & L. Ltd. Forms/C.2118/13.

Appendix I

Programme of Training 58th Coy. M.G. Corps. for week ending – 8th Sept.

	Monday.	Tuesday.	Wednesday.	Thursday.	Friday.	Saturday.
7.30–8 am	Squad Drill without Arms and Saluting Drill.	Squad Drill without Arms and Saluting Drill.		Squad Drill without Arms and Saluting Drill.	Section Drill.	Section Drill.
9–9.50 am	Gun Drill by Sections	Gun Drill by Sections	Route March	General Description	Gun Drill by Sections.	Combined Gun Drill.
10–10.50 am	Squad Drill with Arms.	Gun Mounting Drill		Gun Drill by Sections	I. A.	Stripping.
11–11.50 am	P. T.	P. T.		Mechanism.	Company Drill.	Extended Order Drill.
12 noon–1 pm	Company Drill.	Company Drill.		Extended Order Drill with Guns	Rough Ground Drill.	I. A.
2–3 pm	Inspection of Mobilisation Equipment.	Packing Limbers.	Lecture by C.O. for Officers & N.C.Os. "Modern Developments"	Kit Inspection.	Demonstration of M.G. Barrage Drill.	
[illegible]				Lecture for N.C.Os. Trench Discipline.		[illegible] Capt. Commanding 58th Coy. M.G. Corps

Programme Appendix II

10-30 a.m. 1. 100 Yards Flat (2 heats)

2. Tug of War (1st & 2nd rounds) 1st round 88th F.A. & London R.

others – bye

2nd round Bde. H.Q. & T.M. Bty.

Newfld. & Hants

Worcesters & M.G. Coy

Essex & winner of 1.

3. 220 Yards Flat (2 heats)
4. High Jump
5. 100 Yards (final)
6. Sack Race
7. One mile
8. Old soldiers race

Interval — Dinner

2-30 p.m. 9. Tug of War (semi-final)
10. 440 Yards Flat
11. Long Jump
12. 220 Yards Flat (final)
13. Slow Bicycle
14. Half mile
15. 3 Legged Race
16. Land Boat Race
17. Obstacle Race
18. Relay Race
19. Tug of War (final)
20. Driving Competition
21. Band Race
22. Officers Mule Race

Open to the nine units of 88th Infantry Brigade Group

Appendix III

Programme of Training 88th Coy. M.G. Corps for week ending 15th Sept

	Sunday	Monday	Tuesday	Wednesday	Thursday	Friday	Saturday
7.30–8 a.m.		8.30 a.m. Company Drill with Limbers	Combined Drill		Gun Drill	Mechanism	I.A.
9–10	11.10 Church Parade		I.A.	Packing Limbers etc.	Section Tactical Exercises (Consolidation etc)	Sections attached to Inf. Bns for joint training	Brigade Day Nos 1 & 2 Sections attached to Bns for consolidation Nos 3 & 4 Sections Occupation of successive barrage positions
10–11			Company Drill				
11–12		1 & 2 Sns Mechanism / 3 & 4 Sns Barrage Drill	1 & 2 Sns Stripping Elem. Pts. Direction / 3 & 4 Sns Barrage Drill				
12–1		I.A.					
1–2	No 3 Section Range Practise (General M.G. Course)	3 & 4 Sns I.A. / No 2 Sn	2 & 4 Sns Kit Inspn / No 1 Sn				
2–3		Range Practice (G.M.G.C.)	Range Practise Stoppages & Repetition	March to Herzeele	Lecture by C.O. Trench discip. & reliefs (Offs. N.C.Os & Nos 1.)		
3–4							
4–5	No 1 Section Ditto	No 4 Section Ditto	No 3 Section Ditto				
5–6							
6–7							

J. J. Paskin Capt.
Commanding 88th Coy. M.G. Corps

Secret.

Operation Orders No. M.G. 88/7. Copy No. 9

Appendix IV

By

Captain J. J. Paskin, Commanding,

88th Company Machine Gun Corps,

In the Field 10th Sept. 1917.

Ref: French Map BIXSCHOOTE (20 S.W. 4) 1/10,000.

I. The 88th Infantry Brigade in conjunction with the 86th Brigade on their right and the French on their left on a day and at an hour which will be notified later, will attack and capture the BLUE LINE and GREEN LINE.

II. The 88th Brigade will attack the first objective with the HAMPSHIRE REGT. on the right and the WORCESTERSHIRE REGT. on the left. After the capture of the first objective the ESSEX REGT. on the right and the NEWFOUNDLAND REGT. on the left will pass through the first objective and capture the second objective.

3. Machine guns are allotted to Battalions for consolidation purposes as follows:-

1 Sub-section of No 1 Section	to	WORCESTERSHIRE	REGT.
Do	Do	NEWFOUNDLAND	Do
1 Sub-section of No 2 Section		HAMPSHIRE	Do
Do	Do	ESSEX	Do

4. Units of the 88th Brigade will be formed up N. of the BROENBEEK, previous to the attack, in the formation in which they will advance to the attack. Sub-sections of machine guns will assemble in rear of the last wave of the battalions to which they are respectively attached.

5. M.G. BARRAGE. Nos. 3 & 4 Sections will take part in the Divisional M.G. Barrage.

6. Acknowledge.

J J Paskin

Captain Commanding

88th Coy. M. G. Corps.

Copies to.
1. 88th Inf. Bde.
2. C.O.
3. 2 i/c
4. O.C. No 1 Section
5. " No 2
6. " No 3
7. " No 4
8 & 9. War Diary
10. File

Issued at 12 noon

Copy No. 9

Appendix I, to Operation Orders No. M.G. 88/7.

Ref. TRAINING AREA MAP. 1:10,000.

I The attack will take place on 10th Sept. 1917. Zero hour will be [illegible]

II The Blue & Green lines and Divisional, Brigade & Battalion Boundaries are shown on attached tracing from TRAINING AREA MAP.

III Consolidation. As soon as any position is captured it will be consolidated and will become a line of defence. M.G. fire will be immediately opened on any bodies of the enemy as soon as they appear within range. Sub-sections of No. 1 & 2 Sections will act under the direct orders of the C.Os. of the Battalions to which they are attached for purposes of consolidation. Immediately consolidation is completed they will again come under the orders of O.C. 88th M.G. Coy.

IV Nos. 3 & 4 Sections will form S.O.S. Barrage Groups respectively.
(Barrage) They will fire the barrages [illegible] according to the barrage table. At Zero [illegible] they will cease fire but the guns will remain laid on the line [illegible] which will become an S.O.S. barrage line. [illegible] In the event of the [illegible] on our left and no [illegible] attack developing on our left flank of the Division, fire will be opened on this line.

V M.G. barrage table.

VI Coy. H.Q. will be at the [illegible]

VII Communication will be by runners. Each Section will detail a H.Q. runner. This man will move forward with his Section and will be sent back to Coy. H.Q. as soon as Section H.Q. have been established.

VIII (Acknowledge).

J. J. Parkin
Captain Commanding
88th Coy. M.G. Corps.

Copies to 1. 88th Inf. Bde.
2. C.O.
3. 2 [illegible]
4. 2[illegible]
5. [illegible]
6. [illegible]
7. [illegible]
8 & 9 War Diary
10. File.

Issued at [illegible]

Appendix V.

Programme of Training; 88th Company Machine Gun Corps, for week ending 22nd Sept.

	Sunday 16	Monday 17	Tuesday 18	Wednesday 19	Thursday 20	Friday 21	Saturday 22	Remarks
4.30–8	March from HERZEELE to PLAISTOW CAMP	Gun drill	Gun drill		Gun drill		Gun drill	
9–10		Cleaning guns & equipment	Bay. drill with limbers	I. A.	Bay. drill	I. A.	Mechanism	
10–11		Filling belts	1&2 Barrage drill 3&4 Rough ground drill	1&2 Rough ground drill 3&4 Barrage drill	J.D.	Barrage drill	Bay. drill	
11–12		Inspection of guns & equipt. by C.O.	Mechanism	T.O.E.T.	Range cards	J.D. and Range cards	I. A.	
12–1		Bay. drill	Lecture by Arty. officers "Trench Reliefs"	Packing limbers	Mechanism	Stripping	Lecture officers defence	
9–10			Night operations		Night operations			
10–11								

J. Baskin
CAPTAIN,
COMMANDING 88TH COY. M.G.C.

All training in the neighbourhood of PLAISTOW CAMP. Sect 27.

V

M. G. Barrage Table

Group	A.B.		A2 B2		S.O.S.	
Time of Firing	Z to Z + 40 Min	Z + 40 Min to Z + 1 hr. 30 min	Z + 1 hr. 55 min to Z + 2 hrs.	Z + 2 hrs to Z + 3 hrs. 5 min	First 5 Mins.	Then [illegible] till atta[illegible] is do[illegible]
Rate of Fire	1 belt in 4 min.	Intermitted	1 belt in 4 min.	Intermittent	1 belt per min.	1 bel[illegible] in 4 m[illegible]

Appendix VI

Copy No 10 [illegible] M. T. Coy. Order No [illegible]

[illegible] Commanding [illegible]

[illegible]

[illegible] BELGIUM [illegible]

[illegible]

[illegible] BOX CAMP [illegible]

[illegible] NICHOLS [illegible]

[illegible] BOX CAMP [illegible] BEVERIDGE [illegible]

[illegible] BOX CAMP

[illegible] WELLINGTON [illegible]

[illegible] WELLINGTON CAMP

II [illegible]

[illegible]

J. J. Parkin [illegible]
Captain
Commanding [illegible] M. T. Coy.

ORIGINAL

WAR DIARY

OCTOBER 1917.

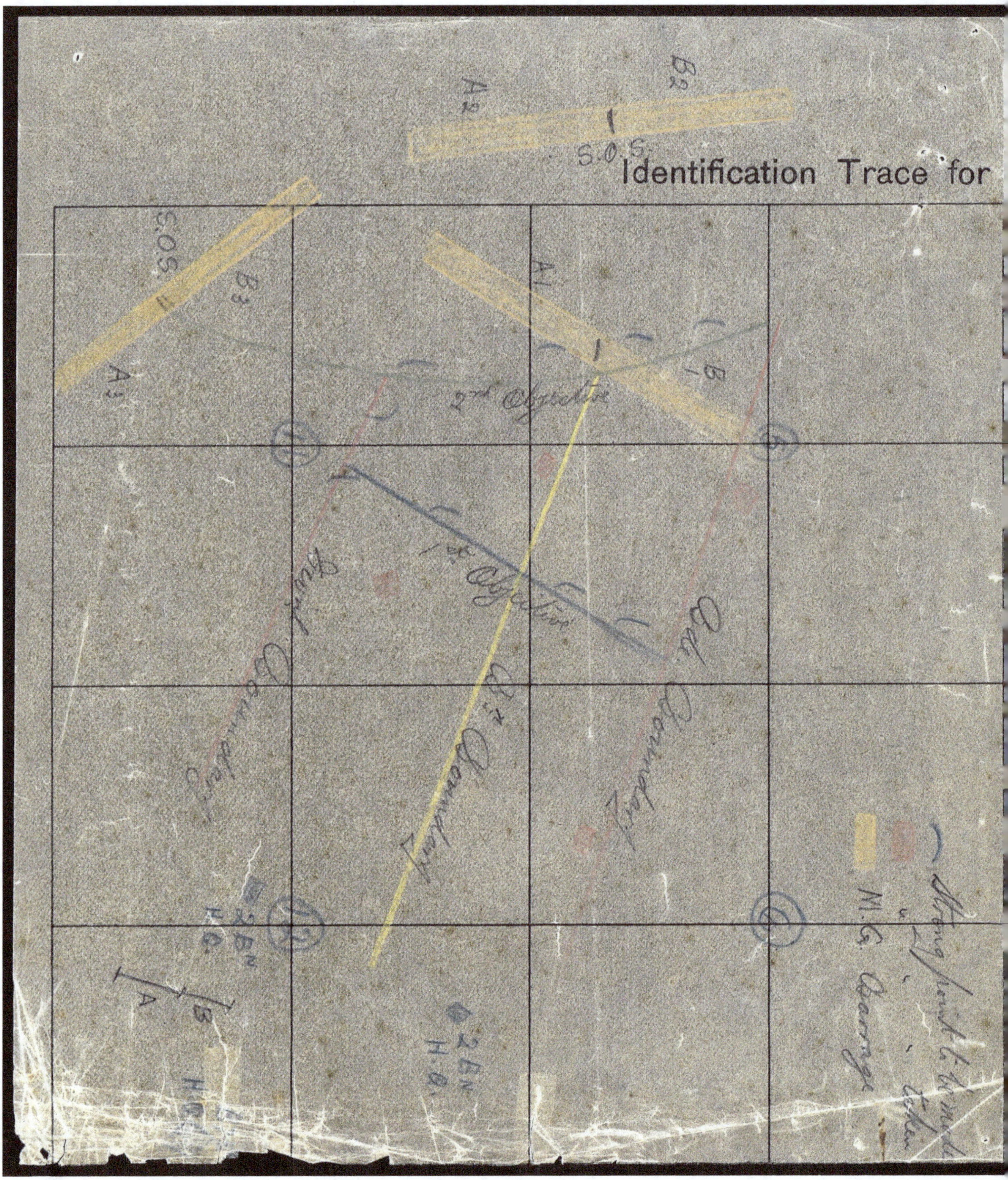

Identification Trace for

Strong point to be made
" " taken
M.G. Barrage

Bde. Boundary
Bn. Boundary
Divl Boundary
1st Objective
2nd Objective
2 Bn H.Q.
S.O.S.
A1 B1 A2 B2 A3 B3

CONFIDENTIAL

WAR DIARY

OF

88th MACHINE GUN COMPANY

FROM 1st October 1917 TO 31st October 1917

(VOLUME No. 17)

Instructions regarding War Diaries and Intelligence Summaries are contained in F. S. Regs., Part II. and the Staff Manual respectively. Title pages will be prepared in manuscript.

Army Form C. 2118.

WAR DIARY

or

~~INTELLIGENCE SUMMARY~~.

(Erase heading not required.)

Place	Date	Hour	Summary of Events and Information	Remarks and references to Appendices
In the field	1 Oct. 1917.		Strength decrease 1 O.R. Countersinking and sandbagging tents at FOREST CAMP.	28/A 11 Central
			Training. (P.T.; Barrage Drill).	
	2/10/17		Strength decrease 1 O.R evacuated. Training (P.T. mechanism, Gun Drill, Immediate action)	
	3/10/17		T2/Lt C.D. MAHLE awarded M.C. for gallantry & devotion to duty in the field.	London Gazette dated 26/9/17.
			Strength increase Lieut B.A. SEQUEIRA from base, and 5 O.R.	
			Training (P.T. Barrage Drill, visual training care & cleaning).	
	4/10/17		Training (Mechanism, lecture on "Consolidation", Immediate action)	
	5/10/17		Move to COPPERNOLLE CAMP.	28/I 16 b 60.90
			Strength Increase 8 O.R. from Inf. Battns	
			Strength Decrease 4 O.R returned to their respective Inf units	
	6/10/17		Preparation for the line. Strength decrease 2 O.R returned to their respective Inf Battns.	Appendices I & II
	7/10/17		Nos. 1 Sub. section of No 2 Section & No 4 Section the sub section of No 2 section relieved 2 guns of the 87 M.G. Coy in forward line	LANGEMARCK MAP 17 d 05.80. & U 1 [illegible]
			2 guns of No 4 Section relieved 2 guns of 87 M.G. Coy Other 2 gun team of No 4 dug emplacements at R1	U 23 a 85.65. Appendix III
	8/10/17.		No 3 & 1 Sections moved into the line	
	9/10/17			"
	10/10/17		Operations.	"
	11/10/17.		Strength decrease. 2/Lt S.C.C. BRYAN wounded, 2/Lt T.E.R FOOT " } 1 O.R Killed. 19 O.R wounded.	"
	12/10/17		Company relieved in the line by the 57th M.G.C. and moved to SASKATOON CAMP.	
	12/10/17		Gun cleaning	
	13/10/17.		Training (P.T. Map Reading.) C.O.s Inspection.	
			2/Lt H. MORRIS and 1 O.R proceeded to BIENVILLERS-au-BOIS as a billeting party	France SHEET 57D.

A5834 Wt. W4973/M687 750,000 8/16 D. D. & L. Ltd. Forms/C.2118/13.

Instructions regarding War Diaries and Intelligence Summaries are contained in F. S. Regs., Part II. and the Staff Manual respectively. Title pages will be prepared in manuscript.

WAR DIARY

or

~~INTELLIGENCE SUMMARY.~~

(Erase heading not required.)

Army Form C. 2118.

Place	Date	Hour	Summary of Events and Information	Remarks and references to Appendices
In the Field	14/10/17		Strength Increase 5 O.R from base	
			Church Parade in the afternoon	
	15/10/17		Strength Decrease 1. O.R. evacuated sick	
			Training (P.T. map Reading Barrage drill)	
	16/10/17		Move to BIENVILLERS-au-BOIS Entrained at PECELHOEK and detrained at SAULTY.	FRANCE SHEET 57D E2
	17/10/17		Arrived in BIENVILLERS-au-BOIS at 5·15 am.	FRANCE SHEET 51C Y7.
	18/10/17		Training (Gun drill, Indication & Recognition Fire Orders)	
	19/10/17		Training (P.T. Visual training Barrage Drill 1.A. Gas drill)	France Sheet 57D
	20/10/17		Training (Route march BIENVILLERS-au-BOIS → SOUASTRE → FONQUEVILLERS → BIENVILLERS-au-BOIS.	
	21/10/17		Church parade in the forenoon	
	22/10/17		Training.	app. III
			Strength Decrease 1.O.R. to U.K. for a course	
	23/10/17		Training	
			Strength Increase 3 O.R. transferred from 227 M.G. Coy: 2, O.R. from 1st Essex Rg. 3,O.R. from 2nd Hants Rg attached for duty	do.
			Strength Decrease 2 O.R. evacuated sick	
	24/10/17		Training	
			2/Lt Barr, 2/Lt Morris & C.S.M. attended gas lecture by D.W. Gas Officer at Croix Commune [illegible]	do
			1 O.R. [illegible] Course C.H.Q. School	St Pol
	25/10/17		Training	
			Strength Decrease 2, O.R. evacuated sick	app III
	26/10/17		Training	
	27/10/17		Training	do
			In the afternoon a football match took place at BARLES-au-BOIS between 'X' Coy 4th Worcestershire Rg & this unit for [illegible] Bde Sports. the 'X' Coy won by 3 goals to nil	do

A5834 Wt. W4973/M687 750,000 8/16 D. D. & L. Ltd. Forms/C.2118/13.

Instructions regarding War Diaries and Intelligence Summaries are contained in F. S. Regs., Part II. and the Staff Manual respectively. Title pages will be prepared in manuscript.

WAR DIARY

or

~~INTELLIGENCE~~ SUMMARY.

(Erase heading not required.)

Army Form C. 2118.

Place	Date	Hour	Summary of Events and Information	Remarks and references to Appendices
In the Field	28/10/17	.	Church Parade.	
	29/10/17		Strength Increase: 3 O.R. attached from 4th Worcestershire Reg. for duty.	
			Strength decrease: Lt B.A. SEQUEIRA to 12th M.G. Coy as T.O.	
			1 O.R. (Sgt. BARRER) to 55 M.G. Coy as C.Q.M.S.	
			Rehearsal for Bde Inspection by G.O.C. Division	
	30/10/17		Training Programme	
	31-10-17		Rehearsal for Bde. Inspection by G.O.C. Division	

J J Paskin CAPTAIN,
COMMANDING 88TH COY. M.G.C.

A5834 Wt. W4973/M687 750,000 8/16 D. D. & L. Ltd. Forms/C.2118/13.

88th Machine Gun Company.

Report on Operations 9th.–11th. Oct 1917.
Ref: Maps {BROEMBEEK / LANGEMARK.} 1:10.000.

I. At 5.20 a.m. on the 9th inst the 88th. Inf. Bde attacked the enemy on the frontage shown on the attached map. The Guards Div. operated on the left of the Bde and the 86th Inf. Bde on the right.

Three objectives were allotted viz. the DOTTED GREEN, DOTTED BLUE and GREEN lines.

II. MACHINE GUNS. The guns of the 88th M.G. Coy. were allotted tasks as follows:–

(1) One sub-section of No 2 Section as garrison of our original front line.

(2) No 4 Section + one section 227 M.G. Coy to form "B" barrage Group [at U 23 a. 05.45] in the Div. M.G. barrage scheme, acting under the orders of O.C. 88th M.G Coy.

At Z + 2 hrs 30 mins. "B" Group to advance to U 17 b. and guns to be laid on S.O.S. barrage line for protection of the GREEN line.

(3) Three sub-sections (No 1 Section and half of No 2 Section) to go forward with attacking troops.

Two sub-sections were to operate in depth on the left flank of the brigade. The remaining sub-section was ordered to advance on the right of the railway in close support to the Infantry.

These sub-sections were to assist in the final consolidation of the ground gained, by taking up positions as follows:–

One sub-section on the left flank of the GREEN LINE; one sub-section in a strong point to be constructed at U 12 d 65.95; the remaining sub-section in the GREEN LINE.

(4) No 3 Section in reserve at U 26 c. 95.20.

(5) Close touch to be kept with Bde H.Q. at MARTIN'S MILL and with D.M.G.O. at VULCAN CROSSING.

III. PRELIMINARY MEASURES.

(a) Nights W/X. and X/Y. A dump of 20.000 rounds S.A.A. was formed at U 23 a. 05.45 for the use of "B" barrage group.

(b). Night X/Y. (i). One Section relieved one Section of the 87th M.G Coy in

positions { U 17d 05.50 / U 17d 10.50 } - These guns afterwards remained for duty as detailed in I (1).
U 23a. 05.45
U 22d. 40.95

II. Gun positions prepared for barrage group "B"

III. Forward dump of belt boxes formed at LANGEMARCK Stn. for use in consolidation.

There was heavy rain during the day and night and limbers stuck in the mud on forward tracks. This entailed much heavy labour for carrying parties. The spirit of determination to perform their allotted task was admirable.

IV. BARRAGE GROUP "B"

Barrage lines were allotted as follows.

Times.	Targets.
Z + 0h 20m. to Z + 0h 40m.	U 12 c.9.8. – U 12 d.5.4.
Z + 0.40 to Z + 1.50.	CAIRO HOUSE – U12d 65.95.
Z + 1.50 to Z + 2.30	V.1.c.00. – V 7a.5.6.

No. 4. Section 88th. M.G. Coy. was in position on Y/Z night and fired the barrage as arranged.

The Section of 227th. M.G. Coy became detached from its officer and in the rain and darkness it was lost till the following morning.

At Z + 2h 30m. both sections moved forward and took up S.O.S. barrage positions at U.17.b.7.1. Here they came under heavy shell fire and one gun was blown up; so the group moved to positions at U.17d.6.7.

V. THE ASSEMBLY: Two sub-sections assembled with the left flank detachment of the NEWFOUNDLAND REGT. and the remaining sub-section with the WORCESTERSHIRE REGT.

VI THE ATTACK The advance to the first objective was accomplished with few casualties and without incidents of note except that our troops and the GUARDS each encroached on the others area: This eventually caused a gap to be left between the WORCESTERSHIRE REGT and the GUARDS. This gap was filled by the NEWFOUNDLAND flank detachment and one sub-section of M.G's. who advanced to the attack on the second objective simultaneously with the troops on their right and left.

The other sub-section of this section then undertook the duties of left flank guard. The remaining sub section advanced in close support to the.

WORCESTERSHIRE REGT.

During the advance one officer became a casualty.

On arrival at the second objective our troops overran our own barrage, and a few casualties were sustained.

VII CONSOLIDATION. While consolidating this objective, particularly the strong point at U12d 65.95, the enemy opened a heavy shell fire. The remaining two officers and many men were wounded and two guns were put out of action.

Sergeant Barker immediately took command of all the guns. He got two guns into action while the others were cleaned.— they had been dropped in the mud when the Nos 1. were wounded.

Sgt Barker re-organised the gun teams and replaced the damaged guns by german M.Gs. that had been captured.

About this time he was visited by the Bde Major who told him that trouble might be expected from the directions of the STADEN railway and the valley of the BROEMBEEK, Accordingly he reorganised the guns in defensive positions 1.2.3.4.5.6A (see attached map), Nos 2 & 4. being captured enemy guns.

There was a gun of the GUARDS Div. at "G". at mid-day our front line was as shown in pencil.

During consolidation all our guns in the line had many targets. These were mainly small parties of Germans moving up to re-inforce the front line and moving to a flank, from shell hole to shell hole. Small parties were also seen frantically digging in.

Whenever a party of Germans was "spotted" it was immediately fired on by our guns. Spare men also did much sniping with rifles. Ranges were short and observation good. Casualties inflicted on the enemy were very heavy and were <u>observed</u>.

At about 5 p.m. an enemy M.G. was spotted in action at V7a.6.2. Single men (Nos 3. of the gun team) were seen to approach this place. They were fired at with rifles as they appeared. When the place was examined through field glasses, 6 German dead were seen to be lying there: The gun itself was engaged by our No 3 gun and was silenced.

Enemy M.Gs. in TAUBE Fm were also engaged, both by Vickers & Lewis guns

During the morning I ordered the reserve section to carry belt boxes to the guns in the front line. Before they arrived at LANGEMARK Stn.

I received news that all three officers who had gone forward had become casualties. The O.C. reserve section (2nd Lieut Morris) immediately volunteered to go up and take charge of the guns in the line. He took his section with him & then sent them back. I immediately sent them up again with a further supply. In all about 80 belt boxes reached the guns in action in the front line. This carrying party passed through heavy shell fire along the railway, and also were sniped at as they approached the front line. In reaching the guns with the second supply of ammunition they displayed a commendable devotion to duty, unaccompanied as they were by an officer.

In addition to making possible continuous harassing fire being kept up by the guns on the enemy, this supply of ammunition for the M.Gs in the line had a very good moral effect on the Infantry, who were very short of ammunition. The knowledge that there were six guns in action with a plentiful supply of ammunition stiffened the defence of the line considerably.

At 5-30 p.m. the enemy counterattacked on the front of the GUARDS Div. and drove them back slightly. Our left flank had to conform. Our front line was then roughly the line of the POELCAPELLE—les 5 CHEMINS road. There were no targets for M.Gs. on our Bde front.

During the night Z/Z+1 three patrols at (10.30 p.m., 11 p.m. & 11.30 p.m) approached the guns, along the railway; our sentries accounted for men in each of these patrols with rifles and revolver. The men of the patrols were wearing clean clothes and new equipment and each man had a bottle full of hot coffee. As the line of the railway seemed to be used as an approach, the NEWFOUNDLAND REGT was requested to provide a post as escort for the M.Gs. there. This request was complied with.

There were no incidents of special interest on Z+1 Day until 5-30 p.m. There was continual sniping and our guns dealt with small parties of the enemy throughout the day. The enemy appeared to be consolidating along the line V7a.30.50 to V7c 10.70. Numerous small parties were seen running to and from the valley of the WATERVLIETBEEK, between the points V7a.80.10. and V7d.70.70. In addition to engaging these with our guns, the occupied localities were pointed out to the artillery who fired on them with shrapnel with effect.

At 5-30 p.m the HAMPSHIRE REGT. carried out a minor operation and captured the House at U12 b 75.50. This attack supported throughout by flanking fire from Nos 2, 3, and 4 guns.

No 6. gun followed up the attacking party and came into action in strong point at U 12 b. 50.50. (6B).

The line then ran approximately as marked in dotted ink.

VIII. Relief. The Company was relieved in the line on the night Z+1/Z+2; the barrage group by 236 M.G. Coy, and the forward guns by 51 M.G. Coy.

IX. REMARKS. The following points are worthy of note:-

α Communication within the Coy was good. Reports on the situation were received early at Coy H.Q. and at frequent intervals.

β There was unusually close liaison with the Infantry, and its value proved.

γ The plans for ammunition supply worked splendidly with the results detailed above.

δ The importance of all N.C.Os and men being made thoroughly conversant with the plan of operations was amply demonstrated.

J.J. Paskin
Capt. Commanding.
88th Coy. M.G.C.

12-10-17.

Koekuit
Langemarck
Namur Crossing
Crescent Pond
Olga Houses
Millers Houses
Conde Ho.
Schreiboom
Chinese House
Blue House
Red House
Eagle House
Station
Martin's Mill
Signal Fm.
Ruisseau Fm.
Denain Fm.
Steenbeek
Broembeek
Kortebeek Fm.
Imbros House
Alouette Fm.
BRITISH FRONT LINE
2 guns 86 M.G. Coy
Coy H.Q.
Bde H.Q.
[Diagrammatic Only]
YARDS
Concreted Emplacement or Dugout
Organised Shell Holes

C O N F I D E N T I A L

W A R   D I A R Y

O F

88TH MACHINE GUN COMPANY

FROM 1st NOVEMBER, 1917 TO 30Th NOVEMBER, 1917

(VOLUME NO. 18)

Original

Instructions regarding War Diaries and Intelligence Summaries are contained in F. S. Regs., Part II. and the Staff Manual respectively. Title pages will be prepared in manuscript.

WAR DIARY
or
~~INTELLIGENCE SUMMARY.~~
(Erase heading not required.)

Army Form C. 2118.

Place	Date	Hour	Summary of Events and Information	Remarks and references to Appendices
BIENVILLERS	1-11-17		Brigade Ceremonial Parade – Inspection by G.O.C. Div. and Presentation of Awards. The Brigade paraded on the open ground N.W. of BIENVILLERS and was inspected by MAJ.GEN. SIR BEAUVOIR DE LISLE in review order, after which hollow square was formed and the recipients formed up in the centre were presented to the G.O.C. and presented by him with the ribbons of their awards. The recipients from this Company were:-	
			2/LT. C.D. MAULE – M.C.	
			" H. MORRIS – M.C.	
			21494. SGT. BOURNE E. M.M.	
			9425 " PURSGLOVE J. "	
			20693 " VEITCH G "	
			18428 CPL (A/SGT) HILL J. "	
			15297 " SPARKS F.J "	
			80457 L/C EVANSON T. "	
			21446 PTE RIDGEWELL J. "	
			After the presentation units marched past in Companies in line, finally the Brigade advanced in review order and gave the General Salute. For the march past of the 88th Machine Gun Company "Colonel Bogey" was played.	

A5834 Wt. W4973/M687 750,000 8/16 D. D. & L. Ltd. Forms/C.2118/13.

Army Form C. 2118.

Instructions regarding War Diaries and Intelligence Summaries are contained in F. S. Regs., Part II. and the Staff Manual respectively. Title pages will be prepared in manuscript.

WAR DIARY
or
INTELLIGENCE SUMMARY.

(*Erase heading not required.*)

Place	Date	Hour	Summary of Events and Information	Remarks and references to Appendices
	2-11-17		Training Programme.	
	~~3-11-17~~		Training Programme. In the afternoon the company football team played the 88th T.M. Bty. team defeating them by 6–0. This was the first round of the Brigade Football League.	
	3-11-17		Training Programme.	
	4-11-17		Sunday. Church Parade at 11.15AM. with 2nd Hants. R.	
	5-11-17		Training Programme. No 3 Section worked a scheme in cooperation with the Essex and No 2 with the Hants. Lt. A.H. Enderby joined Coy. from Base.	
	6-11-17.		The Essex Regt. with No 3 Section gave a demonstration of a company forming a flank guard to an attack.	
	7-11-17.		Training Programme.	
	8-11-17.		Training Programme. In the afternoon the 88th M.G. Coy met the 89th F.A. in the 2nd Round of the 88th Brigade Football Tournament. The M.G. Coy was defeated by 2–0. After the game the visiting team was entertained to tea with some of the M.G. team.	
	9-11-17		Training Programme.	
	10-11-17		"	
	12-11-17		Divine Service in Billets at 11.15AM.	
	13-11-17		The Commanding Officer went by lorry to reconnoitre that part of the line in which the Company is next to be engaged	

A5834 Wt. W4973/M687 750,000 8/16 D. D. & L. Ltd. Forms/C.2118/13.

Instructions regarding War Diaries and Intelligence Summaries are contained in F. S. Regs., Part II. and the Staff Manual respectively. Title pages will be prepared in manuscript.

WAR DIARY
or
INTELLIGENCE SUMMARY.
(Erase heading not required.)

Army Form C. 2118.

Place	Date	Hour	Summary of Events and Information	Remarks and references to Appendices
	12-11-17		A dump for surplus stores and kit was formed at Bde. HQ.	
	13-11-17		Training Programme.	
			Conference of Company (Infantry) Commanders and M.G. Section Commanders at Bde. HQ. to discuss the schemes for the 14th & 15th with the G.O.C. Brigade.	
	14-11-17		Combined scheme with 88th Bde. in an exercise attack on the MONCHY-RANSART RD.	
	15-11-17		The Company took part with the 88th Bde. in a Divisional rehearsal attack in preparation for a coming offensive. The F.M. C in C. was present in person.	
	16-11-17		Surplus kit of Company dumped at Bde. Dump at POMMIER. Transport left to proceed to PERONNE by Road, staying at BAPAUME	
	17-11-17		The Company marched to BOISLEUX-AU-MONT and there entrained for PERONNE, detraining at about 23.20. Thence it marched to MOISLAINS.	
	18-11-17		The Company marched by night to a camouflaged bivouac camp SW of SOREL LE GRAND	
	19-11-17		Sections joined Battalions in accordance with Operation Orders and proceeded to Assembly Positions N. of GOUZEAUCOURT	Appendix I. Operation Order
	20-11-17 21-11-17 22-11-17 23-11-17		} Company took part in operations of 29th DIVN.	App. II Report

A5834 Wt. W4973/M687 750,000 8/16 D. D. & L. Ltd. Forms/C.2118/13.

Instructions regarding War Diaries and Intelligence Summaries are contained in F. S. Regs., Part II. and the Staff Manual respectively. Title pages will be prepared in manuscript.

WAR DIARY
or
INTELLIGENCE SUMMARY.
(Erase heading not required.)

Army Form C. 2118.

Place	Date	Hour	Summary of Events and Information	Remarks and references to Appendices
	23-11-17		The 88th M.G. Coy. was relieved in the line by the 86th M.G. Coy. and went to MARCOING where it was accommodated in cellars recently evacuated by the enemy.	
	25-11-17		Nos 1 & 4 Secs. and half Section of No 3 Sec. proceeded to the road in G 32 A and there constructed barrage positions in the N. bank of the road.	MAP WIERNIES 1:20,000 App III Operation order No M488/11
	26-11-17		The 88th M.G. Coy. relieved the 87th M.G. Coy in the line.	
	27-11-17		Coy in the line - Conditions bad, but enemy activity not excessive	
	28-11-17		The 88th M.G. Coy. was relieved in the line by the 87th M.G. Coy	
	29-11-17		Lt. C.D. Marsh was admitted to hospital suffering from P.U.O. About 5.0 P.M. the whole town was heavily shelled for about two hours. During the remainder of the evening and night shelling was extremely heavy and many gas shells were sent over.	
	30-11-17		During the early morning the Bombardment of the town of MARCOING recommenced with greater intensity than before and it became evident that a Counter Attack might be expected.	

Army Form C. 2118.

Instructions regarding War Diaries and Intelligence Summaries are contained in F. S. Regs., Part II. and the Staff Manual respectively. Title pages will be prepared in manuscript.

WAR DIARY
or
INTELLIGENCE SUMMARY.
(Erase heading not required.)

Place	Date	Hour	Summary of Events and Information	Remarks and references to Appendices
			The [illegible] casualties were suffered by this Company in operations between Nov 20th and Dec. 4th 1917.	
			KILLED.	
			31014 Pte Hinton, E. 20-11-17	
			21427 CPL. FORDHAM E. 20-11-17	
			73076 Pte Webb, E.G. 22-11-17	
			102477 " Ernst, H 30-11-17	
			12761 " Kilner, S. 30-11-17	
			Died of Wounds	
			108757 " Pritchard W. 1-12-17.	
			Wounded.	
			108796 " Warren A.E. } 20-11-17	
			115186 " Booker R. } 20-11-17	
			108659 " Ray F.T. } 20-11-17	
			60691 L/Cpl. Eckley E.P. 21-11-17	
			86569 Pte Cannon A 22-11-17.	
			42064 " Murphy P. 25-11-17.	

A5834 Wt. W4973/M687 750,000 8/16 D. D. & L. Ltd. Forms/C.2118/13.

Army Form C. 2118.

Instructions regarding War Diaries and Intelligence Summaries are contained in F. S. Regs., Part II. and the Staff Manual respectively. Title pages will be prepared in manuscript.

WAR DIARY
or
INTELLIGENCE SUMMARY.

(Erase heading not required.)

Place	Date	Hour	Summary of Events and Information	Remarks and references to Appendices
			108780 Pte Watkins A. J. 25-11-17.	
			21467 " Dowling, W. 26-11-17.	
			114918 " Hunter J. 26-11-17.	
			106072 " Strong W. 30-11-17	
			10135 " Ethelchild A "	
			29536 " Ellis W. "	
			108723 " Rawsthorne H. "	
			21470 " Hodges, W. "	
			84863 " Thorne T. 1-12-17	
			87018 " Pitt W. 2-12-17	
			116797 " Armstrong G. 3-12-17	
			115861 " Roberts S. W. "	
			72005 " Cox F 1-12-17	
			104694 " Connell T. 3-12-17	
			108877 " Yeomans S. 3-12-17	
			~~21470 " Hodges W. 30-11-17~~	

Army Form C. 2118.

Instructions regarding War Diaries and Intelligence Summaries are contained in F. S. Regs., Part II. and the Staff Manual respectively. Title pages will be prepared in manuscript.

WAR DIARY
or
INTELLIGENCE SUMMARY.

(*Erase heading not required.*)

Place	Date	Hour	Summary of Events and Information	Remarks and references to Appendices
			72088 Pte. Pedlingham V. 30-11-17	
			60722 L/Cpl. Bowyer R. 30-11-17.	
			Missing	
			117276 Pte. Ramey L. 20-11-17	
			Casualties among attached men.	
			Wounded.	
			17000 Pte. Everitt C. 20-11-17. Essex Regt.	
			41522 " Costello (Worcs) 22-11-17.	
			4191 " Peacock (Essex) 30-11-17.	
			1783 " Ford, W. (NFLD) 30-11-17	
			203377 " Miller W.G. (Hants) 2-12-17	
			2706 " O'Keefe C (NFLD) 2-12-17	
			Missing.	
			45960 Pte. Hill W. (Worcesters) 20-11-17	
			41033 " Cotton [illegible] " "	

A5834 Wt. W4973/M687 750,000 8/16 D. D. & L. Ltd. Forms/C.2118/13.

Instructions regarding War Diaries and Intelligence Summaries are contained in F. S. Regs., Part II. and the Staff Manual respectively. Title pages will be prepared in manuscript.

WAR DIARY
or
INTELLIGENCE SUMMARY.
(Erase heading not required.)

Army Form C. 2118.

Place	Date	Hour	Summary of Events and Information	Remarks and references to Appendices
			Summary of Battle Casualties – 20 Nov. 1917 to 6 Dec. 1917	

	OFFS.	O.R	ATTD.
Killed.	Nil	5	-
Died of Wounds . .	Nil	1	-
Wounded . . .	Nil	23	6
Missing . . .	Nil	1	2
		30	8

J.J. Baskin
CAPTAIN,
COMMANDING 88TH COY. M.G.C.

A5834 Wt. W4973/M687 750,000 8/16 D. D. & L. Ltd. Forms/C.2118/13.

Copy No. 11

app I

88th M.G. Coy. Orders to M.G. 17 [illegible]

by

Capt. [illegible] Commanding 88 [illegible]

Map BROEMBEEK 1.10000.

1. At "ZERO" hour on "Z" day 88th Inf. Bde will attack DOTTED GREEN DOTTED BLUE & GREEN LINES.

The Guards Division will operate on the left and 16th Inf. Bde on the right.

2. The [illegible] Regt. will attack first two objectives & [illegible] Regt. the final objective.

The flanks of attacking battalions will be protected by flanking detachments.

3. MACHINE GUNS

The guns of the Coy. are allotted as follows:-

A. [illegible] of present front line

One sub-section of No 2 Section at U.17 D1.4.

[illegible] sub-section will be [illegible] for [illegible] as [illegible] is [illegible]

B. BARRAGE No 4 Section will form part of "B" barrage group [illegible] [illegible] [illegible]. They will fire a barrage on [illegible] from positions [illegible] U.22 A1.5 [illegible]. They will subsequently move to & take up S.O.S. barrage positions in U.17 [illegible]

In the event of enemy resistance breaking down completely "B" group must be prepared to move under the orders of [illegible] to the neighbourhood of PASCAL Fm & take up S.O.S. barrage positions protecting the right [illegible]

C. CONSOLIDATION

No 1 Section will [illegible] on the [illegible] flank of the Bde [illegible] [illegible] [illegible] [illegible] & will finally consolidate the [illegible] of [illegible] DOTTED BLUE [illegible] GREEN [illegible] on the [illegible] of the railway & will occupy positions in each objective as it is captured.

RESERVE [illegible] sections in the vicinity of VULCAN CROSSING

The sections will be prepared to participate in the attack on the PURPLE LINE at Z + 9 hours

5. **BATTLE H.Q.**

88 Inf. Bde. ...... MARTINS MILL

88 M.G. Coy ...... LANGEMARCK STATION moving to U.23 A.5.9

6. Dumps of S.A.A. boxes are being established at LANGEMARCK STN and U.23 A.5.9

Coy. dumps { MARTIN'S MILL
PASCAL Fm

7. **ASSEMBLY**

Sections will assemble on Y/Z night behind the WORCESTERSHIRE REGt in our present front line, on their attack frontage.

They will be in position at a time to be notified later.

8. **PRELIMINARY MOVE**

Sections will move to C.2.a.4.7 on the afternoon of Y day, and be used to [illegible] there.

9. COMMUNICATIONS }
RATIONS } as arranged

Capt.

Commanding 88th M.G. Coy.

Copy No. 1 88th Inf Bde
2 D.M.G.O. 29th Division
3 O.C. 88th M.G. Coy.
4 2 i/c "
5 O/C No 1 Sec. 88th M.G. Coy
6 " 2 "
7 " 3 "
8 " 4 "
9 Transport Officer
10 } War Diary
11 }
12 File

SIGNALS.

1. S.O.S. [illegible] rockets bursting in RED [illegible]

[illegible] attack

[illegible] [illegible] [illegible] [illegible] [illegible] [illegible]

[illegible] [illegible] [illegible] [illegible] [illegible] [illegible]

[illegible] [illegible] [illegible] [illegible] [illegible] [illegible] [illegible]

[illegible]

[illegible]

PROVISIONAL AMENDMENTS TO

BARRAGE TABLE

No of Barrage	Time of Firing
[illegible]	Z + [illegible] to Z + [illegible]
[illegible]	Z + [illegible] to Z + [illegible]
[illegible]	Z + [illegible] to Z + [illegible]

Rate of Fire [illegible] [illegible] [illegible] 10 [illegible]

[illegible] { Z + [illegible] to Z + [illegible]
Z + [illegible] to Z + [illegible]

8. [illegible] [illegible] [illegible] [illegible] [illegible] [illegible] [illegible]

[illegible] [illegible] [illegible] [illegible] [illegible] [illegible] [illegible] [illegible]

[illegible] [illegible] [illegible] PURPLE LINE

[illegible] [illegible] [illegible] [illegible] [illegible] [illegible] [illegible]

[illegible] [illegible] [illegible] [illegible] [illegible] at Z + [illegible]

[illegible]

M. G. Barrage Table

Group	No of Barrage	Zero Time	Target	Rate of Fire
A 4 Guns 227 M. G. Coy REITRES F^m	1	0 – 4	NAMOR CROSSING	1 Belt in 4 mins.
	2	+4 – +10	NAMOR CROSSING to 44 K	1 Belt in 4 mins.
	3	+10 – +15	44K to extreme range	1 Belt in 4 mins
B 4 Guns 88 M. G. Coy 4 Guns 227 M. G. Coy. RAILWAY U 25.a.1.6.	4	+15 to +20	U. 12. c. 9. 8 – U. 12. d. 5. 10	1 Belt in 4 mins
	5	+20 to +40	CAIRO HOUSE – U 12. d. 65.95.	1 Belt in 10 mins
	6	+40 to +1.40	V.1.c.0.0. – V 7. a. 5. 6.	1 Belt in 10 mins
C 4 Guns 86 M. G. Coy 4 Guns 227 " U 23 . . 6	4	+15 to +20	U 12 d. 7. 5 – V 7. c. 2. 0	1 Belt in 4 mins
	5	+20 to +40	TAUBE F^m – V. 7. d. 1. 5.	1 Belt in 10 mins
	6	+40 to +1.40	V. 7. b. 2. 3. – V 7. d. 7. 9.	1 Belt in 10 mins

Appendix I.

88.Coy.,M.G.C.
Report on Operations 30-11-17 to 5-12-17.
Ref.Maps 1:20000 Special Sheets NIERGNIES
GOUZEAUCOURT.
@@

The heavy bombardment to which MARCOING was subjected on the night 29/30, made it evident that an attack might be expected. Accordingly at 7.a.m. I sent arunner to Bde.H.Q. to ask if there was any news. I received a negative reply but was told that I should be informed as soon as news was received. At 10.30a.m. I had received no news so I sent an officer to Bde.H.Q.

He found that the assistant Staff Capt. was the only officer there. He was told that the enemy had broken through our lines on the right and were attacking MARCOING from the S.E. I received orders to move with my coy. to L28b central.

I explained this situation to my officers and leaving Lt Nichols to lead the coy. I rode forward to L28b centdal.

At L22d40 I came under M.G. fire so I dismounted and endeavoured to get into touch with the situation. I saw our infantry advancing in extended order towards the ridge in L29c from which rifle and M.G. fire was coming. I met the Bde. Major who told methat our infantry had met the enemy on the outskirts of the village & vere driving him back.

By this time the coy. had arrived. I handed my horse over to the Bde. Major who found it of greatest use in keeping touch with our pursuit.

I ordered Nos. 2 & 3 Sections to push on in close support of the infantry. No.2 Section on the right of the road L28b central - L28d80, and No.3 Section to the left of this road. I sent No.4 sect--ion along the road to support Nos.2 & 3 Sections and ordered No.1 Section to take up defensive posns. along/

along the line L28c34-L28c86.

All spare men were then sent back to the vill--age under the C.S.M. to bring up all belt boxes that had been left behind and also to bring up addit--ional S.A.A. from the Bde. dump. This party showed a remarkable devotion to duty in performing this task, as the village was being very heavily shelled.

No.2 Section on the right of the road worked its way forward via the "Brown Line" and eventually came into action with its 4 guns on the bank of the road about L34d78.

No.3 Section went forward on the left of the road and leaving the HAMPSHIRES caught up the KOSB. These advanced till they reached the ridge running N.E. through L25a00 where they were held up by M.G. fire. They stopped this side of the crest, but 2LT. LYS M.C. pushed two guns forward to L35a23 and dis--persed a party of Germans who were digging in beyond. Later the infantry advanced and established a line through these gun positions. He got his other two guns and two guns of 227Coy. into action on the road bank about L34b74.

2LT.GADSBY, acting on orders from the Brigadier took his section in a N.E. direction and got into action with all 4 guns in squares L29d & L30c, his most forward gun being in chalk pit at L30c96. These guns were in action against large numbers of the enemy advancing over the ridge in G31d and also L36d.

In the afternoon, the reserve section with ammn. dump and Coy.H.Q. moved forward to trench about G28d98, from which the canal valley could be command--ed as far as LES RUES VERTES.

During the night 30/1 it became evident that the enemy was occupying and probably concentrating in in the works in **L35**, so as there was a big gap in the **M.G.** defence of the line, two guns **(SGT. HILL)** were sent from Bde. Res. to positions with the left Coy. of the **ESSEX REG.** about **L29d52** and **2LT.LYS** took two guns from the sunken road at **L34b74** to the junct-ion of the **ESSEX** and **WORCS. REGTS.** at **L35 68.** These guns were got into action in the front line with good fields of fire. Two guns of **No.4** Section were relieved by **87** Coy. and were withdrawn to Bde. Res..

There were in addition a section of 87 Coy. and **3** guns of **86** Coy. in action in squares **L30 & G25; and 2 guns of 227 Coy. at L34d57 firing S.E.** to protect our right flank should line of Div. on our right(which was weakly held) be forced.

1-12-17.

The day was fairly quiet, the chief activity being sniping and **M.G.** fire. The sub-section at **L29d52** was kept busy, dealing with these and it also had many good targets, -parties of **20/30** of the enemy seen moving in square **L35.** It inflicted heavy cas-ualties on these parties. The sub-section in the **NFLD. strong point about L30c05 also engaged similar** targets. It also fired at **3** limbered wagons which appeared for a moment on the ridge, to the **E.** of the **VACQUERIE VALLEY** and which disappeared at the gallop into the valley as soon as we opened fire.

Night 1/2

The only activity in our immediate front was sniping and **M.G.** fire which was replied to by our guns throughout the night. Our line was established as shown AB1, guns of this Coy. being marked in red, the gun at **G25b45** being taken from Bde. Res. and established.

established in post, with a Coy. of the **HAMPSHIRE REG.**

During the night the **86**th. Inf. Bde. whose position in **MASNIERES** had become untenable, retired through our lines.

<u>2-12-17.</u>

Our guns kept up a harassing fire all day against the usual snipers and small parties of the enemy. **A M.G.** on the ridge in **G20**a made communication along road in **L29 & L30** difficult. Enemy were seen digging in N.E. of **MASNIERES**. There was considerable shelling of our positions in **L30 & G25** throughout the day.

The sub-section at **L29**d**52** saw an enemy party carrying what might have been stretchers or **M.G.** mountings, and preceded by a white flag. It immediat-ely opened fire and the party disappeared into a trench.

<u>Night 2/3.</u>

Night was quiet. Our gun at **G25**b**45** was relieved by **87C**oy.

<u>3-12-17</u> (onwards)

From dawn our positions in **L30** and **G25** were heavily bombarded by artillery and **T.M.**s with great destructive effect. At **11**am an infantry attack developed from **LES RUES VERTES**, and the enemy occup-ied our trenches in **G25** and forced an entry into the **NFLD.** strong point at **L30**c**05**. Our line was with-drawn to the **W.** side of the road running **N. & S.** in **L30**. The **M. G.**s in the strong point were contin-uously in action and covered the withdrawal of the infantry.

Our guns at **L29**d**52** brought direct ~~fire~~ enfil-ade fire to bear on the enemy advancing [illegible] In addition our gun at **L28d98 fired indirect into**

the/

the VACQUERIE VALLEY and those at L34d fired in--direct at the ground between the CRUCIFIX and LES RUES VERTES, opening fire whenever firing was heard from the direction of the threatened area.

In the intervals between the periods of act--ivity on the left, SGT. HILL(L29d52) turned his attention to harassing the enemy on hisown front. He saw 2 M. G.s attempting to get into action, the sledge mountings being carried as stretchers. He opened fire on each occasion, killing some of the enemy and dispersing the rest. Neither enemy M. G.s succeeded in getting into action.

During the day one gun at L28d98 was blown up, one at L29d52 was pierced by a bullet, but was patched up with clay and rag and again brought into action. The two in the NFLD strong point were both ~~blown~~ put out action, but before dark 2LT. GADSBY again had 4 guns in action , having salved derelect guns of other companies.

Night 3-4

The situation N. of the canal made it necessary to withdraw our line to AB2, which was done with--out mishap. The gunsin that part of the line which was not withdrawn remaining in action, the others moving to positions shown by BLUE arrows.

Bde. H. Q. moved to L34a34, Coy. H. Q. to L34 Central, and there were three guns in Bde Res. at L28c22, with orders to be ready to protect the N. flank of the Bde. should the enemy cross the canal at MARCOING.

4-12-17.

Our guns in trenches round L29a00 were kept busy throughout the day ,dealing with parties of the enemy attempting to enter MARCOING COPSE. Many good targets were offered at effective ranges and many casualties were inflicted on the enemy.

Night 4-5./

Night 4-5.

The Army Commander decided to withdraw to the "BROWN LINE" -AB3- as main line of defence, with an outpost line about 600yds. in front of it. The outpost line was first established, covered by posts in the line AB2. and a proportion of M. G.s, the remainder being moved to positions in the "BROWN LINE".

At the completion of this move our guns were distributed as shown in pencil on attached map, 12 being in the line and 4 in Bde. Res.

In these positions we were relieved partly by 107M.G.Coy. and partly by 108M.G. Coy.

REMARKS.

During the lulls in the fighting, when both we and the enemy were consolidating our positions, there was ample scope for harassing fire against snipers and the small parties of the enemy continually~~ment~~ mentioned throughout the report. our guns seized every opportunity of inflicting casualties on the enemy in this way. It is a matter for regret that the Lewis guns of the Bde. did not seem equally ~~a~~ alive to the opportunities offered-- the more so as the Lewis gun is eminently suitable for this ~~p~~ purpose, being far handier than the Vickers gun for ~~carrying-about~~ engaging fleeting targets.

J. Paskin Capt.

Cmdg. 88th. Coy. M. G. C.

Appendix I

SECRET.

88th M. G. COY ORDERS No M.G.88/10 A
COPY No [illegible]

by

Capt J.J. PASKIN. Commanding 88th M. G. Coy.

Ref Map 1:20,000. Special Sheets GOUZEAUCOURT and NIERGNIES.

1. On a date and at atime to be notified later, British Troops will attack and capture the BLUE LINE and BROWN LINE. This attack will be made under the protection of Tanks and Artillery and Smoke Barrages.

2. The 29th Division will be in reserve and willbe used for the capture of the RED LINE. The 88th Infantry Brigade will operate on the right and 87th Brigade in the centre.

3. The right flank of the 88th Brigade will be protected by the 59th Brigade(20th Division), operating as follows:
As soon as the BLUE LINE is captured , it will push forward and establish itselfon the line M2d9.7. -- LES RUES VERTES.
It will attempt to seize crossings near C26.B.4.5. and L.24.C.8.5. It will probably protect the right flank of the 88th Brigade by direct M.G. Fire from the squares G.33.B&D.
It will also reconnoitre for crossings over th e Canal in square G.27.C.

4. Preliminary Moves:

Detraining Area.	Staging Area.	Forward Area.
W/X	X/Y	Y/Z.

5.

5. (a). As soon as the assaulting troops (29th Bde) have left our trenches the 88th Inf Bde will occupy the front from R.7D.9.7.-- sunken road in R.8.D. inclusive.

(b). On receipt of orders to move the 88th Inf Bde will advance and cross the BROWN LINE about R.35.c.8.0. It will attack MASNIERES from the S.W. and crossing the Canal will push forward and will establish itself in the RED LINE to the NORTH and EAST of that village.

(c). The junction between the 88th and the 87th Bdes will be the MASNIERES--CAMBRAI Road, inclusive to the 88th Bde.

6. During the advance of the Bde, it will be preceeded by a screen of TANKS.

7. All Objectives gained willbe consolidated immediately and the defence reorganised in depth.

8. On the capture of the RED LINE, the Cavalry will pass through and will operate towardsthe N.E. The road LA VACQUERIE--R.5.Central-MASNIERES will be reserved for their use till they have passed through.

9. MACHINE GUNS are alloted as follows:

No 3 Section to the ESSEX REGT.(Advanced Guard.)

One Sub-Section to push forward and occupy positions to cover Canal Crossing at G.26.b.4.5.

One Sub-Section to act under the orders of the C.O. ESSEX REGT. as circumstances demand. Both Sub-Sections to cross the Canal and assist in the capture of the RED LINE and finally consolidate in depth.

No 4Section . to the WORCESTERSHIRE REGT (Right FLANK Guard.)

This Section will consolidate finally as follows

One Sub-Section SOUTH of the Canal,

One Sub-Section NORTH of the Canal. These Sub-Sections to arrange cross fire across the Valley for the protection of the right ~~of~~ flank of the Brigade.

<u>No 1. Section</u> to the NEWFOUNDLAND REGT.(Left Flank Guard.)

One Sub-Section finally ^To consolidate^ in the square Q.W?.25. b. and to arrange cross fire with asection of the 87th M.G.Coy in position in the square L.30. a.

One Sub-Section to cross the Canal and co-operate in the capture and consolidation of the RED LINE.

<u>No 2 Section</u> in Brigade Reserve.

10. An Aeroplane will fly continuously during the hours of daylight. If it observes an enemy counter-attack developing it will throw out the following signal OVER THE THREATENED LOCALITY:

A Smoke-Bomb, bursting 100feet, below the machine into a parachute flare which descends slowly leaving a trail of brown smoke about 1ft broad.

11. As soon as a Sub-Section has taken up a position , arrangements willbe IMMEDIATELY made to enable it to fire on enemy approaches, (by indirect fire if necessary). FIRE WILL BE OPENED ON THESE LINES IF THE AEROPLANE COUNTER-ATTACK SIGNAL IS OBSERVED.

12. <u>S. O. S. SIGNALS.</u>

On the front of the 3rd Corps: A Rifle Grenade, bursting into 2 green and 2 White Lights.

On the front of the Corps on our Right:Ditto,

On the front of the Corps on our Left:Ditto, but 2 RED and 2 WHITE Lights.

CavalryS.O.S. Signal: A Green1" VEREY LIGHT.

13. <u>AMMUNTION SUPPLY</u>

A series of dumps will be formed on the line and in the vicinity of Brigade Signal Stations and Runner Relay Posts.

~~One sub-section~~ This work will be organised by the T.O.

~~One sub-section~~

One/

One Sub-Section of No 2 Section is placed at his dispesal for this purpose.

14. **COMMUNICATION.**

~~wi~~(a). Coy H.Q. will move forward by bounds with Brigade H.Q.

(b). Full advantage must be taken of the lines of Relay Posts established by Battallions.

(c). As soon as a Sub-Section is established in position, runners will be sent to Coy H.Q. These willthen guide forward runners from CoyH.Q. who willthen be available for communication between Coy H.Q. and Sections.

15. **RATIONS .**

Each Man going into action will carry 2 Days Rations, (viz: for Z Day and for Z plus 1 Day.) in addition to the Iron Rations.

Rations for Z plus 2 Day will be issued onZ plus ~~Q~~ 1 Day.

16. **WATER.**

All Water Bottles to be full at ZERO HOUR. Full Petrol Tins will be dumped forward together with Ammunition as in para 13.

17. **ACKNOWLEDGE.**

J.J. Paskin

Capt:

COMMANDING 88th M. G. COMPANY.

Issued at 23.00
Date: 15-11-17.
Copies to 1. 88th Inf Bde, 2. C.O. 3-6. Section Officers, 7. T.O. 8-9. Diary, 10. File.

4

Appendix 2.

88th MACHINE GUN COY. Report on Operations 20/11/17-23/11/17.

Ref.Map1/20.000 Special Sheets GOUZEAUCOURT & NIERGNIES.

---

1. GENERAL IDEA. British troops were given the task of breaking through the HINDENBURG LINE and forcing crossings over the ST.QUENTIN CANAL at MASNIERES and MARCOINGin order to allow the Cavalry to pass through the break in the enemy line.
2. SPECIAL IDEA . The 88th Inf. Bde. was allotted the following task:-
   (a) To pass through the objective captured by the 20th Divn., and attack the villages LESRUES VERTES and MASNIERES.
   (b) To force the crossings of the canal in L.24.C., G.26.B. and G.27.C.
   (c) To capture the MASNIERES-BEAUREVOIR Line (The RED Line) between the MASNIERES-CAMBRAI Road on the left and the MON PLAISIR Farm on the right, and to form a defensive flan[k] there.
3. PRELIMINARY MOVES.

Night.	By.	From.	To.	Remarks.
V/W	Transport March Route	BIENVILLERS AU BOIS.	BAPAUME.	Brigaded.
W/X	Transport March Route	BAPAUME	MOISLAINS	Brigaded.
	Personnel Tactical Train March Route	BIENVILLERS PERONNE	PERONNE MOISLAINS	Huts.

1.

3. Preliminary Moves/

3. PRELIMINARY MOVES (continued).

Night.	By.	From.	To.	Remarks.
X/Y	March Route.	MOISLAINS	SORREL GRAND .BIVOUAC	Camouflaged Camp.
Y/Z	March Route	SOREL	Assembly Area W. of GOUZEAUCOURT	By Sects with Bns

No wheeled transport was allowed forward of SOREL so that the moves to the Assembly Area and during the battle had to be carried out by means of Pack Transport. 12 additional Pack Ponies were lent by D.A.C. and 9 Pack Saddles were issued by Bde. This made a total of 25 Pack Saddles in the Company. Improvised wooden crates were used with universal saddles on the remainder of the animals.

Each Gun Team was given 2 Pack animals on which were carried :-

(a) Gun, Tripod, Spare Parts Case, 2 spare filled belt in sandbags.

(b) 8 Belt Boxes.

The remaining Belt Boxes and 10,000 rounds S.A.A. moved in rear of the Bde under the Transport Officer to be pushed forward as soon as circumstances would permit.

4. TASKS. Machine Guns were attached to Battallions and allotted as follows:-

Section	Regt to which attached	Sub Section Commander	Tasks.
No 3.	ESSEX (Adv Guard)	2nd Lieut A.F.GADSBY	To push forward and cover crossing of Canal at G.26. B. Central. When

Tasks (cont'd)

4. TASKS. (continued).

Section	Regt to which attached.	Sub-Section Commander.	Tasks.
			Bridge head was established on far side to revert to command of M.G.C.C.
		2nd Lieut E.A.M.LYS. M.C.	To act under orders of C.O. of Essex Regt and assist in establishing Bridge Head in MASNIERES.
No 4.	WORCESTERS (Rt Flank Gd)	Sgt Elfes	To cover crossings in G.27.C. and remain in position to protect the right flank of Bde.
~~No 1.~~	~~NFLAND.~~	2nd Lieut C.D.MAULE. M.C.	To ~~cover~~ act under orders of WORCESTERS. To cross Canal and consolidate RED LINE. (right).
No 1.	NFLAND. (Lt Flank Gd).	2nd Lieut R.BEVERIDGE.	To cover crossings in L.24.C. and remain in position on W. side of Canal.

Tasks (cont'd)

4.-TASKS (continued).

Section	Regt to which attached	Sub-Section Commander	Tasks.
No1.	NFLAND (Lt Flank Gd)	2nd Lieut L.MATHISON	To assist in above and finally to cross Canal and in consolidation of the RED LINE (left)
No 2.	HAMPSHIRE	2nd Lieut H. Morris. M.C.	To assist in capture and consolidation of RED LINE (centre).
	Bde Reserve	Sgt Bourne	To assist transport in ammunition supply.

The ground was extremely favourable for the employment of direct overhead fire , and all M.G.O,s were ordered to give all possible assistance to the Infantry by this means.

M.G.O,s were also ordered to fire at low flying enemy aeroplanes if opportunity offered.

5. ASSEMBLY&FORMING UP.

Sections joined their Bns at SOREL on Y/Z night and after a hot meal moved with them to Assembly positions W. of GOUZEAUCOURT. The reserve sub-section and the pack transport moved with Coy HQ.

Zero hour was 6-20a.m. on the 20th instant.

Soon after Zero the Bde moved up the valley towards VILLERS PLOUICH and as our original front line system became emptied of troops , the 88th Bde occupied/

occupied it between points R.8.D.4.2. and R.14.D.9.7.

When news came through that the BROWN LINE had been captured the order was given for the 88th Inf. Bde. to advance.

6. **THE BATTLE. MACHINE GUN ACTION.**

(a) **Z Day- Advanced Guard ~~Action~~ Section.**

2nd Lt GADSBY moved with W Coy Essex Regt. He became detached from them about L.36.A.55. but made straight for Bdge in G.26.B.Central, taking up positions in house G.26.B.3D.QU17. from which he could command the Bridge. The Bridge had been broken down by a Tank but still offered a possible crossing to individuals. About 3p.m. snipers and a M.G. were firing from houses at G.26.B.6.7. With one gun in a shell hole in the garden at G.26.B.30.25. he silenced them His 2 guns remained, covering Bridge during night Z-Z plus 1.

2nd Lieut Lys.M.C. advanced at first with Bn. H.Q. and then pushed on and caught up the second wave. On reaching G.25.B.85.30. he got both his guns into action and fired with effect over the heads of the first wave on two lines of Germans advancing in G.20.A. After about an hour and ahalf he moved to Bn. H.Q. which had been established at G.26.B.30. He was told later to post a gun at the corner of the hedge at G.26.A.6.2 the other gun remaining at Bn H.Q.

During the night the Essex Regt were ordered to mop up the N.W. Sector of village in which the enemy were still holding out. I ordered 2nd Lt LYS to relieve 2nd Lieut GADSBY'S guns which were guarding Bridge in G.26.B., thus freeing those guns to go forward.

Right Flank Section.

Sgt Elfes moved with W Coy of the Worcester Regt He first occupied positions in G.32.B. and while there, news came through that the leading Coy of the Worcester Regt had crossed the Canal at the Lock in in G.27.B. About 6p.m. he moved with W.Coy and dug in defensive positions at G.26.D.5.3.where he stayed for the night.

2nd Lt MAULE M.C. moved with Y Coy of the Worcester Regt and crossed the Canal at the Lock and eventually took up defensive positions at G.27.D.04 and G.27.A.~~10~~ 8.0.

Left Flank Section.

The complete section moved with C Coy NFLAND Regt at the commencement, 2 guns moving over to D Coy on passing the BROWN LINE.

On nearing the Lock in L.24.C. the NFLAND Regt came under heavy M.G. and rifle fire from rising ground across the Canal and the C.O. NFLAND Regt ordered our guns to open covering fire. On his way back to take up positions for this 2nd Lieut MATHISON met a section of ~~MMU~~ 227th Coy M.G. He got all guns into action near L.30.A.4.7. firing over the heads of the Infy at enemy in squares L.24.A. and G.19.B. This fire was observed and was very effective. The Infy waited until fire was opene and then under ~~cover~~ cover of it rushed the Bridge and lock. As soon as they had crossed , 2nd Lieut MATHISON followed them up with 2 guns again coming into action with one gun at about 50yds range against snipers in house L.24.D.9.5. These snipers were silenced and 2nd Lieut MATHISON was sent back to L.~~24~~30.A.4.3.to cover Bridge. The 4 guns were then dug in there.

The Sub-Section (commanded by 2/Lt MORRIS M.C.) attached to Hampshire Regtmoved with Y Coy as far the BROWN LINE where he became seperated from them. 2/nd Lieut MORRIS worked his way down the Sunken Road to Red House at G.26.C.02. where he met the Brigade Major who told him to go forward with the Worcester Regt to the Bridge. He came into action at the Bridge in G.26.B. Central where one gun was put out of action by a sniper. He then met the C.O. of the Hamps Regt and followed the Bn across the Canal and came

into/

into action at G.27A. 90.20. where the Hampshire Regt commenced to dig in. At this stage one Squadron of Cavalry went through and disappeared over the ridge to the N.E. The Infantry then decided to move up the slope further; 2nd Lieut MORRIS moved with them and finally dug in his remaining gun at G.27.A.60.40.

One Section 227 M.G.Coy had followed up the Brigade and had got into action as shewn on attached map(1). During the night I received a message from the D.M.G.O. placing this Section at my disposal.

Ammunition Supply. As soon as our troops had entered LES RUES VERTES I sent back to the T.O. and ordered him to bring up the Reserve of Belt Boxes and S.A.A. He did this helped by the Reserve Sub-Section, arriving at Coy H.Q. (which had been established at G26.D.19.) about 4p.m. On the way up one mule fell into a trench and had to be shot.

Position on night Z/Z plus 1 was as shewn on attached map(1)

(b) Z plus 1 day.

8 It was decided to continue the attack.

Sergt ELFES crossed the Canal with W Coy Worcester Regt and took positions up in Road bank to the right of SUGAR Factory. This made it necessary to send out another Sub-Section as Right Flank Guard.

Sgt BOURNE was ordered to take up the Reserve Sub-Section, and move along the right bank of the Canal to bridge atG.28.C.20.

He moved (with pack animals)and took up positionsG.34.A.10.25. &G.34.A.20.80. He fired with effect on groups of the enemy in G.28.D. Central. When Companies of the 20th Division attempted to cross the bridge they came under extremely heavy M.G. fire Sergt BOURNE provided covering for this crossing.

2/Lt MAULE (2 guns G.27.D.04.G.27.A.80.)about 1 10a.m

10a.m. saw the enemy advancing over ridge beyond MON PLAISIR Farm. Both guns at once opened fire. Other M.G. and rifle fire was also opened, and the enemy's advance was stopped. A little later he saw M.G's on ridge G.28.B&D. firing on parties of 20th Division who were attempting to cross bridge G.28.C.20. He at once opened covering fire. In the afternoon his other Sub-Section (Sergt Elfes) came up and dug in near him.

During the morning the Hampshire Regt advanced their line somewhat, the flank of one Coy was left in the air, and to cover this 2/nd Lt. Morris moved his gun from G.27.A.60.40. to G.27.A.70.80. As there was only one M.G. in that part of the Line I ordered 2/Lt Beveridge to reinforce with two guns taken from L.30.A. He moved with pack animals and eventually consolidated in positions G.27.A. 90.20.&G. 27.A.90.80. This latter gun fired during the day at parties of the enemy digging in on the ridge in front. 2/nd Lieut BEVERIDGE handed over command of these two guns to 2/nd Lt MORRIS and returned to Coy H.Q.

<u>No. 3 Section</u>.

During the early morning a Company of the Essex Regt, were prevented from advancing up the main street across the Canal by snipers in houses N.E. of the bridge. 2/Lt LYS fired on the roofs of the houses from the top floor of house G.26.B28.24; sniping ceased for the time being.

During the morning 2nd Lt LYS was releived at the bridge by aSub-Section of 227th M.G.Company and moved to positions in G.26.D.covering the bridge and Lock in G.27.C.

2/nd Lt GADSBY'S sub-sectionat Bridge in G.26. B. was relieved (as already stated) by 2/nd Lt LYS to free him to go forward with the Essex Regt across the Canal. He was not required to move till 11-30a.m. when he moved with W Coy across the Canal at/

at G.20.C.33. He occupied positions in houses at G. 20.C.97. and G.20.D.15. and fired on a party of the enemy at G.20.B.17. driving them back and thus enabling the Infantry to advance. They were again checked by snipers in houses on W. side of MASNIERES -CAMBRAI (CAMBRAI) Road, and these had then to be dealt with by our M.Gs. Areport was next received that the Line G.20.B.10.-G.20.B64. was clear of the enemy, so that the Infantry followed by the M.Gs advanced. When they reached the wire in front of this trench a surprise local counter-attack compelled them to fall back. During this retirement a No 1 was killed and the tripod he was carrying was lost. The LineG.20.B.06.S.E. to CAMBRAI Road was then consolidated. At 5-30p.m. the Essex Regt were relieved by S.W.B. and moved over and consolidated LineG.20. B.70.-G21.C.28.

(c) Z plus 2 day.

On the right the day was spent in consolidation our M.Gs firing occasionally on enemy snipers etc on ridge G.28.A&B.

Isent a Sub-Section of 227Coy to occupy positions in G.33.to cover bridge at G.28.C.20' thereby enabling me (later in the day) to send Sgt BOURNE to the relief of 2/Lt GADSBY's sub-section, which had been fighting continuously for three days. In the evening I obtained permission to withdraw the sub-section of 227 Coy from the bridge in G.26. B. and sent them to join their Section Officer, covering ground beyond MON PLAISIR Farm,thereby affording additional protection to the Right Flank of the Brigade.

In the Essex Sector following a bombardment at dawn,snipers and M.Gs opened fire from houses on E. side of CAMBRAI Road in G.20.B. One of 2/nd Lieut GADSBY's guns was out of action but he took the other

gun/

gun to a shell hole at G.20.D80. and from that exposed position he searched the houses, concentrating particularly on the house at G.20.D89. where the enemy was in force. Without this covering fire the positions held by the Infantry would probably have untenable. In the afternoon he was relieved (as detailed) by the Sub-Section withdrawn from bridge G.28.C.20.

(d) Z plus 3 day.

I decided to strengthen our Left in depth by

moving Sgt ELFES (2 guns in G.27.C) to positions at G.20.D.71, and G.20.D.51, with fields of fire directly up the RUMILLY and CAMBRAI roads respectively. The guns were ordered (by the Brigade Major) temporarily to remain in their old positions. Parties of the Worcester Regt had not completely dug in, N. & E. of MON PLAISIR Farm during the night and were receiving considerable attention from snipers on the ridge beyond. Sgt ELFES and 2/nd Lt MAULE's sub-sections in G.27.C. kept these snipers under fire by shooting over the heads of the Infantry. AS a result there was a marked decrease of sniping and the Infantry were then able to consolidate.

7. ANTI-AIRCRAFT FIRING was done by the sub-sections ~~in G.EP.~~ L.30.A. & G.26.D. and by M.G.s of other Coys along road in G.32.B.

8. RELIEF.

The Company was relieved by the 86th M.G.Coy. in the evening of Zplus 3 day, the defence scheme handed over being shown in map(2).

On relief the Coy moved into Divisional Reserve at MARCOING, with Coy H.Q. at L.16.D.63.

9. CASUALTIES.

	K.	W.	M.	Total.
Officers	1	1	-	-

10. Casualties/

9. CASUALTIES. (continued).

	K.	W.	M.	Total.
O.R.	3	6	3	12.

10. NOTES.

(1) The great moral and material effect of direct overhead fire covering, when such is possible, was proved.

(2) Communications from Sections to Coy H.Q.

(a) Via Battalions broke down almost immediately.

(b) By runner direct to Coy H.Q. worked well, possibly because that system is the one habitual to the Coy.

(3) The improvised pack saddlery worked fairly well, no loads being lost.

J Raskin Capt.

Cmdg 88th M.G.Company.

24-11-17.

SECRET.

88th M.G.Coy. Orders No M.G. 88/10 B.
by
Capt J.J.Paskin. Cmdg 88th M.G.Coy.

Addendum and Corrigendum to M. G. 88/10 A.

Para.

1. The attack will take place on 20-11-17.

9. ALLOTMENT OF MACHINE GUNS.

No 3 Section. The sub-section at the bridge G20b45 to remain in position and revert to command of M.G.C.C. when bridge is crossed.

The remaining sub-section to consolidate bridge-head with ESSEX REGT.

No 2 Section. One sub-section to move with HAMPSHIRE REGT and assist in consolidation of centre sector of RED LINE.

J.J.Paskin Capt.
Cmdg 88th M.G.Coy.

XXXX

SECRET

Appendix III

Copy No. 6

In the Field,
26-11-17.

88TH M.G. COY. ORDERS
No. M.G/88/11

REF. MAP. NIERGNIES
1:20,000.

(1) The 88th M.G.Coy. will relieve 87th M.G.Coy. in the line in accordance with Relief table attached.

(2) No 2 Sec. will occupy positions 1, 2, 3 & 4
3 " 5, 6, 7 & 8
1 " 9, 10, 11 & 12.
4 " 13, 14, 15 & 16.

(3) Coy HQ. will remain at L16D6.3 to-night & will move to HQ occupied by 87th Coy. to-morrow morning (L22 D 6.3).

(4). 4 men per gun team only will be taken into the line.

(5) "Relief Complete" will be reported by two runners to present Coy HQ who will then guide ration party to Section HQ's. Rations for succeeding nights will be carried up by reserve men.

Routes to places appointed for meeting guides will be reconnoitred immediately.

②

⑦ - Barrage positions will not be evacuated until arrival of relief

⑧ - Tripods + Belt boxes will be handed over in present positions + others taken over in the line. Copies of receipts to be sent to Coy. H.Q. by the runner reporting relief complete. Code word for "Relief Complete" will be name of Section Officer concerned

⑨. ACKNOWLEDGE.

(Signed) J. J. Parkin,

Captain,

Issued at 15.00 Commanding 88th M.G. Coy.

COPIES

① C.O.

② O.C. Barrage Group.

③ 88 INF. BDE. (for information)

④ File

⑤+⑥ Diary.

Machine Gun Relief   Night 26/27 Nov. 1917

Moves	Guns	From	To	Guides	Time	Remarks
1	6 (88 M.G. Coy) Nos 2 & ½ No 3	Reserve L16 D 6.3.	Line 1.2.3.4.5&6	Railway Bdge L 23 C 05.80	4.30 p.m	
2	6 (87 M.G. Coy)	Line 1.2.3.4.5&6	Barrage Posn 632 A	to move with No 1		On relief
3	6 (88 M.G. Coy) ½ No 3 & No 1	Barrage (L 32 A)	Line 7.8.9.10.11.12	Railway Bdge L 23 C 05.80	8.0 P.M.	On relief
4	4 (87 M.G. Coy)	Line 7.8.9 & 10	Barrage Positions	Lock L 24 C 80.45	9.30 P.M.	On relief
5	2 (87 M.G. Coy)	Line 11 & 12	Reserve			
6	4 (88 M.G. Coy)	Barrage Positions	Line 13.14.15 & 16	Lock L 24 C 80.45	10.30 P.M.	On relief
7	4 (87 M.G. Coy)	Line 13,14,15 & 16	Reserve			

N.B. With reference to moves 4 & 6 Guides will be on N. Side of Canal.

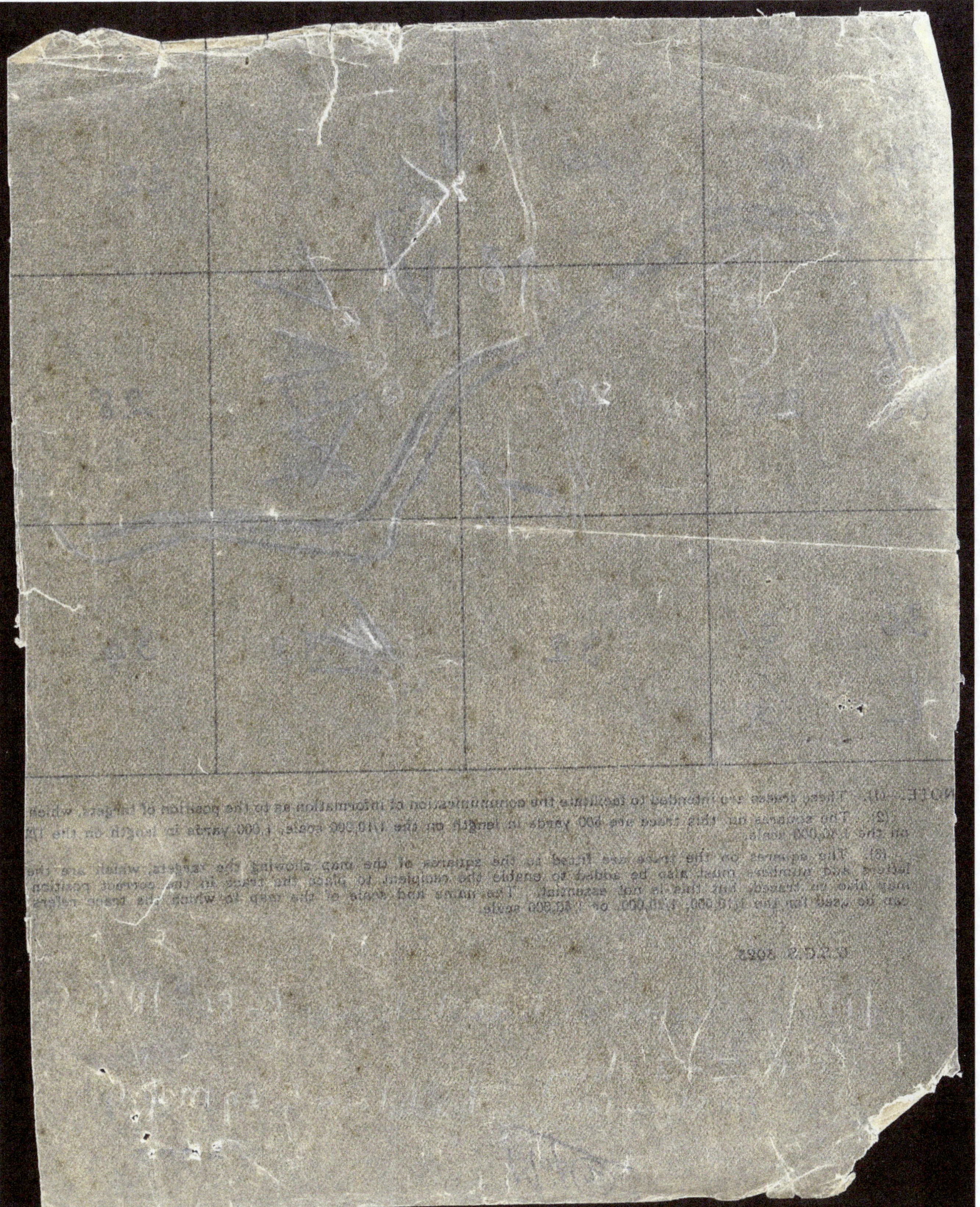

Confidential

War Diary

of

88th Machine Gun Coy

88/89

From 1st Decr. 1917 To 31st Decr. 1917

(Volume No. 19)

88 M.G. Coy
Vol 21

Original Copy

Army Form C. 2118.

Instructions regarding War Diaries and Intelligence Summaries are contained in F. S. Regs., Part II. and the Staff Manual respectively. Title pages will be prepared in manuscript.

WAR DIARY
or
INTELLIGENCE SUMMARY.

(Erase heading not required.)

Place	Date	Hour	Summary of Events and Information	Remarks and references to Appendices
MARCOING	1-12-17 / 4-12-17		The Coy. was engaged with the 88th Brigade in driving back the enemy from MARCOING, defending the right rear of the 29th Division and moving back to a new line. See Report on Operations 30-11-17 to 5-12-17 (Appendix I) attached.	I Report on Operations 30-11-17 to 5-12-17.
	5-12-17		The Coy. was relieved in the line by a Company of the 36th Divn. and marched to RIBECOURT where a hot meal was served at about 7.0 AM. About 9.0 AM the Company marched to ETRINCOURT and entrained there at 7.0 PM. At FREMICOURT at about 11.0 PM. the train ran into a shell hole in the line and was brought to a standstill. A new train was wired for and the troops detrained, unloaded and entrained again. This train arrived at MONDICOURT about 8.0 A.M. and the Coy. marched thence to its billeting area at WARLUZEL.	
	6-12-17		The Transport which had moved by road joined the Company in billets, after having left RIBECOURT on the 4th staging at SOREL LE GRAND the night of the 4th/5th and at BAPAUME the night of the 5th/6th.	

Instructions regarding War Diaries and Intelligence Summaries are contained in F. S. Regs., Part II. and the Staff Manual respectively. Title pages will be prepared in manuscript.

WAR DIARY
or
INTELLIGENCE SUMMARY.
(Erase heading not required.)

Army Form C. 2118.

Place	Date	Hour	Summary of Events and Information	Remarks and references to Appendices
WARLUZEL	7-12-17		Reorganization of Company.	
	8-12-17		Paying – out.	
	9-12-17		Sunday.	
	10-12-17		Baths & Refitting. LT R. C. Evans joined Coy.	
	11-12-17		Refitting	
	12/12/17			
	13/12/17			
	14/12/17		LT J F Nichols leave to U.K	
	15/12/17		Paying-out & Baths	
	16/12/17		Church Parade	
	17/12/17			
	18/12/17		Move to Blangerval by March Route 2Lt Barr returned from IV Army School Course	
	19/12/17		Move to Wamin by March Route 2LT Mathieson returned from short leave to U.K.	
Sains les Fressin	20/12/17		Move to Sains-les-Fressin by March Route.	
	21/12/17		Training Programme.	
	22/12/17		Training Programme	
	23/12/17		2LT Singleton admitted to Hospital. 2LT Burridge took over duties as Transport Officer	
	~~24/12/17~~ 24/12/17		~~Church Parade~~	
	25/12/17		Xmas day	
	26/12/17		Training Programme.	

A5834 Wt. W4973/M687 750,000 8/16 D. D. & L. Ltd. Forms/C.2118/13.

Army Form C. 2118.

WAR DIARY
or
INTELLIGENCE SUMMARY.

(*Erase heading not required.*)

Instructions regarding War Diaries and Intelligence Summaries are contained in F. S. Regs., Part II. and the Staff Manual respectively. Title pages will be prepared in manuscript.

Place	Date	Hour	Summary of Events and Information	Remarks and references to Appendices
SAINS	27/12/17		Training Programme.	
les	28/12/17		Training Programme.	
	29/12/17			
FRESSIN	30/12/17		Church Parade. Capt J. Paskin proceeded on short leave to U.K. LT J. F. Nichols returned from leave.	
	31/12/17		Training Programme.	

[signature]
~~CAPTAIN,~~ Lt.
COMMANDING 88TH COY. M.G.C.

A5834 Wt. W4973/M687 750,000 8/16 D. D. & L. Ltd. Forms/C.2118/13.

C O N F I D E N T I A L

W A R D I A R Y

OF

88TH MACHINE GUN COMPANY

FROM 1st January, 1918 TO 31st January, 1918

(VOLUMEN NO. 20)

""""""""""""

Vol 22

Instructions regarding War Diaries and Intelligence Summaries are contained in F. S. Regs., Part II. and the Staff Manual respectively. Title pages will be prepared in manuscript.

WAR DIARY
or
~~INTELLIGENCE SUMMARY.~~

(Erase heading not required.)

88TH COMPANY, MACHINE GUN CORPS. No. Date 31-1-18

Army Form C. 2118.

Original

Place	Date	Hour	Summary of Events and Information	Remarks and references to Appendices
SAINS-LEZ FREZZIN	1-1-18		Training Programme carried out as far as weather conditions – about six inches of snow, and a hard frost – made this possible. A party was detailed to work at clearing the road between the Coy and Brigade HQ at TORCY, but as the road was "snowed up" to a depth of 5 to 7 feet, the task was found impossible and a cross country track alongside of the road had to be resorted to.	
	2-1-18		Training Programme. The Coy was visited by the Bde Major of the 88th Inf.Bde. A message from Bde notified the awards below mentioned and conveyed congratulations of Corps, Division and Brigade Commanders. Capt. Parkin J.L. – – M.C. PTE PHILLIPS – – M.M. CPL. RICHARDS – – M.M. L/CP. WEBB – – M.M. PTE SMITH – – M.M. L/CP. GELLATLY – – – M.M. PTE DOYLE – – – M.M.	

A5834 Wt. W4973/M687 750,000 8/16 D. D. & L. Ltd. Forms/C.2118/13.

(2)

Instructions regarding War Diaries and Intelligence Summaries are contained in F. S. Regs., Part II. and the Staff Manual respectively. Title pages will be prepared in manuscript.

WAR DIARY
or
INTELLIGENCE SUMMARY.
(Erase heading not required.)

Army Form C. 2118.

Place	Date	Hour	Summary of Events and Information	Remarks and references to Appendices
	2-1-18		A cablegram conveying congratulations of the officers of the Company was despatched to Capt. Perkin on leave in U.K.	
	3-1-18		The Company paraded at 9.0 AM & moved off by march route at 9.15 AM. to the TILQUES area. The Transport moved with the Company. The Coy. reached LE BERGUET at 7.0 PM. and billeted there for the night. Stragglers – one	MAP HAZEBROUCK 5A
	4-1-18		The Company moved off at 8.45 and completed move arriving at VAL D'ACQUIN at 2.30 P.M. There were no stragglers and the march was extremely well carried out having regard to the difficulties of the road which were extremely heavy for vehicles.	
	5-1-18		Cpl J. Moore No 21512 proceeded to G.H.Q. 2nd Physical & Bayonet course at St Pol. Cpl J. Coldman ~~[illegible]~~ No 54929 return from course with appointment as instructor 510th (London) Field Coy R.E.	
	6-1-18		Divine Service. Church Parade of Nos 88, 87 and 227 conducted by MAJ. HUNKIN, S.C.F.	
	7-1-18		Training Programme – training Summer Ser.	
	8-1-18		Training Programme – A simple tactical scheme; work much hampered by severity of weather.	

A5834 Wt. W4973/M687 750,000 8/16 D. D. & L. Ltd. Forms/C.2118/13.

(3)

Instructions regarding War Diaries and Intelligence Summaries are contained in F. S. Regs., Part II. and the Staff Manual respectively. Title pages will be prepared in manuscript.

WAR DIARY
or
INTELLIGENCE SUMMARY.

(Erase heading not required.)

Army Form C. 2118.

Place	Date	Hour	Summary of Events and Information	Remarks and references to Appendices
	11-1-18		Practice for Brigade Ceremonial Parade	
	12-1-18		The Brigade paraded at 10.0 AM for inspection by the G.O.C. Division and presentation of New Year Honours & awards in connection with operations on Nov. 20th 1917. The following were the recipients from this Company.	
			CPL. RICHARDS } Military Medal.	
			" WEBB. }	
			PTE DOYLE }	
			" PHILLIPS }	
			" SMITH }	
			In addition the following decorations were awarded for operations (88th Bde. B.R. 15 of 10-1-18	
			MILITARY CROSS.	
			2/Lt. A.F. GADSBY.	
			D.C.M.	
			18422 SGT. J. HILL.	
			42081 C.S.M. H. MAGGS.	
	13-1-18		Church Parade at VAL D'ACQUIN. 2/Lt. J.F. Bishop went by motor lorry with Bde. Party to make a preliminary reconnaissance of forward area to which Bde. will shortly move	

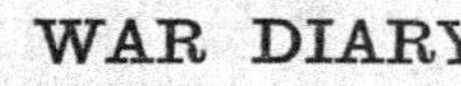

Instructions regarding War Diaries and Intelligence Summaries are contained in F. S. Regs., Part II. and the Staff Manual respectively. Title pages will be prepared in manuscript.

(4)

WAR DIARY
or
INTELLIGENCE SUMMARY.
(Erase heading not required.)

Army Form C. 2118.

Place	Date	Hour	Summary of Events and Information	Remarks and references to Appendices
	14-1-18		Training Programme.	
	15-1-18		The Coy took part in a Brigade Tactical Scheme at BARBINGHEM. The very bad weather, heavy rain made the work extremely difficult.	
	16-1-18		Transport moved by road to new area.	
	17-1-18		Coy moved by march route to WIZERNES leaving ACQUIN at 2.0 AM, and entraining for BRANDHOEK arriving up about 11.0 AM.	
	18-1-18 19-1-18		Coy remained in hutment camp at BRANDHOEK.	MAP 28 N.W. [illegible] Belgium
	20-1-18		Coy moved to Camp at REAOEND, [illegible] E of YPRES. [illegible] the Coy moved into support with [illegible] at [illegible]	
	21-1-18 to 27-1-18		Coy remained in support without any incident of importance arising. During this time all the officers of the Company reconnoitred the routes forward and all Section officers reconnoitred the positions in the line.	
	28-1-18		The Coy moved into the line in accordance with Coy Orders M. G. 88/11.	Appendix I. Op. Orders M.G. 88/11

A5834 Wt. W4973/M687 750,000 8/16 D. D. & L. Ltd. Forms/C.2118/13.

Instructions regarding War Diaries and Intelligence Summaries are contained in F. S. Regs., Part II. and the Staff Manual respectively. Title pages will be prepared in manuscript.

(5)

WAR DIARY
or
INTELLIGENCE SUMMARY.
(Erase heading not required.)

Army Form C. 2118.

Place	Date	Hour	Summary of Events and Information	Remarks and references to Appendices
			The strength and employment of the officers of the Company on going into the line was as under:-	
			C.O. Capt J.J. Parker M.C. Fwd HQ	
			i/c No 1 Sec 2Lt L. Mathieson	
			No 2 Sec " R. Rees	
			3 { " E.A.M. Hoggs, M.C.	
			{ " A.F. Gadsby, M.C.	
			4 { Lt R.C. Evans	
			{ 2Lt J.W. Ferguson.	
			At Rear HQ.	
			2 i/c .. Lt J. Pritchard	
			T.O. .. 2Lt R. Beveridge.	
			Relief .. " H. Morris, M.C.	
	30-1-18		Casualties in the line were two OR wounded (one M.G.C. and one HANTS attached). Reliefs (about 6 to 8 men per section) were sent up and hot soup was successfully sent up in the improvised hay packs. In addition to aid in the prevention of Trench Foot clean socks at the rate of one per man per day were	

A5834 Wt. W4973/M687 750,000 8/16 D. D. & L. Ltd. Forms/C.2118/13.

Instructions regarding War Diaries and Intelligence Summaries are contained in F. S. Regs., Part II. and the Staff Manual respectively. Title pages will be prepared in manuscript.

WAR DIARY
or
INTELLIGENCE SUMMARY.
(Erase heading not required.)

Army Form C. 2118.

Place	Date	Hour	Summary of Events and Information	Remarks and references to Appendices
			Sent up.	
	31-1-18		Reliefs at an average of two men per team were sent up the line and a considerable amount of work in improving & constructing shelters and emplacements was carried out	
			The following decorations were awarded in addition to those already noted	
			C.S.M. [illegible] } D.C.M. Operations 30.11.17	
			18428 Sgt. [illegible] Hill }	
			Lt. A. F. Eadsby M.C. "	
			New Years Honours:-	
			22693 Cpl. Hatch G. D.C.M. } London Gazette 24.12.17	
			24394 Sgt Smith S. Mentioned in Despatches }	
			J. J. Baskin CAPTAIN, COMMANDING 88TH COY. M.G.C.	

A5834 Wt. W4973/M687 750,000 8/16 D. D. & L. Ltd. Forms/C.2118/13.

Appendix I. Copy No 7

88th M.G.Coy. Orders No. M.G.88/11.

1:10000. 27/1/18.

1. The 88th M.G.Coy will relieve the 86th M.G.Coy in the lineon the night 28/29 Jan.
2. Approximate Locations of Sub-Sections of guns will be as follows :-

No. 1 Section.	No. 2 Section.	No. 3 Section.	No. 4 Section.
V30d 40, 10	D6 b45, 00.	V 5d0/0 (To moveto V29d 90,90)	D4 b40, 40.
V30 c55, 25.	D5 c 55, 05.	(V29 d25, 55	D4 b 40,40.
		(V29 c85, 80.	WALLEMOLEN.

Locations of section H.Q. will be Notified later.

3. Guides will meet Sections at WATERLOO at times to be notified later.
4. The Code word for"relief complete" will be the name of the Section Officer concerned.
5. Lists of Trench Stores taken over at each position will be sent to Coy. H.Q. with the first morning report.
6. Reports will be rendered daily to Coy. H.Q. as follows:-
   - 8a.m. 1. Intelligence Report.(6a.m. to 6a.m.)
     2. Work Report.
     3. Morning Report.
     4. Casualty Return.
     5. Certificate that during the 24 hours, each man has removed his boots, rubbed his feet and changed his socks.
   - 4a.m. & 4p.m. Situation Report.
7. Section Officers will report daily to the C.Os in whose areas their guns are situated and whose fronts they cover.viz.
   - No. 1 S.O.will report to C.O. Rt. Bn.and C.O.Lt. Bn.
   - " 2 " " " " C.OsGOUDBERG & BELLEVUE DEFENCES.
   - " 3 " " " " C.O. Lt. Bn. & C.O. GOUDBERG DEFENCES
   - " 4 " " " " C.O. BELLEVUE DEFENCES.
8. RUNNERS. 4 H.Q. runners will proceed in advance to Coy H.Q. They will leave their kitthere and will join their Sections at WATERLOO. On completion of relief a H.Q. runner and a Section runner will be sent to Coy H.Q. by each Section .Section runners will then rejoin their Sections.
9. The following locations are published for information :-

Bde H.Q.		GALLIPOLI.	
Coy. "		LAAMKEEK.	D10 b6,5.
Rt.Bn."		D5 c05	
Lt " "		D4 a25, 40.	
GOUDBERG DEFENCES H.Q.		D5 a3 9.	
BELLEVUE " "		D4 d05 20.	
R.A.P.s		MOSSELMARKT	V29 c63.
"		WATERLOO	D9 a3 4.
"		ZONNE REDOUBT	D13 a6 6.
S.A.A. DUMPS	Adv Div Dump	SPREE FARM	C18 d34
	Bde Dumps	KANSAS	D13 a29.
		WATERLOO	D9 a39.
		BELLEVUE	D4 d33.
R.E.DUMPS	Adv Div Dumps	BILGE	C23 a63.
		SPREE	C18 d12.
		MONS	in D15 b where Tramway crosses No.6 Track(U frames revetting material and duckboards only)

10. 4 men per gun will be taken into the line. The remainder of Sections will remain in camp at DEAD END and will be available for inter/section reliefs. Rolls of Sections by Gun Teams showing proposed reliefs to be submitted to Orderly Room by 6p.m. 27th inst.

11. <u>RATIONS.</u> Two days rations and water will be taken into the line. Thereafter two days rations and water will be delivered every other day at WATERLOO at 6p.m. Sections will detail parties to draw rations at this point.

12. <u>PUTTEES.</u> will NOT be worn in the trenches. Each man will take 5 sandbags into the line, one of which will be worn round each leg in place of a puttee.

13. It is notified for information that it is a Court Martial offence

a. To use the Light Railway tracks as foot roads.

b. To remove wodd(revetting, duckboards etc.) from existing trenches.

14. There will be an inter-section relief on night 1/2 Feb. as follows"- Nos. 2 and 4 Sections will relieve Nos. 3 & 1 Sections respectively.

Positions to be reconnoitred by S.O.s concerned in advance in orderto preserve continuity in work.

15. Acknowledge.

COPIES.
1. C.O.
2 -5 S.O.s
6 File.
7&8 War Diary.
9. D.M.G.O. (For Information.)
10. 88th. Inf. Bde. (For Information.)

Issued at 5.0 PM

Capt.
Commanding 88th. Coy. M.G.C.

29TH DIVISION
88TH INFY BDE

88TH LT TRENCH MORTAR BTY
JLY - DEC 1916

29th Division.

88th Infantry Brifade.

88th LIGHT TRENCH MORTAR BATTERY

J U L Y 1 9 1 6

1

Dec "

HEADQUARTERS,
88th INFANTRY BDE.
No. B. 540
Date.

Headquarters,

29th Division.

Reference your A.723 of 12th instant; 88th Trench Mortar Battery's War Diary for month of July, 1916 herewith.

[signature]
Captain,
for/Brigadier General,
Commanding 88th Brigade.

14th August, 1916.

Army Form C. 2118.

Vol 1

Instructions regarding War Diaries and Intelligence Summaries are contained in F. S. Regs., Part II. and the Staff Manual respectively. Title Pages will be prepared in manuscript.

WAR DIARY
or
INTELLIGENCE SUMMARY

(Erase heading not required.)

88th Trench Mortar Battery

Place	Date	Hour	Summary of Events and Information	Remarks and references to Appendices
France In the Field	July 1st	1916	Acting under Divisional Operation Orders (8) eight guns of the Battery at 7.20 am opened rapid fire on the enemy trenches, from emplacements made at the end of a tunnel about 110 yds long driven out from No 6 Sap. Owing to the ground rising a little in front of the emplacements and the heavy Enemy machine gun fire, little observation of the effect of the fire could be done. Firing continued until 7.30 am when in accordance with orders cease fire was ordered so as not to shell on our men as they advanced. Number of shells fired about (1200) twelve hundred. About 9 am judging our attack was not successful fire was opened again with four (4) guns which fired about (100) one hundred in all. About 6 pm the Battery left No 6 Sap and proceed to Thurles Dump, where defensive positions were reconnoitered to be taken up in case of attack by the enemy. Casualties (1) one Sergeant Killed. The following Officers took part in the battle. Captain Vicars-Miles 2nd Hampshire Regt, Lieut. H. Rendell Newfoundland, 2/Lieut. F. A. Day 16th Middlesex Regt, 2/Lieut. R. O'Niel 10th North Staffords, 2/Lieut. A. B. Nicholls Essex Regt, 2/Lieut. R. E. S. Gregson 2nd Hampshire Regt.	

2449 Wt. W14957/M90 750,000 1/16 J.B.C. & A. Forms/C.2118/12.

Army Form C. 2118.

Instructions regarding War Diaries and Intelligence Summaries are contained in F. S. Regs., Part II. and the Staff Manual respectively. Title Pages will be prepared in manuscript.

WAR DIARY
or
INTELLIGENCE SUMMARY
(Erase heading not required.) 88th Trench Mortar Batteries

Place	Date	Hour	Summary of Events and Information	Remarks and references to Appendices
France in the Field	July 2nd	1916	About 4 P/m orders were received to return to our position in No 6 Sap and to support the attack we were to make next day. About 12 P/m these orders were cancelled and the Battery returned to Thurles Dump.	
	3rd		One Battery (4 Guns) relieved the 84th Trench Mortar Battery in Piccadilly.	
	4th To 16th		These days were spent in recovering shells from No 6 Sap tunnel and the tunnel in front of Mary Redan, helping to clean trenches and recovering and carting away dead bodies.	
	14th		Relieved by 84th Trench Mortar Batteries, going back and taking up tents, vacated by them in Acheux Wood.	
	18th To 22nd		Quiet. Thorough inspection of kits, Gas Helmets, rifles etc to make up any damaged received since July 1st.	
	23rd		Moved from ACHEUX to BEAUVAL on foot	
	24th To 26th		Quiet. Routine drill.	
	27th		Entrained at CANDAS for POPERINGHE.	

2449 Wt. W14957/M90 750,000 1/16 J.B.C. & A. Forms/C.2118/12.

Army Form C. 2118.

Instructions regarding War Diaries and Intelligence Summaries are contained in F. S. Regs., Part II. and the Staff Manual respectively. Title Pages will be prepared in manuscript.

WAR DIARY
or
INTELLIGENCE SUMMARY
(Erase heading not required.)

88th Trench Mortar Batteries

Place France	Date	Hour	Summary of Events and Information	Remarks and references to Appendices
In the Field	July 28th	1916	O C reconnoitered trenches and emplacements to be taken over from the 16th Infantry Brigade.	
	29th		Moved up by train to Ypres and four (4) Guns moved up to Railway Wood and took over from 16th Infantry Brigade (8) Eight guns in dugouts in Ypres.	
	30th		Four guns moved up to positions in HAMPSHIRE Lines commenced digging defensive emplacements quiet day.	
	31st		Quiet. Engaged in cleaning and getting ammunition up to line.	

J.H. Rendell Lieut
for O.C. 88th Trench Mortar Battery

2449 Wt. W14957/M90 750,000 1/16 J.B.C. & A. Forms/C.2118/12.

29th Division.

88th Infantry Brigade.

88th LIGHT TRENCH MORTAR BATTERY

AUGUST 1 9 1 6

C O N F I D E N T I A L

W A R D I A R Y

of

88th TRENCH MORTAR BATTERY

FROM 1st August, 1916 to 31st August, 1916.

(VOLUME No. 2.)

88 Trench Vol II

94

Instructions regarding War Diaries and Intelligence Summaries are contained in F. S. Regs., Part II. and the Staff Manual respectively. Title Pages will be prepared in manuscript.

Army Form C. 2118.

WAR DIARY
or
INTELLIGENCE SUMMARY

(Erase heading not required.) 88th Trench Mortar Battery

Place	Date	Hour	Summary of Events and Information	Remarks and references to Appendices
~~France~~ BELGIAN	AUGUST 1916			
In the Field	1st		Quiet day. Engaged in repairing emplacements casualties nil.	
	2nd		Quiet day. Engaged in clearing and carrying ammunition up to line. Casualties nil.	
	3rd		Quiet day. Casualties (1) one O.R. wounded (1) one admitted to hospital.	
	4th		Quiet day. Casualties nil.	
	5th		Quiet day. Casualties (1) one O.R returned to duty with his Regiment.	
	6th		Quiet day. Casualties nil.	
	7th		Quiet day. Fired (12) twelve rounds at small enemy working party in front of RAILWAY WOOD. Received 88th INFANTRY BRIGADE operation orders No. 23 containing orders for relief by 86th INFANTRY BRIGADE.	
	8th		Relief by 86th INFANTRY BRIGADE cancelled. Enemy released GAS at 10.40 PM and shelled heavily during it. The guns in the line stood to in case attack should follow. One shell dropped in one of the emplacements and wounded (3) three men. Casualties Captain Vicars Mil... A. L. W slightly gassed (1) one O.R gassed and died. (3) Three O.R wounded and gassed.	

2449 Wt. W14957/M90 750,000 1/16 J.B.C. & A. Forms/C.2118/12.

Instructions regarding War Diaries and Intelligence Summaries are contained in F. S. Regs., Part II. and the Staff Manual respectively. Title Pages will be prepared in manuscript.

WAR DIARY
or
INTELLIGENCE SUMMARY
(Erase heading not required.)

88th Trench Mortar Batteries

Army Form C. 2118.

Place	Date	Hour	Summary of Events and Information	Remarks and references to Appendices
BELGIAM In the Field	AUGUST 9th	1916	Enemy shelled the RAMPARTS at YPRES from 5 A/M to 9 A/M. Rest of the day quiet. Casualties (2) two O.R wounded.	
	10th		Quiet day Casualties (1) one O.R sick (effect of the gas) admitted to hospital.	
	11th		Quiet day fired (13) thirteen rounds at enemy machine gun in front of H.19. Casualties (1) O.R. admitted to hospital sick.	
	12th		Enemy shelled RAILWAY WOOD. (25) Twenty five rounds fired by Battery while our Artillery was retaliating. Casualties nil.	
	13th		Quiet day. Casualties nil.	
	14th		Quiet day. Improving cover on emplacement and making shell recesses Casualties nil.	
	15th		Quiet day. (3) Three rounds fired at small enemy working party in front of H.19. Improving emplacements. Increase of (14) fourteen O.R to complete establishment. Casualties nil.	
	16th		Gas alarm which turned out false. During alarm the battery stood to but did not fire. Increase Lieut. S. J. Griggs (1st ESSEX REGT) and (1) one O.R Casualties nil	

Instructions regarding War Diaries and Intelligence Summaries are contained in F. S. Regs., Part II. and the Staff Manual respectively. Title Pages will be prepared in manuscript.

WAR DIARY
or
INTELLIGENCE SUMMARY

Army Form C. 2118.

(Erase heading not required.) 88th TRENCH. MORTAR. BATTERIES

Place	Date	Hour	Summary of Events and Information	Remarks and references to Appendices
BELGIAN.	AUGUST 1916 14th		Quiet day. Casualties (1) one O R admitted to hospital sick. Increase (1) one O.R. rejoined Unit from hospital	
	18th		Quiet day. Received 88th Infantry BRIGADE operation orders No 24 containing orders for relief by 86th INFANTRY BRIGADE on 19th inst. Casualties nil.	
	19th		Relieved by 86th TRENCH. MORTAR BATTERIES on night of 19th/20th. Two Officers and 7 seven O.R remained behind until night of 20th to help relieving Unit. On completion of relief BATTERY entrained at YPRES and detrained at BRANDHOEK and proceeded to Camp C O group.	
	20th		Resting and cleaning up generally.	
	21st		SUNDAY. (holiday.) resting.	
	22nd		Began training as per programme attached	
	23rd To 25th		As per programme.	
	26th		Day of Assault at Arms 88th Infantry BRIGADE. (1) one O. R admitted to hospital sick.	
	27th		Received 88th BRIGADE operation order No 25 to relieve the 86th TRENCH MORTAR BATTERY night of 28th/29th	

2449 Wt. W14957/M90 750,000 1/16 J.B.C. & A. Forms/C.2118/12.

Army Form C. 2118.

Instructions regarding War Diaries and Intelligence Summaries are contained in F. S. Regs., Part II. and the Staff Manual respectively. Title Pages will be prepared in manuscript.

WAR DIARY
or
INTELLIGENCE SUMMARY

(Erase heading not required.) 88th TRENCH. MORTAR BATTERIES

Place	Date	Hour	Summary of Events and Information	Remarks and references to Appendices
BELGIUM	AUGUST 1916			
In the Field	28th		Relieved 86th TRENCH MORTAR BATTERIES Relief completed at 1.30 A/M 29th inst. Casualties (2) Two O.R's admitted to hospital Sick. Increase (1) one O.R. rejoined from hospital.	
	29th		Quiet day. Weather bad with rain thunder and lightning. Enemy ~~discharged~~ reported to have discharged gas between 11.0 and 11.30 p/m,	
	~~30~~		we wore our gas helmets for (20) twenty ~~minutes~~. Apparently a false alarm. All gun teams stood to. Casualties nil.	
	30th		Quiet day. Weather bad raining all day. Casualties (1) one O.R.	
	31st		Quiet day. Weather, fine. Fired (3) three rounds of T.M. Ammunition at supposed machine gun position in Enemy's front line opposite DUKES. STREET.	

H. Rendell Lieut.
O.C. 88 Trench Mortar Battery

2449 Wt. W14957/M90 750,000 1/16 J.B.C. & A. Forms/C.2118/12.

88th Trench Mortar Batteries.

Time	Sunday	Monday	Tuesday	Wednesday	Thursday	Friday	Saturday	Sunday	Mon.	Tues
6.30 a/m to 7.30 a/m		Running and Physical Exercises.								
9.30 a/m to 10.45 a/m	Holiday	Inspection of Kits, rifles, gas helmets and S.A.A.	Practice squad in mounting and aligning Gun.	Squad drill with arms if possible.	Practice ranging and rapid fire if possible.	Training of special class.	Training of special class		Training of special class	Ditto.
11.0 a/m to 12.30 p/m		Training special class.	Training special class.	Training special class	Training special class	Gas helmet drill squad drill	Ranging and rapidity of fire if possible		Holiday	
2.0 p/m to 4.0 p/m		Lecture on Gas. Gas drill.	Lecture on Stokes Gun. Gas drill.	Lecture on necessity of cleanliness. Practice ranging	Ranging and rapid fire if possible	Gun drill with mounting and aligning	Gas drill Lecture on care of arms		Lecture on complete inspection of Trench Warfare Kit, Gas helmets, ranging and rapid fire. Guns. etc.	

In the Field.

31st August 1916

J.H. Rundell Lieut

Commanding 88th T.M. Bts.

"(29th Division.

88th Infantry Brigade.

88th LIGHT TRENCH MORTAR BATTERY

SEPTEMBER 1 9 1 6

Army Form C. 2118.

WAR DIARY
or
INTELLIGENCE SUMMARY

(Erase heading not required.) 88th Trench Mortar Battery

Instructions regarding War Diaries and Intelligence Summaries are contained in F. S. Regs., Part II. and the Staff Manual respectively. Title Pages will be prepared in manuscript.

Place	Date	Hour	Summary of Events and Information	Remarks and references to Appendices
BELGIAM.	1st SEPT. 1916		During gas attacks on enemys lines last night which took place at 1.30 A.m, we fired from three of our positions between S.21 and MUDDY LANE opening fire at 2.10 A.m. We sent over (165) one hundred and sixty five shells on to enemys' front line but am unable to say with what results, observation being impossible. Weather fine. Casualties (1) one O.R. wounded and (1) O.R. very slightly wounded but remained at duty. (Gas was only discharged from RAILWAY. WOOD).	RIGHT SUB SECTO
	2		Quiet day. commenced digging fion defensive emplacements on CAMBRIDGE RD. LINE Carried (40) forty boxes to F.11.) (120) one hundred and twenty shells. During the afternoon enemy active with TRENCH MORTARS, we replied effectively with (20) twenty rounds, from our position in SUNKEN RD.	RIGHT Sub. SECTOR
			Considerable activity by Enemys' TRENCH MORTARS on right of BATT. front. One gun team from emplacement on top of	LEFT SUB-SECTO

2449 Wt. W14957/M90 750,000 1/16 J.B.C. & A. Forms/C.2118/12.

Instructions regarding War Diaries and Intelligence Summaries are contained in F. S. Regs., Part II. and the Staff Manual respectively. Title Pages will be prepared in manuscript.

WAR DIARY
or
INTELLIGENCE SUMMARY
(Erase heading not required.)

88th Trench MORTAR BATTERY

Place	Date	Hour	Summary of Events and Information	Remarks and references to Appendices
BELGIUM	2nd SEPT. 1916		DUKES. ST. registered on top of trees, where enemy snipe from at night, and fired (3) three rounds, registering one direct hit. The team employed in building emplacements in CAMBRIDGE RD. Casualties nil.	LEFT SUB SECTOR
	3.		Enemy reported to have discharged gas. It turned out to be false. We bombarded violently for about (30) thirty minutes. (57) fifty seven rounds were fired in retaliation to enemy's rifle grenades and trench mortars, on enemy's front line in front of H.19. and H.20. Weather misty with rain. Casualties nil.	RIGHT SUB SECTOR.
	4		Quiet day. Work is continuing on defensive Emplacements in CAMBRIDGE RD. (7) Seven rounds were fired at enemys' front line.	LEFT SUB SECTOR
			(55) Fifty five rounds were fired in retaliation. Weather very misty with slight showers. Casualties nil.	RIGHT SUB SECTOR
	5		Quiet day. (65) Sixty five rounds fired on Enemy's front line in retaliation for their trench mortars. Carried (150) One Hundred and fifty shells to H. 11. Weather fine. One O.R. from hospital. Casualties nil.	RIGHT SUB SECTOR

2449 Wt. W14957/M90 750,000 1/16 J.B.C. & A. Forms/C.2118/12.

Instructions regarding War Diaries and Intelligence Summaries are contained in F. S. Regs., Part II. and the Staff Manual respectively. Title Pages will be prepared in manuscript.

or

INTELLIGENCE SUMMARY

(Erase heading not required.)

88th TRENCH. MORTAR. BATTERY.

Place	Date	Hour	Summary of Events and Information	Remarks and references to Appendices
BELGIUM	6th SEPT. 1916		Quiet day. We fired ~~(32.) thirty rounds~~ (53) fifty three rounds during night and (32) thirty two rounds between 10.0 a/m and 11-30 a/m on morning of 4th inst in retaliation. Weather fine. Casualties nil.	RIGHT SUB.SECTN
	7.		Quiet day (175) one hundred and seventy five rounds were fired in retaliation for enemy trench mortars and rifle grenades. Weather fine. Casualties nil.	RIGHT SUB SECTN.
	8		During bombardment covering the firing of a we fired (73) seventy three rounds. Everything has been unusually quiet since. Weather fine. Casualties (1) one O.R. wounded	LEFT SUB.SECTN
			Quiet day. Fired (10) ten rounds.	RIGHT SUB.SECTN
	9		Quiet day. Weather fine. Casualties nil.	
	10		Quiet day. Fired (23) twenty three rounds in retaliation of enemy trench mortars following the registering of our heavy guns. Weather showery at 12 midnight. Casualties nil.	RIGHT SUB.SECT.
	11		Quiet day (6) six rounds fired	RIGHT
			Quiet day. Early in the evening the enemy sent over three trench mortars.	LEFT SUB.SECTN

2449 Wt. W14957/M90 750,000 1/16 J.B.C. & A. Forms/C.2118/12.

Instructions regarding War Diaries and Intelligence Summaries are contained in F. S. Regs., Part II. and the Staff Manual respectively. Title Pages will be prepared in manuscript.

or

INTELLIGENCE SUMMARY

(Erase heading not required.) 88th TRENCH. MORTAR BATTERY

Place	Date	Hour	Summary of Events and Information	Remarks and references to Appendices
BELGIUM	11th SEPT.	1916	Shells into the GULLY doing no damage. we retaliated immediately from our position in the Gully with (15) fifteen rounds with good results (6) six direct hits into the enemy's trench were recorded. Trench boards and other trench material were blown into the air. We blew in his parapet in one or two places. Later in the evening he sent over another Trench Mortar Shell, we retaliated with (3) three rounds with good results. Weather showery. Casualties nil.	LEFT SUB. SECTOR.
	12.		Quiet day (45) forty five rounds fired in retaliation for Enemy Trench Mortars and Rifle Grenades. Weather Misty. Casualties nil.	
	13.		The Enemy sent over Trench Mortar shells into the GULLY, we retaliated immediately firing (16) Sixteen rounds with good results. Early in the Evening he carried out a furious bombardment lasting Several minutes with light and heavy Mortars on the GULLY and Trench leading from GULLY to CRATER damaging it in several places. We replied immediately firing (17) Seventeen rounds eventually silencing him. The enemy appeared to be firing from two	LEFT SUB. SECTOR.

2449 Wt. W14957/M90 750,000 1/16 J.B.C. & A. Forms/C.2118/12.

Instructions regarding War Diaries and Intelligence Summaries are contained in F. S. Regs., Part II. and the Staff Manual respectively. Title Pages will be prepared in manuscript.

or

INTELLIGENCE SUMMARY

(Erase heading not required.) 88th TRENCH MORTAR BATTERY.

Place	Date	Hour	Summary of Events and Information	Remarks and references to Appendices
BELGIUM	13th Sept 1916		Guns in the same position which position we have located. This light mortar appears to fire a shell similar to our Stokes shell, the casing of which is made of similar material to that used for his bombs. Weather misty Casualties nil.	
	14		Quiet day (9) nine rounds fired in retaliation. Work is proceeding on new emplacements. Weather fine Casualties nil.	
	15		Quiet day. Enemy sent over two Trench mortars during morning and afternoon, we retaliated at once (47) forty seven rounds were fired. Weather fine and cold. Casualties (2) two O.Rs from hospital (1) one O.R. to hospital sick.	
	16		Registered during the day firing both in morning and afternoon. During the bombardment (186) One hundred and eighty six shells we fired, one gun being put out of action soon after zero, by the base plate sinking (2) two feet and bending so that it was impossible to fire more from the gun	R. Sub Subsection
			During the bombardment we fired (75) Seventy five rounds. Weather fine. Casualties (1) one O.R. admitted to hospital sick.	L. SUB SECTOR.

2449 Wt. W14957/M90 750,000 1/16 J.B.C. & A. Forms/C.2118/12.

Instructions regarding War Diaries and Intelligence Summaries are contained in F. S. Regs., Part II. and the Staff Manual respectively. Title Pages will be prepared in manuscript.

or

INTELLIGENCE SUMMARY

(Erase heading not required.) 88th TRENCH MORTAR BATTERY.

Place	Date	Hour	Summary of Events and Information	Remarks and references to Appendices
BELGIAM.	17th Sept	16	Quiet day. Enemy has been heard quite distinctly using a pick and shovel underground in the entrance to the GULLY. This noise has been heard during the day and night and looks as if he were mining. (15) fifteen rounds fired. Weather fair Casualties nil.	L. SUB. SECTOI
	18.		Enemys Trench Mortars active. Heavy bombardment by Trench Mortars and other shells from 7.50 pm to 8.30 pm. Gun Emplacements in SUNKEN RD knocked in (57) fifty seven rounds were fired. Weather Showery Casualties 1. (one) O.R. Killed.	
	19		"E" Camp Training as per programme Weather fair Casualties nil.	
	20		"E" Camp Training as per programme Weather fair. Casualties nil	
	21		"E" Camp Training as per programme Weather fair Casualties nil.	
	22		"E" Camp Training as per programme Weather Cold Casualties nil.	
	23		"E" Camp Training as per programme Weather fine Casualties (1) one O.R. to hos	Sick
	24		"E" Camp Training as per programme Weather fair Casualties (3) three O.R. to Complete	Battery
	25		"E" Camp Training as per programme Weather fair Casualties (2) two	O.R. to Complete
	26		"E" Camp Training as per programme Weather fair Casualties nil	
	27		"E" Camp Training as per programme. Weather fine. Casualties Lieut. H RENDELL NEWFOUNDLAND REGt evacuated to hospital Sick. (2) Two O.R. to hospital Sick. An hostile aeroplane flew over	

Instructions regarding War Diaries and Intelligence Summaries are contained in F. S. Regs., Part II. and the Staff Manual respectively. Title Pages will be prepared in manuscript.

or

INTELLIGENCE SUMMARY

(Erase heading not required.) 88th TRENCH MORTAR BATTERY.

Place	Date	Hour	Summary of Events and Information	Remarks and references to Appendices
ELGIAM.	27th Sept. 1916		C. Camp. no limbs were dropped. LIEUT. S. J. GRIGGS 1st ESSEX REGT assumed charge of	Battery
	28		Training as per programme. Moving up under 88th Infantry Brigade Operation Order No. 30 Copy No 9 to relieve 86th Infantry BRIGADE on night of 28/29th in the RIGHT and LEFT SUBSECTOR respectively. Casualties 2 LIEUT BARROW-SIMONDS and (1) one O.R. joined Battery for duty (3) three O.Rs. admitted to hospital Sick. Weather fine	
	29th		Quiet day. Preparing eight gun Emplacements at H.19. right of the SUNKEN RD.	
			Prepared Emplacements and roofed them in with timber, corrugated iron, and Sand bags, Each Emplacement being Suitably Camouflaged. Carried (600) six hundred Bombs to RAILWAY WOOD. weather fine. Casualties (1) one O.R. to hospital Sick.	
	~~30~~		~~Quiet day up to 6 p.m. [illegible] and with the Second round [illegible] on the Enemy TRENCH.~~	

2449 Wt. W14957/M90 750,000 1/16 J.B.C. & A. Forms/C.2118/12.

Instructions regarding War Diaries and Intelligence Summaries are contained in F. S. Regs., Part II. and the Staff Manual respectively. Title Pages will be prepared in manuscript.

~~WAR DIARY~~ or

INTELLIGENCE SUMMARY

(Erase heading not required.) 88th TRENCH MORTAR BATTERY.

Place	Date	Hour	Summary of Events and Information	Remarks and references to Appendices
BELGIUM	30th Sep 1916		During raid carried out by Lancashire Fusiliers of the 86th Infantry BRIGADE we fired according to programme, commencing at 8.15 p/m and finishing at 9-30 p/m.	
			We fired from (8) eight positions in RAILWAY WOOD between SUNKEN RD. and right of DIVISIONAL SECTOR firing (338) three hundred and thirty eight rounds.	
			Enemys' retaliation weak, consisting principally of Trench Mortars (MINNIEWERFER). Remainder of night quiet. Weather fine. Casualties Nil.	
			Under orders from BRIGADE time was put back (1) one hour at 1.0 a/m according DAYLIGHT SAVING BILL.	
			A.J. Ainger [illegible] Lieut	

Programme of Training

Time	Tuesday 19th	Wednesday 20th	Thursday 21st	Friday 22nd	Saturday 23rd	Sunday 24th	Monday 25th	Tuesday 26th	Wednesday 27th	Thursday 28th
7.0 a/m to 7.30 a/m.				Running	and		Physical	Exercises		
9.0 a/m to 10.45 a/m.	Inspection of kit, rifles, gas helmets, and S.A.A.	Practice speed in mounting and aligning guns [illegible]	Squad drill with arms if possible.	Practice ranging and rapid fire if possible	Route March.	Holiday	Practice Battery in new drill movements	Practice in making defensive gun emplacements	Route March	Complete inspection of kit, rifles, gas helmets, Stokes mortars, and huts.
11.0 a/m to 12.30 p/m	Cleaning of guns and S.A. Amm.	Baths for Battery.	Practice in mounting guns with [illegible] respirators on.	Training. Battery in new drill movements			Drill with Stokes guns	Lecture on use of Stokes mortars in bombing enterprises.		Practice speed in mounting and aligning guns.
2.0 p/m to 4.0 p/m.	Cleaning area of huts.	Lecture on Stokes gun. Gas drill	Lecture on necessity of cleanliness. Practice ranging	Practice in putting on box respirators in marching order.	Feet inspection. Lecture on Gas by Gas N.C.O.		Lecture on French Standing Orders.	Gas helmet drill. Lecture on map reading.	Feet inspection. Lecture on Sanitation	Lecture on recent copy of "Information given by prisoners of war"

19th September 1916

[signature] Capt.

Commanding 88th T.M.Bty.

29th Division.

88th Infantry Brigade

88th LIGHT TRENCH MORTAR BATTERY

OCTOBER 1 9 1 6

Instructions regarding War Diaries and Intelligence Summaries are contained in F. S. Regs., Part II. and the Staff Manual respectively. Title Pages will be prepared in manuscript.

WAR DIARY
or
INTELLIGENCE SUMMARY

Army Form C. 2118.

Vol 29

(Erase heading not required.) 88th TRENCH MORTAR BATTERY.

Place	Date	Hour	Summary of Events and Information	Remarks and references to Appendices
BELGIAM.	1st October 1916.		Very quiet day nothing to report. Weather fine. Casualties nil.	
	2		Quite day, fired three rounds at enemy's front line. Received 88th INFANTRY BRIGADE Operation order No. 31, copy no. 10, dated 2nd October 1916. The 165th INFANTRY BRIGADE will relieve the 88th INFANTRY BRIGADE in the RIGHT SECTOR of the 29th DIVISIONAL LINE on the night of the 4/5th & 5/6th Oct., reliefs as under:- The 165th TRENCH MORTAR BATTERY will relieve the 88th TRENCH MORTAR BATTERY, who will on relief proceed to POPERINGHE. Weather fair. Casualties nil.	
	3		Quite day. Nothing to report. Weather misty. Casualties nil.	
	4		Were relieved by the 165th INFANTRY BRIGADE, TRENCH MORTAR BATTERY at 10.30 P.M. & marched to billets in POPERINGHE. Billets good.	
	5		In billets at POPERINGHE. Cleaning mortars. Weather fine. Casualties nil.	
	6		In billets at POPERINGHE. Cleaning mortars. Weather fine. Casualties 1 O.R. hospital.	
	7		Marched to PROVEN STATION & entrained for SALEUX at 10.00 P.M.	
	8		Arrived SALEUX at 11.30 P.M. being brought from there to CORBIE by motor lorry. All men were in billets by 5.30 P.M. Billets good. Received wire from BRIGADE with instructions to be ready to move on the 10th inst.	

2449 Wt. W14957/M90 750,000 1/16 J.B.C. & A. Forms/C.2118/12.

Instructions regarding War Diaries and Intelligence Summaries are contained in F. S. Regs., Part II. and the Staff Manual respectively. Title Pages will be prepared in manuscript.

Army Form C. 2118.

WAR DIARY
or
INTELLIGENCE SUMMARY

(Erase heading not required.) 37th. TRENCH MORTAR. BATTERY.

Place	Date	Hour	Summary of Events and Information	Remarks and references to Appendices
FRANCE.	9th Oct.	1916	Received orders from BDE HEAD.QRS at 11.00 p/m to be ready to move at 12. MIDNIGHT. Battery left CORBIE at MIDNIGHT, conveyed by motor Lorry to S. 22. D. 9.4. Weather fine, Casualties nil.	
	10		Baggage left CORBIE at 9.0 a/m arriving at S. 21. D.9.4. at 2.30. p/m. Battery took up its quarters at S. 21. D. 4.5. men being put into dug-outs. Took over two (2) guns and (50) fifty rounds from 35th BDE 12th DIVISION. Weather fine - Cold Casualties nil.	
	11		Conference at BDE. HEAD QRS. at 3.0 p/m. and received orders to move to advance BDE. HEAD QRS, S. 12. B. 88. where men were put into dug-outs. Weather fine - Cold. Casualties (2) two. O.Rs. admitted to hospital (Sick).	
	12.		Operations carried out 2.5 p/m. in which we did not take part. (543) Five hundred and forty three rounds dumped at BDE. HEAD. QRS. S. 21. B. 88. Weather fine - Cold. Casualties nil.	
	13.		(600) Six Hundred rounds dumped at BDE HEADQRS. S. 12. B. 88. bringing total to (1143) one thousand one Hundred and forty three rounds. Weather fine - Cold - Casualties (1) one O.R. admitted to hospital (Sick.)	

2449 Wt. W14957/M90 750,000 1/16 J.B.C. & A. Forms/C.2118/12.

Army Form C. 2118.

Instructions regarding War Diaries and Intelligence Summaries are contained in F. S. Regs., Part II. and the Staff Manual respectively. Title Pages will be prepared in manuscript.

WAR DIARY
or
INTELLIGENCE SUMMARY

(Erase heading not required.)

88th TRENCH MORTAR BATTERY.

Place	Date	Hour	Summary of Events and Information	Remarks and references to Appendices
FRANCE	14th OCT	1916	Received orders for (1) one gun to go into line. Emplacements dug in Gird Support TRENCH. Weather fine - Cold - Casualties Nil.	
	15.		Heavily shelled between 3 pm and 5.0 pm at S.12.B.5.5. Several rounds dropped on S.12.B.4.8. Rounds [illegible] at S.12.B.8.8. (2.303) Two thousand three hundred and three. Enemy observation balloons very active. Weather fine - cold. (2) two O.Rs. admitted to hospital Sick.	
	16		Quiet day. Weather wet - cold. Casualties One O.R. to hospital (Sick)	
	17		Quiet day Weather Wet - Cold Casualties (1) one O.R. to hospital (Sick)	
	18		Quiet day Weather Cold Casualties 2nd Lieut R. O'Hall to hospital (Sick)	
	19.		Quiet day received 88th INFANTRY. BDE. operation order No 36 Copy No 8. Weather Wet. Cold. Fired (78) seventy eight rounds. Casualties (3) three O.Rs. Wounded.	
	20/ /21		Quiet day relieved by the 87th BDE TRENCH MORTAR BATTERY and proceeded to BERNAFAY WOOD. HOSTILE AEROPLANES flew over Camp near BERNAFEY WOOD	
	22		Quiet day. Weather fine Cold Casualties (2) two O.R to hospital (Sick)	

2449 Wt. W14957/M90 750,000 1/16 J.B.C. & A. Forms/C.2118/12.

Instructions regarding War Diaries and Intelligence Summaries are contained in F. S. Regs., Part II. and the Staff Manual respectively. Title Pages will be prepared in manuscript.

WAR DIARY
or
INTELLIGENCE SUMMARY

(Erase heading not required.) 88th TRENCH MORTAR BATTERY

Army Form C. 2118.

Place	Date	Hour	Summary of Events and Information	Remarks and references to Appendices
FRANCE	23	1916	Quiet day, Weather fine - Cold Casualties nil.	
	24		Quiet day. Received 88th INFANTRY BRIGADE Operation Orders No 37 Copy No 12, containing orders to move at half an hours notice if required. Weather wet Cold Casualties nil.	
	25		Quiet day. Complete inspection of Kit, Guns, Etc. Weather Wet Casualties	nil.
	26		Quiet day. Found working party of (1) one Officer and (30) thirty O.R.s making new Road at LONGUEVAL FLERS ROAD. Weather Wet Casualties	nil.
	27		Quiet day. Found working party of (1) one Officer and (30) thirty O.R.s at LONGUEVAL FLERS clearing Road. Weather wet Cold Casualties	nil.
	28		Quiet day. Found working party of (1) one Officer and (30) thirty O.R.s at LONGUEVAL FLERS clearing Road. Weather Showery Casualties	nil.
	29		Quiet day. Found working party of (1) Officer and (30) thirty O.R.s at LONGUEVAL FLERS clearing ROAD. Received 88th INFANTRY BRIGADE orders to move from BERNAFAY WOOD TO POMMIERS REDOUBT. Weather wet - Cold Casualties nil	
	30		Quiet day. MOVED from BERNAFAY Wood at 10.30 A/m and proceeded to POMMIERS ~~[illegible]~~ CAMP. Received 88th INFANTRY BRIGADE Operation Orders No 39, Copy No 9. Containing orders to proceed to VILLE by march route via FRICOURT, MEAULTE, VILLE. Weather wet - Cold Casualties: Lieut R. O'NEILL ~~[illegible]~~ 4th Worcester Regt discharged from hospital for duty with BATTERY.	
	31		Quiet day. Moved from POMMIERS CAMP at 10.0 A/m by MARCH ROUTE. Weather wet cold Casualties (1) one O.R. from hospital.	

2449 Wt. W14957/M90 750,000 1/16 J.B.C. & A. Forms/C.2118/12.

29 DIVISION
88 INFANTRY BRIGADE
BRIGADE TRENCH MORTAR BATTERY
NOV. 1916 MISSING

29th Division.

88th Infantry Brigade.

88th LIGHT TRENCH MORTAR BATTERY

DECEMBER 1 9 1 6

Instructions regarding War Diaries and Intelligence Summaries are contained in F. S. Regs., Part II. and the Staff Manual respectively. Title pages will be prepared in manuscript.

WAR DIARY
or
INTELLIGENCE SUMMARY.
(*Erase heading not required.*)

Army Form C. 2118.

Duplicate

88th Trench Mortar Battery.

Place	Date	Hour	Summary of Events and Information	Remarks and references to Appendices
FRANCE	1st December 1916		Very quiet day Operation Orders No. 49 & 50 of the 88th Bde were received. 87th TRENCH MORTAR BATTERY will relieve 88th TRENCH MORTAR BATTERY on the 3rd Dec. Heavy shelling took place by both sides between 5-30 P.M. and 7.0 P.M. but no damage to our emplacements. Weather foggy Casualties Nil	
	2nd		Received Operation Order No 51 of the 88th Bde. Very little shelling. We finished our Gun emplacements during the last 24 hours Weather Misty Casualties (1) one O.R. Wounded. Shrapnel Face.	
	3rd		Battery moved from TRONES WOOD to BRIQUETERIE CAMP. during the day Weather dull Casualties (1) one O.R. Hospital. Sick. from Div. Schl of Instruction.	
	4th		Hostile Aerial activity in vicinity of MONTABAN. Battery paraded for Clothing Inspection at 10·30 A.M. rest of day cleaning up camp. Weather fine. Casualties. 10 Men returned from Div Sch. of Instruction.	
	5th		Quiet day. Found party of 1 Officer & 30 men for Road Repairing Weather wet Casualties Nil.	
	6th		Found party of 1 Officer & 60 men for work: unloading trucks from 8·0 A.M. until 4 P.M. Weather dull Casualties ~~Nil~~ (1) one O.R. Hospital Sick.	
	7th		Found working party 1 Officer 30 O.R.'s Weather Dull Casualties Nil.	

A5834 Wt W4973/M687 750,000 8/16 D. D. & L. Ltd. Forms/C.2118/13.

Instructions regarding War Diaries and Intelligence Summaries are contained in F. S. Regs., Part II. and the Staff Manual respectively. Title pages will be prepared in manuscript.

WAR DIARY
or
INTELLIGENCE SUMMARY.
(Erase heading not required.)

Army Form C. 2118.

Duplicate

88th Trench Mortar Battery

Place	Date	Hour	Summary of Events and Information	Remarks and references to Appendices
December	8th		Received 88th Inf. Bde Operation Order to move into billets at Ville on the 9th. Weather dull. Casualties Nil.	
	9th		Battery marched from the BRISETERIE CAMP to VILLE. Billets good and arrived at 4 P.M. Weather: Rainy. Casualties Nil.	
	10th		Cleaning up Equipment and Clothing etc. Weather dull. Casualties Nil.	
	11th		[illegible] paraded for [illegible] at 10.0 A.M. and issue of Clothing etc at 2.0 P.M. Received 29th Division Administrative Orders Copy No 4 at 8.0 P.M. Weather dull. Casualties one O.R. to hospital sick. 2 two O.R.'s rejoined battery from Hospital.	
	12th		Battery paraded for Gun inspection at 10.0 A.M. Received 88th Inf. Bde Operation Order No 51 [illegible]. Battery will entrain at Edgehill at 2.0 P.M. on the 14th inst for MOLLIENS VIDAME resting the night of the 14th at HANGEST. Officers Kit etc will proceed by Motor Lorry. Weather Dull. Casualties Nil.	
	13th		All Trench Stores sent by Lorry to CORBIE. Weather Dull. Casualties one O.R. rejoined.	
	14th		Battery paraded at 11.30 A.M. and marched to Edgehill. Entrained at EDGEHILL at 2.0 P.M. arrived at HANGEST at 6.0 P.M. Marched from HANGEST to MOLLIENS VIDAME arriving in billets at 9.0 P.M. Weather Rainy. Casualties Nil.	

A5834 Wt. W4973/M687 750,000 8/16 D. D. & L. Ltd. Forms/C.2118/13.

Instructions regarding War Diaries and Intelligence Summaries are contained in F. S. Regs., Part II. and the Staff Manual respectively. Title pages will be prepared in manuscript.

WAR DIARY
or
INTELLIGENCE SUMMARY.
(*Erase heading not required.*)

Army Form C. 2118.

Duplicate

88th Trench Mortar Battery

Place	Date	Hour	Summary of Events and Information	Remarks and references to Appendices
DECEMBER	15		Battery cleaned up Billets all day Weather Dull Casualties Nil	
	16		Battery paraded at 10.0 a.m. for Kit Inspection, at 11.0 a.m. Rifle, bayonet, Equipment, ammunition, and Gas Helmet Inspection. Battery paraded at 2.0 P.M. for issue of Clothing, Boots and necessary kit. Casualties Nil.	
	17		Battery paraded at 9.15 AM to attend Church Service at HOTEL DE VILLE MOLLIENS VIDAME. Rest of the day a holiday. Weather dull Casualties Nil.	
	18		Battery paraded for Baths at 10.0 a.m. Weather fine Casualties Nil	
	19		Battery paraded for ROUTE MARCH. Distance [illegible] miles. Dress Marching Order. Weather dry and cold Casualties Nil.	
	20		Battery paraded at 10.0 a.m. and proceeded to training ground. 10.15 a.m. Physical Training Handling of Arms and Saluting Drill. Weather dry Casualties Nil.	
	21		Battery paraded at 10.0 a.m. for Physical Training, Squad Drill, and Saluting Drill. Weather Rainy Casualties Nil.	
	22		Battery paraded for ROUTE MARCH at 10.0 a.m. Weather fine Casualties Nil.	
	23		Battery paraded at 10.0 a.m. and proceeded to training ground for physical training. 11.30. Billet & Kit Inspection by C.O. Weather Rainy Casualties Nil	
	24		Holiday. Weather fine. Casualties Nil	
	25		Holiday. Weather fine. Casualties Nil.	
	26		Battery paraded at 9.45 a.m. and proceeded to Fourth Army School of	

A5834 Wt. W4973/M687 750,000 8/16 D. D. & L. Ltd. Forms/C.2118/13.

Army Form C. 2118.

Instructions regarding War Diaries and Intelligence Summaries are contained in F. S. Regs., Part II. and the Staff Manual respectively. Title pages will be prepared in manuscript.

WAR DIARY
or
INTELLIGENCE SUMMARY.
(Erase heading not required.)

Duplicate

88th Trench Mortar Batt.

Place	Date	Hour	Summary of Events and Information	Remarks and references to Appendices
FRANCE	26		School of T. Mortars at VAUXEN AMIENOIS in motor lorries arriving at the school at 1.0 PM Billets Good. Weather fine, Casualties Nil.	
	27		Battery paraded at 8.30 AM. for instructions on Stokes Gun & Shell Gun Drill, Check Stores, and lecture by Capt Price R.A. Weather dull Casualties Nil.	
	28		Battery paraded at 8.30 AM Running drill, Check Stores, Gun drill, Detail, and Special lecture to Officers and N.C.Os on Ranging Weather dry cold. Casualties Nil.	
	29th		Battery paraded at 8.30 AM. Parades for the day:- Advancing over trenches, Marching Drill, Gun Drill, Fired 100 Practice rounds and Special Lecture to Officers and N.C.O.s on Lines of Fire. Weather Rainy Casualties Nil.	
	30		Battery paraded at 8.30 AM Cleaning Guns and Shells, Gun Drill and lecture on Organization. Weather Rainy Casualties Nil.	
	31.		Battery paraded at 8.30 AM. Preparation of Ammunition, Marching & Gun Drill, Fired 50 rounds Weather Rainy Casualties Nil.	

A5834 Wt. W4973/M687 750,000 8/16 D. D. & L. Ltd. Forms/C.2118/13.

www.ingramcontent.com/pod-product-compliance
Lightning Source LLC
Chambersburg PA
CBHW080803010526
44113CB00013B/2319
* 9 7 8 1 4 7 4 5 2 4 6 9 8 *